A TRAILS COUNTRY GUIDE

GREAT LITTLE
MUSEUMS
OF THE MIDWEST

CHRISTINE DES GARENNES

TRAILS BOOKS
Black Earth, Wisconsin

Library of Congress Control Number: 20011097360
ISBN: 1-931599-08-4

Editor: Stan Stoga
Graphic Designer: Jennifer Walde
Photos: Christine des Garennes; page 126, The Museum of Miniature Houses;
page 150, The Museum of Holography
Maps: Mapping Specialists
Cover Designer: John Huston
Cover Photo: The Museum of Holography

Printed in the United States of America.
07 06 05 04 03 02   6 5 4 3 2 1

Trails Books, a division of Trails Media Group, Inc.
P.O. Box 317 • Black Earth, WI 53515
(800) 236-8088 • e-mail: books@wistrails.com
www.trailsbooks.com

CONTENTS

Introduction

When people talk about the middle of America, they often allude to it in homey terms such as "Midwestern values," "the Heartland of America," "the Bread and Butter of America." But what do these phrases really mean? What are Midwesterners all about anyway?

One way in which we can get a sense of the Midwest's character is through its museums. Everyone knows about such magnificent places as Chicago's Field Museum of Natural History or its Art Institute. But what about those smaller, specialized museums run by the local historical society or collectors of items such as cookie jars or pedal cars? These places, many of them curious and off the beaten track, can provide an informative and entertaining glimpse into the Midwestern psyche. A look at the some of the places in this book, for example, reveals that Midwesterners cherish resort culture and outdoor activities like boating and fishing (head to Mikkelson's Boat Museum in Minnesota or Wisconsin's National Freshwater Fishing Hall of Fame and Museum); we like our cars and cruising down a long stretch of highway (stop by the Elwood Haynes Museum in Kokomo, Indiana); we are tough and admire fellow tough folks (check out the hockey and wrestling halls of fame); we appreciate farmers and rural heritage (visit Iowa's American Farm Implements Heritage Museums and the National Farm Toy Museum); we love to create things of beauty (drop by Rudy Rotter's Museum of Sculpture in Wisconsin); we are fiercely proud of Midwesterners who have achieved fame and fortune (sample the two McDonald's museums in Illinois that honor founder Ray Kroc); and we have a distinctly offbeat sense of humor (witness the Mount Horeb Mustard Museum or the Museum of Questionable Medical Devices, among others).

I hope this book helps readers appreciate the incredible variety of Midwest museums. And I hope it motivates you to get out on the open road and visit as many of them as possible. The book includes some places that fall into the traditional definition of a museum—essentially a building and organization that collects and preserves items of historical, scientific, or artistic value. (For example, the Indiana Medical History Museum educates visitors about how medicine was practiced in the first half of the 20th century.) But who's to say that Elmer's Auto and Toy Museum in Fountain City, Wisconsin, a hodgepodge collection of basically anything with wheels, from pedal cars to bookmobiles, does not have any value (though you will certainly get a kick out of visiting it)? And what about the Mount Horeb Mustard Museum? Why does mustard rate its own museum? One answer is that it, and other museums like it, are poking a little fun at the expense of the big boys. Also, they're just plain fun to visit.

You will enjoy these venues even more if you get to know a little about the people behind them. This book attempts to do that. Ed Krueger of Ed's Museum in Wykoff, Minnesota, didn't invent anything and he never served as governor or senator, but everything he collected in his lifetime was dear to him, from his photos of Hollywood beauties to his dead cat in a shoe box. So make tracks to museums focused on people like "Dick Tracy" cartoonist Chester Gould or 3M founder John Dwan (both excellent small museums), but also spend an afternoon at Mike Bjorn's Fine Clothing Store and Museum in Kenosha, Wisconsin, or Lucille Hodges-Bromerek's Cookie Jar Museum in Lemont, Illinois. In this book I've also tried to introduce you to some of the collectors, curators, proprietors, and others who turned their obsessions and some may say strange hobbies into reality and are now sharing them with us. Many of these wonderful folks are as entertaining as the museums themselves.

Acknowledgments

Thanks go out to Jean Cole and her Cole Clothing Museum, which made me much more appreciative of the modern swimsuit. Thanks to Ben Winter, whose museum showed me how tough it was to be a farmer 50 years ago. (Ever sat on a metal tractor seat for hours?) Thanks to Bob McKay, of the Museum of Questionable Medical Devices, I will never fork out $80 for a gas grill igniter masking as a medical cure-all for headaches or allergies.

Thanks to all the collectors who candidly shared their stories with me (and sometimes met me at unusual hours); the many visitors' bureaus and chambers of commerce that shared suggestions and dug up phone numbers for me; state tourism agencies for aiding me in research; fellow museum visitors who racked their brains for tips (that lengthened my list and pointed me in the direction of places like the smallest church in the world); Nina, whose class shaped my offhanded idea for a book into a legitimate proposal; Randy and Teri for their devotion to Main Streets and back roads; Jeff for nonstop enthusiasm; Mom and Dad for hauling the family to the Midwest years ago; Jen, Dave, Jim, and Kate for making road trips in a station wagon memorable (Dave for playing tour guide with me); and Geoff, my favorite Wisconsinite, who opened my eyes to the beauty and wonderful nuttiness of the Midwest.

1 WISCONSIN

Outsider Art, Big Fish, and a Little Hocus-Pocus

1. Mike Bjorn's Fine Clothing Store and Museum, Kenosha
2. Kenosha Military Museum, Pleasant Prairie
3. Spinning Top Exploratory Museum, Burlington
4. International Clown Hall of Fame, Milwaukee
5. The Angel Museum, Beloit
6. Chalet of the Golden Fleece, New Glarus
7. Mount Horeb Mustard Museum, Mount Horeb
8. Rollo Jamison Museum and The Mining Museum, Platteville
9. Aliens and Oddities Museum, Poynette
10. American UFO and Sci-Fi Museum, Wisconsin Dells
11. Deke Slayton Memorial Space and Bike Museum, Sparta
12. Elmer's Auto and Toy Museum, Fountain City
13. Prairie Moon Sculpture Garden and Museum, Fountain City
14. Woodcarving Museum, Shell Lake
15. National Freshwater Fishing Hall of Fame and Museum, Hayward
16. Wildlife Museum and Moccasin Bar, Hayward
17. Peshtigo Fire Museum, Peshtigo
18. Hamburger Museum and Hall of Fame, Seymour
19. Rudy Rotter's Museum of Sculpture, Manitowoc
20. Houdini Historical Center and Outagamie County Historical Museum, Appleton

Mike Bjorn's Fine Clothing Store and Museum
Kenosha

A former art teacher, Mike Bjorn and his wife, Judy, opened Mike Bjorn's Fine Clothing in 1981 with $10,000. It began as a traditional menswear store. "But after a few years in the business, we said to each other, 'Let's turn it into a tourist attraction,'" Bjorn remembers.

Tourist attraction, indeed. All around the store and museum you'll find examples of Bjorn's kitschy and festive personality, from the conga drum reportedly used by Desi Arnaz in "I Love Lucy" to the $.95 straw hats. A zeppelin painting ("Doesn't exactly suit a dining room, but it's perfect for the store, right?" he says), gold spray painted carousel ponies, and stuffed ducks are among the many items dangling from the store's ceiling. Toward the rear of the building you'll find The Diana (as in the late Princess of Wales) dressing room stocked with London newspapers. And a few doors down you'll find the "Over-18" dressing room plastered with photos of the "special ladies" of former American presidents. Marvel at Mike Bjorn's collection of cups used by celebrities like Dennis Rodman. And try not to stare too long at the infamous poster of Farrah Fawcett found in the bedroom of practically every teenage boy in the 1970s. One wall recognizes political figures such as Richard M. Nixon and Martin Luther King Jr. and another wall containing hundreds of newspaper clippings documents the closings of independently owned and operated, downtown-located menswear clothiers.

You won't find Mike Bjorn's among the names of stores that shuttered. He and his business are an anomaly among menswear stores (and museums for that matter). In a former dime-store building in downtown Kenosha, the Bjorns sell men's clothing at dime-store prices. They don't have plans to jet off to Capri for an early retirement anytime soon, but they are faring quite well. And it's quite obvious they have fun running their business. Take one advertisement that ran in the local paper: "Prom blinky light belly button jewelry—Yes!! Now you can light up the dance floor!!!" Bjorn's is stocked with tuxedos ranging from basic black to yellow-striped zoot suit and fur-accented tuxes, "The finest selection of tuxedos in the world," he claims. Although it is not billed as a tuxedo museum, Bjorn's could be called one because of the many tuxes you'll find there, powder blue ones from decades ago to modern black tuxes.

It's difficult to determine where the store ends and the museum begins (or vice versa). Folks stopping by to ogle at the Pee Wee Herman dolls may also purchase a prom blinky light. Or maybe the guy trying on a sport coat will stay a while longer to admire Bjorn's taxidermy display. (Really, where else can you model a pair of dress shoes under the watchful eye of a stuffed duck?) Some items you'll want to look for are the masks (including Gorbachev and Franken- stein ones) and a string bass reportedly played on the *Titanic*. Speaking of the *Titanic*, Bjorn sells, ahem, iceberg water his grandfather supposedly harvested from the berg the *Titanic* ran into.

The Bjorns conduct business a bit differently than mall-based menswear shops. For one thing, Bjorn flaunts the competition with copies of their ads laminated and dangling from the ceiling. "If I don't have what customers are looking for, I'll send them to the right place. Why not keep the money in town?" he explains. Because Mike and Judy buy in bulk, they sell items at dirt-cheap prices. All ties are $.95, oxford shirts are $10; sport coats are $39. You can buy a tux or suit for $59. And, big men cheer: Bjorn's sells shoes up to a size 20.

Not surprisingly, Bjorn abhors places he calls "Blah-Marts" and is down- town by choice. Dressed in a black suit accented with a purple tie, Bjorn is the unofficial mayor of downtown Kenosha. Since the store and museum opened years ago, he has been a central figure in rebuilding Kenosha's downtown; for example he supported bringing a trolley to the area. It was a logical business decision to operate the store downtown because the rent is cheaper and the buildings have much more character. Because they are not forking out a lot of dough for overhead they can sell clothing at inexpensive prices, he says.

A drummer for decades, Bjorn is also a big supporter of high school music programs. If you're looking for music-themed ties, this is the place; one wall is crowded with trumpet- and trombone-patterned ties. Even if you're not shopping for ties, amuse yourself for hours by scouring his extensive collec- tion. He has ties for practically every occasion.

5614 6th Avenue, Kenosha
(262) 652-0648
Open year-round: Monday through Friday from 10 a.m. to 5:30 p.m.;
Saturday from 10 a.m. to 1 p.m.
Free admission

2 Kenosha Military Museum
Pleasant Prairie

By now you've probably come to expect roadside oddities while crossing the Wisconsin state line: the world's largest scrap metal collection, the world's largest mustard collection, the world's largest angel collection. Even though you may no longer guffaw at billboards advertising watermelon seed spitting contests, you might still be surprised to see, halfway between Milwaukee and Chicago, rows of giant, almost menacing-looking Sherman tanks and Sikosky helicopters.

"It's a hobby, an expensive hobby," says Joyce Sonday with a laugh. She and her husband, Mark, a Vietnam veteran, are collectors of military vehicles—large military vehicles. Their museum, the Kenosha Military Museum, consists of military vehicles ranging from World War I jeeps to Desert Storm tanks, most of which are set up on cement blocks on a flat piece of land overlooking I-94.

Billed as the largest privately owned and operated military museum in the Midwest, the Kenosha Military Museum contains a World War I howitzer (a cannon), a World War II landing craft, M-48 Patton tanks, an M-41 Walker Bulldog tank, and an experimental hovercraft, among many others pieces. The largest and perhaps most daunting of the vehicles are two heavy lift helicopters, which seem to have just landed in the yard; you almost expect soldiers to rush out of them. The Sondays also have a riverboat patrol boat from Vietnam

Famous Wisconsin Natives

- Actor Don Ameche, born in 1908 in Kenosha
- Writer Hamlin Garland, born in 1860 in New Salem
- Actress Heather Graham, born in 1970 in Milwaukee
- Musical entertainer Liberace, born in 1919 in West Allis
- Artist Georgia O'Keeffe, born in 1887 in Sun Prairie
- U.S. Supreme Court Chief Justice William H. Rehnquist, born in 1924 in Milwaukee
- Actor Spencer Tracy, born in 1900 in Milwaukee
- Baseball player and comedian Bob Uecker, born in 1935 in Milwaukee
- Author Laura Ingalls Wilder, born in 1867 in Pepin
- Playwright Thornton Wilder, born in 1897 in Madison
- Architect Frank Lloyd Wright, born in 1867 in Richland Center

and a number of Sherman tanks for you to investigate. Go ahead, peer through the windows and examine the patrols. Each vehicle has a sign posted nearby listing the vehicle's dimensions, its horsepower, where it was built, and in which war it was used.

Military vehicles are quite the rage among collectors right now, and there is a huge market for these vehicles, which are bought and sold daily for thousands of dollars. Sonday, dressed in jeans and an olive drab T-shirt, pulls out a few trade magazines, tank catalogs, and helicopter catalogs, and points to a photo of a Sherman tank. "That goes for $65,000. But you have to pay to transport the thing here," she says. "That can get expensive." As if $65,000 for a tank isn't enough. The Sondays had to ship some of the vehicles they bought from European dealers to the United States, a process that took months. And before rolling them out on U.S. soil, the vehicles had to be thoroughly cleaned—even between the tracks of the tanks—because of customs regulations.

In order to finance the purchase of big-ticket items like helicopters and Hummers, the Sondays frequently lend their vehicles to movie and television production studios. You may recognize a few of their tanks. One of them was used in the filming of *Saving Private Ryan* and another was seen in *Courage under Fire*.

For people who have never fought in a war or served in the armed forces, and for whom the only images of war they have come from history books or movies, a visit to this museum can be an eye-opening experience. These machines are tough, and so were the people who drove and rode in them in the middle of a desert or jungle. Take some time to walk through the museum building and examine photos of some of these soldiers. The bulk of the military collection is outside, but you'll find plenty of military artifacts inside the museum building—photos, uniforms, dog tags, photos, and mess kits.

The museum attracts a wide variety of visitors, from children fascinated with tanks to veterans who were actually at the helm of such vehicles. The place is busiest in August when the Oshkosh Experimental Aircraft show is held. A few tanks and one helicopter have been set aside for folks who want to climb up on them. Looking for military souvenirs? The gift shop has a wide variety of items for sale.

11114 120th Avenue (from I-94, exit at Highway 165), Pleasant Prairie
(262) 857-3418 or 857-7933
www.kenoshamilitarymuseum.com
Open year-round, Wednesday through Saturday 9 a.m. to 5 p.m.;
Sunday 10 a.m. to 5 p.m. Closed during inclement weather.
Admission charged

3 Spinning Top Exploratory Museum
Burlington

Located in an aging, nondescript building on Main Street in Burlington, a quaint Wisconsin town with its antiques shop and ice cream parlor, the Spinning Top Exploratory Museum is the only one of its kind in the world, a place devoted entirely to objects that whirl, gyrate, and pivot. The museum is like a "discovery zone" that emphasizes hands-on fun. Imagine being let into your grandparents' attic and allowed to play with whatever you found for hours. (You'll want to sit cross-legged on the museum floor and spin tops into the night.) Visitors don't walk around staring at exhibits in the Spinning Top Exploratory Museum. They attend a program produced by owner Judith Schulz, a program that includes time to check out her top collection and time to spin a few tops yourself.

With her floor-length floral skirt and floppy straw hat wrapped with a peach scarf, Schulz is a lady straight out of a 1970s-era Walt Disney movie (think Angela Landsbury in *Bedknobs and Broomsticks*). Schulz, who was a latecomer to the world of tops—she got her first top 20 years ago—simply started collecting tops because they were fun. She was having so much fun that she got a little caught up in her newfound hobby. One day she had a $5 top, the next, she had 6,000 of them, including an 1876 centennial top worth hundreds of dollars. In 20 years, Schulz has become a top expert. (Her official title is Top Lady.) In addition to working on Bob Clark films like *A Christmas Story* and *My Summer Story*, she tossed tops for the short-lived television show "Superfudge," based on the Judy Blume book.

Schulz's program lasts about two hours. (You'd be surprised at how easy it is to get caught up in those spinning, buzzing gyroscopes.) For the first few minutes of the show, she introduces herself and runs down the rules of the museum. (For example, do not put your feet on the wooden benches.) She also explains the show's agenda and the museum's layout, which consists essentially of game tables and display cases. Visitors watch a quick video, not about the history of tops or the museum, but of Schulz (you only see her hands) playing with a ton of tops.

After the video, head over to a few tables set up with about 30 different tops that everyone can play with. While you play with the tops, Schulz walks around helping people who are unfamiliar with how some of the more complicated tops work. During playtime, visitors can also check out the display cases filled with tops, top games, and yo-yos ("return tops"). The museum has flip-over tops, gyroscopes, peg tops, bracket tops, snake tops, glass tops, and even a few Pokémon tops. You'll see wooden tops from the 1800s and tops that companies such as Cracker Jack gave away as prizes. You'll also find out how peg tops, whip tops, and tulip tops work.

Calling All Chocoholics

Every second weekend in May, Burlington—self-proclaimed "Chocolate City, U.S.A."—is a virtual Shangri-la for chocolate aficionados. Though Nestlé has its origins in Switzerland, the company operates a factory in Burlington, Wisconsin, and it has been the pride and joy of its residents for decades. So why not celebrate the cacao seed? Not only does Nestlé come out in full force for the annual **Chocolate Fest** (at the 2000 event they built a king-size bed out of milk chocolate), but all the local sweet shops sell their goods: chocolate-covered pretzels, strawberries, turtles, and ice cream. The festival also has the usual carnival attractions like Tilt-A-Whirl rides, shooting galleries, and fireworks. And although this event celebrates chocolate, this is also Wisconsin: There's no shortage of brat and cheese stands. For more information, call (262) 763-6044.

After playtime, Schulz performs a number of top tricks, demonstrations that elicit much oohing and aahing. The show is not overtly academic, but nevertheless Schulz frequently quips about centripetal force and the possibility of a fourth or fifth dimension. (She is a former teacher.) She engages everyone in her audience, addressing people by name (visitors wear name badges) and inviting many to help her with her top tricks, such as ringing a bell every time she flips a top off a tray, onto her hand, and onto a paddle. During her presentation, Schulz will pick up a few of her more rare tops, ones from the Czech Republic or Malaysia, and note, "Toys are our common language."

Want to learn more? Schulz offers yo-yo classes, top spinning, and top optics classes. She also builds and paints her own tops, which you can buy in the gift shop. The Spinning Top Exploratory Museum holds an annual yo-yo contest in April.

533 Milwaukee Avenue (Highway 36, located next to the Teacher Place and
Parent Resource Center), Burlington
(262) 763-3946
Call for hours
Admission charged
Children three years old and younger are not allowed in the museum.

International Clown Hall of Fame
Milwaukee

"Humor is an essential factor in human life," explains Kathryn O'Dell, director of the International Clown Hall of Fame. When you infuse laughter into your life, you feel better, body and soul, she says. Watching a clown act is one way people can bring more laughter to their lives. Or they can head over to Milwaukee's Clown Hall of Fame, where the motto is "Let the laughter loose." Not only does the hall of fame infuse laughter into the lives of Milwaukee-area residents by sending clowns to hospitals and nursing homes, it also opens its doors to visitors who wish to learn about the history of clowning, see pictures of famous clowns, and look at some zany outfits.

Clowning is considered to be the oldest known performance art and clowns have long been a part of Wisconsin's history, so it is only fitting that their hall of fame be located here. In the mid-1800s, many circuses wintered in Wisconsin, perhaps one of the more well known being the Ringling Brothers Circus in Baraboo. Many clowns who were part of the circuses made Wisconsin their homes when they were not out touring the country. You'll find plenty of circus museums around the world that contain clown exhibits, but the hall of fame's staff believes the Milwaukee museum is the only one in the world specific to clowns.

The museum, now housed in Milwaukee, got its start in 1986 in Delavan, a town west of the city that was a gathering place for clowns in the 19th century. Years ago, a man named Gareth Betts from the University of Wisconsin–Extension in Walworth County thought the town should establish a museum to honor the town's clown history. In 1997 the museum moved to Milwaukee in order to reach a larger audience and to expand their outreach programs.

International Clown Hall of Fame, Milwaukee

The hall of fame's exhibit is colorful and larger-than-life, but the clown retrospective is also surprisingly serious, a thoughtful tribute to the clown presence in Wisconsin. You will find photographs of clowns from the early part of the century, photos of clowns during their inductions into the hall of fame (with and without their make-up), and autographed photos. Posters advertising clown shows also don the walls. The collection includes clown costumes from the early 1900s (mannequins have been dressed up in clown gear) and props like a giant popsicle, hammer, and camera. The museum also has a legion of oversize shoes on display. The item most people are drawn to in the museum, according to O'Dell, is the self-portrait of Emmett Kelly, done in charcoal. Composed from 1968 to 1969 and worth around $17,000, the drawing is on permanent loan to the museum.

After you've examined the many portraits of the clowns on view in the museum, take about 15 minutes to watch an informative video that tells the life stories of the hall's first inductees: Red Skelton, Lou Jacobs, Emmett Kelly, Mark Anthony, Felix Adler, and Otto Griebling.

The exhibits currently on view in Milwaukee's Grand Avenue Mall represent about 10 percent of the hall of fame's entire collection. The other pieces are in storage, awaiting the museum's transition to another larger downtown Milwaukee locale by the end of 2002.

Afraid of clowns? If so, you're not alone. "A lot of children are afraid of clowns. I think it's because their gestures are so large," offers Nancy Schier, the office manager and membership director of the hall of fame. But rest assured, the museum is definitely not a frightening place. The museum does arrange clown shows for children, but surprisingly, most of the museum's visitors happen to be adults who collect clown memorabilia. Call the museum for more information on the shows.

Want to discover the clown within you? University of Wisconsin–La Crosse hosts a Clown College every summer.

161 West Wisconsin Avenue (lower level of the Grand Avenue Mall), Milwaukee
(414) 319-0848
www.clownmuseum.org
Open year-round, Monday through Friday from 10 a.m. to 4 p.m.
Admission charged

While in the Area Make a Cheesy Stop

Yes, there are a gazillion roadside cheese shops with mammoth cheese signs or gorilla-size mice hugging chunks of Swiss in Wisconsin, but the **Oasis Cheese and Gift Shop** off I-90 in Janesville is special. First of all, you can't miss this store. The signs are Las Vegas large and shout, "Oasis!" "Turn Here!" "Cheese!" "Motel!" And even if you miss these Wal-Mart–size signs, you can't miss Leena, the brown and white cow statue that has greeted visitors to the store for 20 years. Try the smoked string cheese or cheddar in the shape of University of Wisconsin mascot Bucky Badger.

5 The Angel Museum
Beloit

The time: mid-morning. The day: a sunny Saturday in April. The scene: An ethereal figure dressed in a shimmery aqua-blue gown complete with silver lamé angel wings, flutters in between glass display cases. The character: Not an actual seraph, but close to it: meet Joyce Berg, angel collector. Though she is not the sole person responsible for putting together The Angel Museum in Beloit, and she only stops by occasionally, it is Berg whom most people associate with the museum. Probably because 7,000 of the approximately 7,600 angels on display are hers. (And there are thousands more angels in her collection than those 7,000.)

Maybe it was the television show *Touched by an Angel*. Maybe it was John Travolta strapping on a pair of huge white wings for his role in the film *Michael*. Whatever the reason, angels have been the new, new thing since the early 1990s. Not the case with Berg, though. For the last 30 years she has accumulated 12,000 angels—and counting. About 7,000 of Berg's angels are showcased in The Angel Museum, in addition to approximately 600 angels donated by Oprah Winfrey, who received thousands in the mail when she mentioned on her show that she had a difficult time finding African American angels in stores.

The story behind the museum is twofold. In 1995 Berg ran out of room in her house for her angels and was looking for a place to stockpile them. At the same time residents were rallying together to save Saint Paul's, a nearly century-old church, from being torn down in the name of redevelopment along the Rock River. The way Berg tells the story is that she was driving along Pleasant Street one day and a ray of light shone on the front door of the church. She knew she had found a home for her angels. Hundreds of Beloit citizens raised money for the church's renovation and its conversion to the present-day eclectic angelic museum.

As visitors enter the museum, they are immediately transported into a halcyon orb of tinkling music, soft white lights, and trilling female volunteers who steer visitors to Berg's very first angel: a figurine with two cherubs playing on a seesaw. All the angels are displayed in crowded cases according to their origin and the material of which they are made. The museum has straw angels, china angels, wood angels, pewter angels, Smurf angels, Lego angels, a Rosa Parks angel, angels from Japan, angels from Mexico, and angels from New Jersey. The staff has even compiled an angel hunt game for visitors, challenging them to find such figurines as the smallest angel and the angels wearing cheeseheads. (This is Wisconsin after all.)

As you look at all these angels, light trickles in from stained glass windows. Men who come with their wives to the museum rest on the benches and chat about the church's arching ceiling. Everyone grins.

"I get goose bumps when I talk to some visitors," says the museum's curator Nora Gard. "I have heard a lot of stories about angels. I believe that, for the most part, people who are absorbed by the museum and by angels must have had an experience," she says, not revealing whether she or Berg believes in angels. Some earthly magic has been known to happen at the museum: A man once proposed to his wife here. "People are happy when they come here," Gard says, recalling a time when 15 motorcyclists stopped by because they had heard about the museum's Harley-Davidson angel. "We allow each visitor to interpret the artifacts in any way they want to. We're not changing a religious or philosophical viewpoint but enhancing it."

656 Pleasant Street, Beloit
(608) 362-9099 www.angelmuseum.com
Open May to September, Monday through Saturday from 10 a.m. to 5 p.m.;
October to April, Tuesday through Saturday from 10 a.m. to 4 p.m.
Admission charged

While in the Area
Visit Foamation Inc.

If you weren't living in the Midwest in 1995, you probably missed hearing about how a foam cheesehead purportedly saved Wisconsinite Frank Emmert's life. The story goes that while flying home from a Packers game in a small private airplane, the plane encountered some rough weather while over Stevens Point and crashed. Before the plane crashed, instead of grabbing a pillow, Emmert braced himself with his beloved foam cheesehead. Emmert survived, but not without a few broken bones and bruises. His head, however, was a-okay. "Maybe God is a Cheesehead, too" read one newspaper headline.

You can pick up one of those corn-colored foam cheeseheads at any Wal-Mart in Wisconsin. But if you're in the Milwaukee area, be sure to stop at the **Foamation factory outlet store,** run by the people who created these cheesy items. Not only can you get a cheesehead at a lower cost—about $12—you also will have your choice of a slew of other foam products to don at a Packers game, or, if you are so inclined, at non-Packer functions. Among the other items you can buy are cheesehead earrings, cheesehead neckties, cheesehead fez, sombreros, coasters, cheeseheads for your car antenna (to complement the Packer flag that everyone driving an evergreen truck displays), and a Cheez-it cracker cushion. Nonspecific Wisconsin accessories available are Billy Bob Teeth and a pink pig hat (yes, that's right: a plump, smiling foam pig hat).

Since the summer of 2000, the Foamation guys, Ralph Bruno and Chris Becker, have been offering Ducks tours of the area from their outlet, located a few yards from Lake Michigan. The Foamation outlet store is open year-round, Monday through Friday from 8 a.m. to 4 p.m. It is located at 3775 South Packard Avenue in St. Francis. For more information, call (414) 481-3337 or (800) FOAM FUN.

6   Chalet of the Golden Fleece
New Glarus

New Glarus is a charming—almost too charming—town about 25 minutes southwest of Madison, with clean streets, finely brewed beer, and many buildings designed with a Swiss look to them. One of the more prominent Swiss-style houses in New Glarus is the Chalet of the Golden Fleece, a museum that boasts an exotic collection of antiques and tchotchkes. Built in 1937 by the town dandy, Edwin Barlow, the chalet resembles a Swiss Alps cottage with its flower boxes and slate shingle roof. It was converted to a museum nearly 50 years ago.

The medley of antiques in the Chalet of the Golden Fleece used to belong to Barlow, a bachelor who had the rough life of never having to hold down a job. Barlow spent his days traveling around the world and buying some swell knickknacks. He never married and when he died in 1955 he donated his house and everything in it to New Glarus.

Before he died, Barlow set up the house the way he wanted it to appear and even wrote up the tour that the museum guides would read to visitors. When he donated the house and its contents to the village, the stipulation was that nothing be added or taken away from the house. This is one man's collection, arranged and explained by him. Nothing has changed since he gave it to the town, museum staff says.

Hopefully your tour guides will be local ladies of Swiss descent who actually knew Barlow. They will gladly spend more than an hour walking through the rooms, diligently reading the guide word-for-word from index cards. If you tour the house on a quiet day, the women may chat about their schoolgirl days when they used to hang out in the basement of this house. For example, after classes they would stage musical shows for Barlow and on Friday nights he would invite all of New Glarus's teens over for dances.

Apart from the fine china and scarf collections, the museum has curious items you wouldn't expect to find in a faux Swiss mountain cottage museum in a small and largely rural Wisconsin town. For example, the collection includes a pocket watch once owned by Louis XVI, a pair of 2,000-year-old Etruscan earrings, and parchments with Gregorian chants on them. Barlow was able to pick up most of these items, worth oodles of money now, for a fair price during the Depression years when museums had to unload a few items in order to keep afloat. You'll find a number of Swiss antiques: traditional costumes, a porcelain tile stove, and wood carvings. Also interesting is the building itself—a replica of a Bernese Mountain Chalet—with its deep brown stained wood walls and rocks and logs on the roof.

Throughout the tour, you'll learn all about the man behind the chalet and its collection. Born in Milwaukee, Edwin Barlow was adopted by New Glarus resident Clara Bosworth Mathers when he was a young man. Related to shipping magnates, Bosworth was well-off, and so would be her adopted son. For a while Barlow worked as a producer in the New York theater scene, but he spent most of his time traveling the world, rubbing shoulders with the elite. He crossed the Atlantic Ocean 63 times in an ocean liner and circled the globe two times. He was invited to Queen Elizabeth's coronation and Grace Kelly's wedding.

"He wasn't in one place for very long. With the lifestyle he led, he didn't have time to marry and raise a family," points out the museum's curator Helen Altman. Barlow would reside in his chalet for about six to eight weeks a year, and then be off to who knows where. But Barlow was certainly fond of little New Glarus. Why else would he leave the town his valuable antiques collection?

618 2nd Street, New Glarus
(608) 527-2614
Open daily May 1 to October 31 from 10 a.m. to 4:30 p.m. Bus and group
tours are welcome anytime by appointment.
Admission charged

While in the Area
See New Glarus for Polka,
Parades, and Mettwurst

New Glarus, known as "Little Switzerland" because 150 immigrants from the Swiss canton of Glarus founded the settlement in 1845, is proud of its ethnic heritage. The town holds its annual Heidi Festival in mid-June—complete with yodeling and girls with braids—and a Wilhelm Tell Festival the first week in September. Both festivals have plays, parades, and polka music.

New Glarus also has a number of specialty sausage shops. One of them is **Ruef's Meat Market**, which makes and sells landjaegers, mettwurst, kalberwurst, and has a "brat of the week," is located at 538 1st Street. For more information, call (608) 527-2554.

Another is **Hoesly's Meats**, which specializes in dried beef, European-style cold cuts, bacon, ring bologna, as well as sausage and brats. Hoesly's is located north of New Glarus off Highway 69 at 219 Industrial Drive. For more information, call (608) 527-2513.

And while you're in the New Glarus area, don't forget to stop by the **New Glarus Brewery**. They brew year-round and seasonal beers. Edel-Pils, Uff-Da Bock, and Staghorn are local favorites. Tour the brewery and savor the free samples. It's a few miles north of downtown New Glarus at County W and Highway 69. For tour times, call (608) 527-5850.

15

7 | Mount Horeb Mustard Museum
Mount Horeb

The day the Boston Red Sox lost the 1986 World Series was a sad, sad occasion for Massachusetts native Barry Levenson. That day, Levenson, then a lawyer living in Mount Horeb, thought he'd get a new hobby, since watching losing baseball teams wasn't cutting it. He decided to become a collector of some sort, and later that evening, while strolling down the condiment aisle at his local grocery store, he heard a voice tell him, "If you collect them, they will come." Thus was born the Mount Horeb Mustard Museum, which houses the largest mustard collection in the world, according to Guinness World Records. As of the summer of 2001, he had more than 3,500 mustards.

Throughout the last several years, Levenson and his museum have been featured on the Oprah Winfrey television show and written about in the *Chicago Tribune*. He was even a guest once on National Public Radio and during the interview belted out a song about the magnificence of mustard. Despite his notoriety as mustard devotee, Levenson has yet to take his curatorship any more seriously than absolutely necessary. The museum is not exactly kitsch—he does sell $10 French mustards—but it is not even close to being staid. He has display cases of porcelain and glass mustard pots (check out the glass slipper), pots from France to Japan, and plenty of mustard paraphernalia (don't miss the mini–Oscar Meyer Weinermobile). Antique posters advertising mustard decorate the walls, and the cabinets are stocked with mustards from around the world spanning decades. (Glance over the labels and learn how to say mustard in five different languages.)

While you're there, make sure you sample some mustards and watch a film about the history of mustard and the museum, appropriately entitled "Mustardpiece Theater." (Does the narrator's smooth voice sound familiar? It's James Earl Jones.)

When asked about ketchup, the "other condiment," and whether he has ever considered starting a complementary museum nearby, Levenson doubles over in his chair as if he has been socked in the stomach.

"We don't concern ourselves with the lesser condiments," he says, in a "Pardon me, do you have any Grey Poupon?" voice.

Speaking of Grey Poupon, Levenson has named his institute of higher mustard education "Poupon U." Pull up the museum's Web site and read about a class on the "Endodynamics of Mustard Management." If you ask, Levenson will even sing the school's fight song, although sometimes he'll break out into song simply because he is feasting on mustard and enjoying it. Obviously the atmosphere of the museum is fun. Quite a change from his former job in the courtroom.

"I looked at it as entertainment, as playing a role," Levenson says of his lawyer days. He still gets his share of playing and providing entertainment as head of the museum. And Levenson's "mustard happens" attitude seems to influence his visitors. As you leave the museum, chances are a car will pass by and a boy who had just finished stuffing his face with free samples of mustard and pretzels will wave his recently purchased "Poupon U" pennant from the window.

Barry and Patti Levenson sell gift boxes for fans of international mustards or pretzel-dipping mustards. Pick out a jar from about 400 mustards in the store or order from their extensive (and amusing) catalog. Try the Aviator Amber Ale Mustard or Austrian Krensenf mustard from a tube. Buy a mustard pot and start a collection of your own or purchase some mustard-making supplies. How about relaxing in a mustard herbal bath? And finally, there are numerous Poupon U sweatshirts and pennants available for purchase. If you can't get enough, consider gathering with fellow mustard lovers at the museum for National Mustard Day, usually held the first Saturday in August.

100 East Main Street, Mount Horeb
(608) 437-3986 or (800) GET-MUST
www.mustardmuseum.com
Open daily from 10 a.m. to 5 p.m. Closed Wednesday in January and
February.
Free admission

8 | Rollo Jamison Museum and The Mining Museum
Platteville

Sure, there are plenty of old mines to tour in the United States, but in Platteville, Wisconsin, you can clamber through a lead mine, hop aboard a little train pulled by a 1931 mine locomotive, tour a mining museum, and check out the head-turning collection of a local man all in less than two hours. Located within a few feet of each other, the Rollo Jamison Museum and The Mining Museum are housed in two renovated schoolhouses atop a hill overlooking Platteville. The museums, especially the Rollo Jamison, are very hands-on. "Now feel this," "Now play this," "Now grind this," seem to be the museums' mantras.

Who *was* Rollo Jamison, you might wonder while pulling up to the museum bearing his name in downtown Platteville. Was he someone you read about in that Wisconsin history class you took in junior high school? After all, to have a museum—a fairly large one at that—named after you, you have to have been a high-ranking someone, right? A Civil War colonel? A lumber baron?

As it turns out, Jamison was a jack-of-all-trades kind of man, someone who did nothing extraordinary other than amass a collection of antiques as a kind of homage to the working man. But by the time you have finished viewing bits of his collection and watching a video in which he reflects on his life, you'll wish you could have met the man.

Diorama of boxing squirrels at the Rollo Jamison Museum, Platteville

Born in 1899 in nearby Beetown, Rollo Jamison left school after fourth grade to take care of his family after his father left. As a child he picked up Native American arrows around his farm, kept them, and built a little collection. Throughout the years, he added slot machines, dentist's tools, and clocks to his collection, among many other items. He didn't search for rare European paintings or sculpture, but rather the tools used by common folk. Touted as the world's largest one-man collection, Jamison said he had more than a 100,000 items (although museum archivists put that number closer to 20,000). For decades Jamison lived in his Beetown trailer and exhibited his wares in a Quonset hut on his property, often explaining and demonstrating the use of the items to visitors; the current museum staff follows this tradition. While most museums display their antiques behind a rope, guides at the Rollo Jamison Museum invite visitors to take a seat on a player piano bench and pump the pedals to the music or heave a yoke over their shoulders.

In addition to learning about life in the early 20th century, visitors discover much about the man behind the collection. Jamison helped organize a letter-writing club during World War II in which residents gathered at a pub and wrote letters to local soldiers without any family. He saved a placard that hung on the wall of the pub—"Write to the boy's [sic] in the service"—with names of his boys still on it. He also saved the velocipede he rode to Chicago from Beetown to see the world's fair in 1933. (The journey took a week.) And there's the tape recorder he purchased in 1947 to interview interesting Wisconsinites (not for a radio show, but for his own interest). One of the interviewees was a 104-year-old man, the last known Civil War veteran in Wisconsin. While working for a local civil defense unit, Jamison frequently carried a walkie-talkie. To improve reception he fastened an antenna to the top of a helmet. Look around the museum closely. Yes, that is a taxidermist's diorama of fighting squirrels literally dressed as boxers in a ring. That really is an electricity machine where, for a small fee, you get a little shock—good for the health. And those wreaths? One is made out of family members' hair (they made these when they couldn't afford family portraits) and another is made out of chicken feathers. Isn't it amazing what people did before television?

When Jamison was shopping around his collection to towns and museums during the last few years of his life, he decided on the city of Platteville because officials agreed to never break up the collection and to call it the Rollo Jamison Museum. The museum opened in the Platteville schoolhouse in June 1981. He died at age 81, a few months after the museum's opening event. Before moving on to the next museum, have a seat and watch the short video on Jamison that was shot a few months before he passed away. While brushing away a tear and speaking though a respirator, Jamison, after talking about his years of collecting, says, "I can say I've done all I wanted to do in life."

On to the mining part of the tour. Before the schoolhouses and the museums stood on the hill on Main Street, the Bevans lead mine was located here.

Discovered in 1845 by Lorenzo Bevans, it used to produce more than two million pounds of lead in a year. And it wasn't the only mine in the area. In the late 1800s, southwestern Wisconsin was teeming with lead and zinc mines. Although only lead was mined at the Bevans mine, curators have set up an exhibit on zinc mining, too.

The Mining Museum is fairly small and includes basic exhibits about the uses of lead—from lead paint to lead crystal—as well as exhibits on mining history going as far back as Native American mining techniques.

The best part of the tour is actually trekking down the stairs into the drippy and cool mine. Dummies dressed like miners (no helmets in those days) are poised in action, digging with their picks. The guide will hand you a drill steel and an auger and invite you to climb into a bear hole for a few moments. (Imagine spending nine hours crouched in these holes as the workers did 150 years ago.) Guides explain how lead and zinc were mined and discuss the various jobs involved in mining. The guys with the riskiest jobs were trimmers, who were the first men in the mine after the blasting the previous evening. They would knock down loose rock for the muckers to shovel and drop into buckets or cans. Tour guides also point out how the miners kept the roof from caving in on them (initially rock piles; lumber and roof bolts later on) and how they carved tunnels before dynamite (gunpowder). Expect to see the usual mine accessories like buckets and "torpedoes," which were used to transport miners in and out of the mines. And did you know that mules were brought down into the mines in order to help transport the heavy rocks? During those pre-PETA days, animals could be housed in a stable down in the mine for up to nine months.

After climbing back up the stairs into the daylight, visitors will ride for a few minutes around the museum campus in a noisy train similar to the one miners would ride into mines. The original cars, much heavier and with splinter-ridden wooden seats (and which were presumably much louder), are on view outside.

If you are thinking about touring the mine, keep in mind there are steps—90 of them—that you must climb up and down.

While you're in the area, take a few minutes and browse the Roundtree Gallery, which features works from local artists. It is located above The Mining Museum. Admission to the gallery is free.

405 East Main Street, Platteville
(608) 348-3301
Open daily May through October from 9 a.m. to 5 p.m. Group tours are available year-round by appointment.
Admission charged

9 Aliens and Oddities Museum
Poynette

Visit the Aliens and Oddities Museum on a gray day at dusk when few people are milling about and you could get the creeps. The museum, located in the MacKenzie Educational Center near Poynette, is a small shedlike building in the woods, off a wooded trail near the pond and tower (next to the much less surreal logging museum). The museum does not contain formaldehyde-soaked Martians with tentacles and bulging eyes and elongated foreheads. Instead you'll find a stuffed chukar partridge and a melanistic mutant pheasant, species alien to Wisconsin. No creatures from outer space here, but some are just as freaky, like the two-headed fetal pig.

Most of the animals in the little museum are those that look perfectly normal—they just aren't native to Wisconsin—animals like the chukar (a brown partridge) and fish like the brown trout and coho salmon. It is an exhibit about the Department of Natural Resource's attempts to stock the rivers and ponds with fish for the fisherman and the woods with birds and animals for the hunters. For each animal or fish on display, the staff has explained when the species was introduced and whether the introduction was successful. Another case shows immigrant and native weeds to Wisconsin.

The museum's oddities, which are defined for visitors as "animals with traits not normally occurring in nature," are hermaphrodites (having male and female characteristics) and deformites, such as the two-headed fetal pig and four-legged pheasant. You'll see a hermaphrodite deer skull—with one antler—and a few albino animals like a deer, porcupine, and woodchuck, as well as melanistic (black) animals.

If you're not interested in alien or odd animals, stroll over to the easier-to-swallow conservation museum, also on the grounds of the MacKenzie Educational Center. Look for the statue of Paul Bunyan at the entrance to the barn.

W7303 County CS (located in the MacKenzie Educational Center, off the nature trail near the tower in the woods), Poynette
(608) 635-8110
Open daily 8 a.m. to 4 p.m.
Free admission

While in the Area Admire the Big "M"

Don't miss the big "M" made by University of Wisconsin–Platteville Mining School engineering students in the 1930s. It's made of limestone chunks and located a few miles northeast of town off County B.

10 American UFO and Sci-Fi Museum
Wisconsin Dells

Had enough of water slides and putt-putt golf in Wisconsin Dells? As the theme song to *Star Wars* blasts, take a tour around the mazelike American UFO and Sci-Fi Museum in downtown Wisconsin Dells. Expect lots of re-creations: the humongous, locuslike alien from the 1996 movie *Independence Day* and an alien dummy levitating an abducted man. With mannequins donning costumes from sci-fi flicks like *Planet of the Apes, Star Trek,* and *Terminator,* and a wax recreation of an alien autopsy thought to have occurred after the alleged Roswell accident, the museum is a hoot for sci-fi buffs and UFO hunters.

The museum is a pet project of Ray Radelia, a sci-fi movie fan from Chicago. When he realized he had a collection large enough for a museum and that the tourist town of Wisconsin Dells was lacking in such a museum, he carted his stuff to town. The museum opened in 1999 and will be moving to a larger space at the end of 2002.

Wax figures performing an alien autopsy at the American UFO and Sci-Fi Museum, Wisconsin Dells

"We have a passion for this kind of stuff, to put it lightly," says the museum's manager David Hankey about the *Star Trek* paraphernalia and wax aliens. Hankey gravitated toward the museum because of his interest in UFOs. Feel free to talk with him about UFO sightings and check the map of these sightings in Wisconsin to see if you live near any of them. If you're looking for information on the Roswell incident—which was when a flying saucer reportedly crashed in New Mexico—the museum houses videotaped interviews and plenty of newspaper clippings that date back to the 1940s, when the crash supposedly occurred. (Hankey's belief is that the incident was indeed a UFO crash, but his bias is not apparent in the exhibit.) You also can read about crop circles and natural phenomena like the northern lights. And check out sci-fi movie ticket stubs and many autographed pictures of sci-fi actors.

740 Eddy Street, Wisconsin Dells
(608) 253-5055
www.ufomuseum.com
The museum will be moving to a larger exhibit space at the end of 2002, but the phone number will remain the same. Open daily Memorial Day through Labor Day from 9 a.m. to 9 p.m.; weekends only in April, May, September, and October. Admission charged

---

Some Wisconsin Firsts and Facts

- The **first successful kidney removal** in the world was performed in Milwaukee. The operation was performed by Dr. Erastus Wolcott in 1861.

- Margarethe Schurz started the **first kindergarten** in Watertown in 1856.

- The **first practical typewriter** was designed by Christopher Latham Sholes in Milwaukee in 1867.

- The **first ice cream sundae**—vanilla with chocolate syrup—was served at Ed Berner's soda fountain in Two Rivers in 1878.

- The **first electric trolley** ran in Appleton in 1886.

- The **first Ringling Brothers circus** was staged in Baraboo in 1884.

- Although Jackson, Michigan, may dispute Ripon's claim to fame, you can tour a schoolhouse in Ripon where the **Republican Party** reportedly was founded in 1854. The Little White Schoolhouse is located on Blackbourn Street (look for the signs) in downtown Ripon. For more information, call (920) 748-4730 or 748-6764.

- Ninety-five percent of the **ginseng** produced in the United States is grown in Wisconsin. It has been harvested primarily in the Wausau area for the past one hundred years.

- **Jim the Groundhog**, spring weather prognosticator for Wisconsin, lives in Sun Prairie.

- The Elm Farm Ollie Fan Club celebrates the **first flight of a cow** in an airplane. During the St. Louis International Air Exposition, on February 18, 1930, some intrepid souls milked Ollie in the plane and parachuted down bottles of her milk.

Deke Slayton Memorial Space and Bike Museum

Sparta

Although Sparta is a small town of about 8,000 people, it has its very own museum complex, which is located in a former Masonic Temple that dates back to the 1920s. The temple's first floor is packed with Monroe County history and the second floor manages to pay homage to two of Sparta's loves. The Deke Slayton Memorial Space and Bike Museum, started in 1999 by Slayton fans and bike enthusiasts, plugs the town's favorite pastime, bicycling, and the town's favorite son, astronaut Donald "Deke" Slayton.

Start your visit to the museum by "meeting" Donald Kent Slayton and reading about his childhood in western Wisconsin. Author Tom Wolfe portrayed the astronaut as a proud, tough, honest man of integrity in *The Right Stuff*, Wolfe's story about America's first astronauts. Sparta's museum characterizes Slayton in a similar vein—as a courageous, all-American, go-after-your-dreams type of guy. Though he excelled during astronaut training, Slayton was often passed over for many of the early flying missions because of a rare heart condition. But his motto was "Decide what you want to do, then never give up until you've done it." Slayton was determined to fly in space. Finally, in 1975, as part of the first cooperative space mission with Russia, known as the Apollo Soyez Test Project, his dream came true. It was the only time he'd reach outer space.

Born and raised in Monroe County, Donald Slayton (he didn't become known as Deke until he was in the service) signed up with the U.S. Army Air Corps one month after he turned 18 years old. (See high school photos of the grinning optimist in the display cases.) While in the air corps he learned how to fly a plane despite not having his left ring finger, which he had lost in a farm mishap. During World War II, Slayton flew in 56 combat missions in Europe. After returning to the United States, with flying still on his mind, he went on to earn a degree in aeronautical engineering from the University of Minnesota.

After being selected as a Mercury astronaut (his Mercury space suit, looking like it weighs 100 pounds, is on view), Slayton became actively involved in the nation's space program. He acted as chief astronaut and was in charge of crew assignments on *Apollo 11* and *Apollo 13*—notice Slayton's flight checklist books such as the ASTP rendezvous and docking checklist. Throughout his years of service, he received many awards, proclamations, and letters from presidents ranging from Nixon to Reagan, thanking him for his service. Many of these awards and letters are on view in the museum. Take some time to read over newspaper articles recounting the astronaut's training and various space missions on which he was involved. There's also an article about Slayton's friend and fellow Mercury astronaut Gus Grissom, who died during a training exercise.

Slayton passed away in 1993 at age 69, six years before the museum opened. His brother still lives in the area and usually drives the float carrying the life-size statue of Deke (in his astronaut suit) for the annual Butter Fest parade.

Kids should get a kick out of the museum's spaceshiplike playroom complete with puzzles and videos about space missions. And don't miss the Apollo "space couch," an uncomfortable-looking astronaut seat, on loan from NASA.

Since Sparta is known as the bicycling capital of America, it is only natural that staff devotes the other half of the museum to bicycles. Stroll, drive, or pedal through town and you will at some point pass a professional bicyclist donned in neon state-of-the-art road gear or a group of six year olds with bikes outfitted with ribbons and bells. Sparta loves to play up its connection to bicycling (a number of bike trails intersect in Sparta). Just take a look at Ben Biken, reportedly the world's largest bicycle, at the corner of Wisconsin and Water Streets.

The bike museum chronicles the evolution of the bicycle, starting from a Boneshaker replica built by local high school students to a human-powered racing recumbent. Begin your tour by checking out the replica of the Draisine Boneshaker, thought to be the first bicycle ever built. Inventor Baron Karl Drais von Sauerbronn called his apparatus a hobby horse or swiftwalker. Visitors walk around the perimeter of the museum and follow major developments in the history of the bicycle. There are high wheelers or velocipides (usually only seen at carnivals or ridden by Shriners at parades); practical bicycles such as cargo cycles found at factories and shipyards, some

Deke Slayton Memorial Space and Bike Museum, Sparta

used to transport 200 to 750 pounds of items; and a 1930 delivery bike with wooden rims. (Did you know the UPS, or the United Parcel Service, started delivering packages via bicycles in 1907?) Have a look at antique bicycle accessories like kerosene lanterns that were strapped to the bike and used as headlights, old bicycle license plates, and advertisements for bike brakes.

Some bikes might induce a chuckle—such as the popular Famolares from the 1970s, banana-seat bikes from the 1980s, and Ole Red, a bike belonging to Dan Castellaneta, the voice of television cartoon dad Homer Simpson. Other bikes might make you say, "Huh?" such as an ice bicycle with studded tires developed in Hungary. And some bikes might inspire you, such as a racing and touring bicycle ridden by Sparta resident and bike shop owner Olga McAnulty, the woman to first finish the Alaskan Iditasport in 1994. (McAnulty biked 200 miles in 60 hours and four minutes in −20-degree-Fahrenheit temperatures and 50-mile-per-hour winds!) The staff also has included a small exhibit on Wilbur and Orville Wright, who built bicycles before airplanes.

200 West Main Street, Sparta
(888) 200-5302
www.spartan.org/dekeslaytonmuseum/
Open mid-April to mid-October, Monday through Saturday from 10 a.m. to 4:30 p.m.; mid-October to mid-April, Monday through Friday from 10 a.m. to 4:30 p.m., and the second Saturday of each month from 10 a.m. to 2 p.m.
Admission charged

While in the Area
Take a Side Trip from Sparta

- Want to tour the Sparta area via bike or kayak? Tag along with Olga McAnulty, the Iditasport champ, or Tom McAnulty at **Outspokin Adventures** for a tour of a cranberry bog, an Amish settlement, or many other places. For more information, call (608) 372-0777 or visit the Web site at www.outspokinadventures.com.

- Ever wonder where those giant fiberglass cows, Big Boys, and water slides come from? For some kicks, wander through the backyard of **F.A.S.T. (Fiberglass Animals Shapes and Trademarks) Corporation**, located on the outskirts of Sparta on Highway 21. See hundreds of molds including a frog, hippo, and gladiator. For more information, call (608) 269-7110.

Plastic molds for various figures at the F.A.S.T. Corporation, Sparta

12 Elmer's Auto and Toy Museum
Fountain City

The Midwest boasts many antique automotive museums (especially in Indiana, see sidebar on page 115), and if you happen to be driving through Fountain City on a late, hot Friday afternoon in the summer you may consider skipping Elmer's Auto and Toy Museum. After all, you have to chug up a pretty big hill and drive along a few rural roads in order to get there. But know this: As you drive up Eagle Bluff toward the sprawling museum that Elmer and Bernadette Duellman have set up on an old farm homestead, a spectacular view of the river valley below awaits you.

The best way to get to Elmer's is to head northwest from Fountain City on Highway 95 and County 6, take a left onto Elmer's Road, and another left onto the driveway named "Bernadette's Road." (Yes, the streets are named after the Duellmans; they've been a part of the community for a while.) You'll pass Elmer's Salvage (with about 9,000 to 10,000 cars, it's one of the largest in the Midwest) and you'll notice that some of it has spilled over onto the museum campus—and some of the museum has spilled over to the salvage company. (Do you see the old bookmobiles and a school bus stuffed with antique pedal cars?)

Inside Elmer's Museum, Fountain City

The Duellman's collection of basically everything that has wheels is something else. The museum consists of five buildings (and these are not small buildings—these are barns that formerly housed hundreds of cattle and hundreds of hay bales) that contain antique cars, motorcycles, pedal cars, toys, toys, and toys. If you're lucky, the Duellmans may even invite you into their home to see the 1929 Model A Ford Phaeton inside their living room, the doll collection, and bald eagle that was stuffed more than 100 years ago.

Married in 1962, Elmer and Bernadette have been seriously collecting for about 35 years. As of the summer of

While in the Area
See the Sights of Fountain City

When Fountain City was founded in the mid-1800s it was primarily a German settlement. While trading and farming in the area, residents discovered an abundance of spring water, which they didn't let go to waste, and breweries sprung up; about 100 years ago the town had six of them. Unfortunately none of them still exist, but you can see bottles of the beers that were brewed in town and other local artifacts at the **Fountain City Historical Museum.** A highlight is its impressive arrowhead collection. Local hardware-store owner Roscoe Stoll received many of these arrowheads from farmers who found them while working the land. Many passed them on to Stoll, who in turn donated his pieces to the museum. The collection contains about 1,700 Indian artifacts dating from thousands of years to 100 years ago. Located on the first block of Main Street in Fountain City. For hours and more information, call (608) 687-7541.

The house at 440 North Shore Drive (look for signs along Highway 35) has a dodgy history. In 1901 a boulder tumbled from the bluff above, crashed into the house, and killed Elizabeth Tobler. In 1995 a 55-ton boulder somersaulted into the house. No one was injured in 1995, but the newly remodeled house was damaged. If you'd like to stop by the **Rock in the House,** call (608) 687-3553.

2001, their collection contained 100 cars, 500 pedal cars, and thousands of toys. Elmer started the salvage business in 1962 and Fountain City's Conoco station and a used-car company in subsequent years. The museum opened to the public in the early 1990s.

Visitors, who tend to be car aficionados, often repeatedly exclaim, "Cool! Wow! Amazing!" and utter, "This is the collection of one couple?" as they meander around the museum. Sometimes it hits Bernadette how vast she and her husband's collection is—usually when she's dusting the minicars and signs. And it's not uncommon for her to discover something—a Rolls Royce, for example—that wasn't there a few weeks ago. Just a little something Elmer picked up at an auction.

"He's loved wheels all his life," Bernadette grins as she eyes a line of race flags in one barn. Elmer and Bernadette met, surprise, surprise, during a car race. And one of their favorite cars in the museum is a 1958 Chevy that Elmer used to drag race. When they met, he was drag racing with the Chevy. He eventually sold it, kept track of the owners, and years later found himself buying it back again.

The three warehouse buildings contain muscle cars (for example, a 1969 Dodge Charger Daytona with 304 miles), luxury cars (a 1946 V12 Lincoln

Continental), antique cars (1932 Ford Model B), whimsical cars (a Dodge Fantasy van made from seven vans and a motorhome), thrifty cars (a two-cylinder 1972 Honda that gets 54 mpg owned by former Nascar driver Marvin Panch), and vintage and modern motorcycles, wagons, and carriages such as a mail carriage. Notice the signs: "Don't touch me. I'm not that kind of car!" and "'61 Pontiac–Sharp!"

One barn contains 1930s-era midget racers and pedal airplanes dating from 1913 through the 1940s including a Lindbergh doll with the *Spirit of St. Louis* pedal plane. And remember those green and white G-man cruisers with toy machine guns mounted on the front? What about Red Racer wagons and sleds? Elmer has restored many of these toys, though some remain in the condition in which he found them. Another building is full of Japanese tin cars and an entire wall of shelves is stocked with mini-Greyhound buses. Other amusing miscellany items include a dogsled built by the Duellman's sons while they were Boy Scouts, an ice cream truck that plays Bruce Springsteen, and a vintage car carousel Elmer purchased a number of years ago that is reminiscent of a 1950s-era theme park. Don't miss the 1936 Ford Windshield that was lying on a workbench for a while, had oil spilled on it, and leaked into the cracks of the broken Safe-T-plate glass inside. Voilà! Three-dimensional oil art.

For those of you who are toy collectors, Elmer has written a price guide to antique toys for sale. Pick up a copy at the museum.

W903 Elmer's Road, Fountain City
(608) 687-7221
Open two weekends a month from May to October, from 9 a.m. to 5 p.m. Call to check dates. Special arrangements can be made.
Admission charged

13 | Prairie Moon Sculpture Garden and Museum
Fountain City

Heed the advice of a man that lived to be 100 years old: Do not always sit in the shade. Get a hobby. And don't be afraid to start a new hobby late in life, say, in your 70s. Herman Rusch's hobby happened to be collecting antiques and building cement sculptures. You can read Rusch's hand-written treatise on "how to live a long and youthful life"—which includes his advice to "get a hobby," "like people," and "be friendly"—at the Prairie Moon Museum, located in a former dance hall abutting the Mississippi River.

Rusch was a farmer, collector, fiddler, sculptor, and ruminator. He was a man who embraced life, spoke his mind, and when he saw something beautiful, by golly, he snatched it up and put it in his museum. While out for walks in the Fountain City area, he picked up many natural sculpture, particularly trees and vines that grew and wound around one another. "See how they get along? Why can't people be like that?" Rusch mused on a piece of paper placed in front of two vines woven together. These vines are on view inside the museum, along with a few of his other writings, portraits, and collectibles.

Born in 1885 in northwestern Wisconsin, Rusch grew up farming on his parents' farm. Eventually he and his wife took it over. But he was not a hermit.

Prairie Moon Sculpture Garden and Museum, Fountain City

Like What You See?
Outsider Art

Outsider art, art practiced by people who didn't go to art school and who worked in other professions, is prevalent throughout the Midwest, particularly in Wisconsin. Here are a few folk-art sites to stop by on your travels through the Dairy State.

Scrap-metal sculptures at Forevermore, Baraboo

- **Forevermore**, a gargantuan scrap-metal sculpture garden described as "home, a piece of heaven" by Eleanor Every, wife of salvager sculptor Dr. Evermore, is located just off Highway 12, opposite the Badger Army Ammunitions Plant, a few miles south of Baraboo. No phone.

- "Few things in life are done just for the joy of doing them . . . Welcome to **Gloria Hills**,"reads the sign welcoming visitors to a sculpture park in Green Lake. Fred Schwartz, another obsolescence junkie, opens his Gloria Hills sculpture park to visitors by appointment only. (Although you can drive by and get a good look at it from the road.) Situated on rolling green acres at County A and County K in Green Lake, the park contains fish and animal-like creatures as well as cars posing as works of art. To arrange a tour, call (920) 748-3720.

- Fred Smith is no longer alive, but his **Concrete World** is still kicking thanks to the many area friends who have volunteered to trim the grounds and keep the hundreds of concrete creatures and their keepers clean. Like the Prairie Moon project, Smith's Concrete World was a Kohler Foundation project. Concrete World is located off Highway 13 in Phillips. For more information, call (800) 269-4505.

- The Midwest is home to many grottos, but not many can impress like the **Dickeyville Grotto**, the work of Father Matthias Wernerus. Built in five years, the grotto, gardens, and shrines were made with petrified wood, glass, stalagmites, rock crystals, and more seashells than you can collect in a summer. The grotto is located on the grounds of Holy Ghost Parish on Highway 61 in Dickeyville. For more information, call (608) 568-3119.

- German immigrant Ernest Hupedon was a self-taught artist who painted houses and anything he could get his hands on in return for food and lodging. One of his projects was painting woodland scenes for the Modern Woodmen of America's hall in Valton, a small community west of the Wisconsin Dells. The hall has been turned into a museum now called **Painted Forest**; it houses a few of Hupedon's paintings on bottles and plates and mementos from the MWA, a fraternal insurance group. For directions and more information, call (608) 983-2352.

- Also see **Rudy Rotter's Museum of Sculpture** on page 50.

Rusch frequently played his fiddle at local fairs and was often seen about town. In the 1950s, after farming for more than 40 years, he decided to give sculpture a go. He had no experience and wasn't exactly a young buck. (He was 73 years old.) Still, Rusch rented and eventually purchased the former Prairie Moon dance pavilion and stocked it with his original creations as well as things—fossils, antique tools, wagon wheels—that struck him as interesting.

To beautify the place, he constructed concrete planters and a nearly 300-foot-long concrete fence, accented with little jewel-like scraps that stuck his fancy—bottle caps, glass shards, shells, you name it. He dipped his paintbrush in buckets of dazzling gold and red paint, further accenting the structures. Over the years he built a watchtower, a rocket to the stars, or "sunspire," and many other curious items. He also purchased some sculpture for his backyard, such as one of a Norwegian hunter fighting a bear and an Indian on a horse, from Howard Landsverk. Feel free to stroll around the garden for as long as you like. Luckily, most of Rusch's original sculpture still remain on the grounds.

Local students plant flowers every year and volunteers touch up any chipping paint or replace any stones that may have fallen off.

"Beauty creates the will to live," was Rusch's response to folks asking about why he created the garden and museum. It wasn't a very practical place, after all, and it was no longer a dance hall. Just a pretty place for people driving along the Great River Road to stop at, stroll around with their necks craned and eyes shimmery from the topaz-coated birdbath at sunset. Constructing sparkly sculptures that pointed to the sky and collecting farm machinery was also a good way to kill old-age boredom, Rusch told the many visitors, reporters, and fellow artists of his project. Eventually attracting the attention of gallery curators, his work was shown in a Minneapolis art museum in 1974. As he spent more and more time at the museum, Rusch moved a trailer to the site and lived there, in full view of the brassy prairie moon painted on the south side of the museum. By the time he reached 89 years old, he had more than 40 pieces of sculpture arranged in the museum and its backyard.

In 1979 Herman decided he wanted to spend more time fishing and sitting in the sun. He auctioned off most of his antiques and a few of his sculpture. He died in 1985, shortly after his 100th birthday.

In the 1980s the property's new owners used the dance hall as a dog kennel, which, needless to say, didn't exactly make the place as welcoming as it was in Rusch's day. But in 1992 the Kohler Foundation, a Wisconsin organization that works to preserve and promote "outsider art" such as Rusch's, purchased the museum and restored the pavilion to the way he'd had it. The organization cleaned and retouched the remaining statues and donated it to the township of Milton in 1994.

The dance hall, once filled with Rusch's creations and antiques, now contains a few local artifacts, such as an antique fire hose, and some found-object sculptures created by area artists. One room, designed by the foundation and looking very much like a professional gallery—with stained hardwood floors and artistic lighting—contains photographs of Rusch and a few of his collectibles, like the vines, that he didn't auction off. His writings and a few newspaper clippings about himself and the museum have been framed, and family mementos like his wife's wedding dress have been placed in glass display cases.

Located off Highway 35 (look for the signs), halfway between Cochrane and Fountain City
(608) 687-8323 or (608) 687-9874
The gardens are always open; the museum is open most days and evenings. Call ahead and volunteers will meet you to take you through the museum. Donation suggested

14 | Woodcarving Museum
Shell Lake

The story of Christianity, told in ponderosa and sugar pine, unfolds for visitors in a roadside museum in Shell Lake, Wisconsin. Beyond a museum rope, a wooden apple dangles from the mouth of the devil (posing as a snake) before Adam and Eve. Take a few steps, fast-forward a few millennia, and there are Mary and Joseph trekking to Bethlehem, taking refuge in a barn. Farther along your museum stroll, Jesus preaches in the temple, and there he is again, spreading out a meal of bread and wine for his friends. Turn around and Judas is suspended from a noose, Jesus nailed to the cross, and Jesus resurrected. For visitors unfamiliar with Old and New Testament stories, carver Joseph Barta chiseled out explanations in wooden stands such as, "Job was sick, covered with sores, but determined to follow God's will and recovered, prosperous as ever."

Joseph Barta was a man devoted to Christianity and to wood. Working for a period of roughly 30 years, he built up the largest collection of wood carvings done by one man: 100 life-size carved wood figures and more than 400 miniature animals and figurines, according to Barta's niece-in-law Maria McKay, the museum's owner. Before working on the life-size religious carvings, Barta was a high school teacher who spent his free time chiseling out hundreds of miniature animals and figurines.

A wall of display cases features these minianimals, including monkeys lined up in *National Geographic* style to show man's evolution. Look closely and you'll notice some carvings are silly: There's a monkey smoking a pipe and reading a book, a monkey with a bow and arrow, and a monkey striking karate poses. In another case white-tailed deer leap, sniff the air, and nibble grass. With these figures, Barta was learning how to carve body movement and expressions—and he was just having fun. Notice the ample women in bikinis brushing their hair.

For his life-size statues he had ponderosa and sugar pine shipped in from the Northwest, all two-by-fours, and was careful to remove any knots that would have created holes in the statues.

Barta's most celebrated piece is the Last Supper, which called for more than 25,000 pieces of wood. Leonardo da Vinci's *Last Supper* painting is flaking in Milan, but Barta's Last Supper rendition will last for many, many years to come, thanks to that hardy wood, McKay says. He spent four and a half years carving The Last Supper, with two of those years devoted to Jesus's face. "How do you show the expression of love, sorrow, forgiveness, and betrayal?" McKay ponders. Indeed, all of the figures have different expressions on their faces. For example, a pregnant Mary on the donkey has a strained look about her and a postbirth Mary has a peaceful expression. And the details are just amazing: lifelike toenails on the people and textured coats of fur on the animals.

Before he became a North Woods carver, Barta was an athletic guy who grew up in Algonquin, Illinois. He went off to the University of Illinois, played baseball, and coached for a little while. Eventually he headed to Spooner, Wisconsin, in the 1940s to teach math and physical education. During the evenings and weekends, Barta started fiddling with wood and took quite a liking to it. In 1951 he quit teaching and began devoting more time to wood carving. He built a workshop and spent the rest of his days carving away, moving from miniatures to life-size figures of Jesus, Mary, and Joseph. Eventually he opened his own museum in Spooner, beckoning travelers heading up north to see the "story of Christianity told in wood."

He ran the workshop and the museum until his death in 1972 at age 68. Barta never married and his nephew Andrew McKay, and McKay's wife, Maria, took over. For a while in the early 1980s, the McKays relocated the museum to Florida only to bring it back to the more appropriate North Woods. In 1989 they built the current building in Shell Lake and have been open every spring and summer since.

539 Highway 63, Shell Lake
(715) 468-7100
Open daily May 1 through October 30 from 9 a.m. to 6 p.m.
Admission charged

Like What You See?
Carving 'em Up

• Wood-carvers passing through Chicago suburbs should stop by the **Midwest Carver's Museum** in South Holland, Illinois, to muse over the more than one thousand carvings by local and international artists. For more information, call (708) 331-6011.

• Ah. The life of a North Woodsman. Get a glimpse of it at **Carl's Wood Art Museum** located at 1230 Sundstein Road in Eagle River, Wisconsin. Attractions include a replica of a trapper's cabin, wood carvings of a 14-foot grizzly bear, giant chair, cowboy boots, and numerous other sculptures. For more information, call (715) 479-1883 or visit www.carlswoodart.com.

• The **Carmelite Visitors Center** in Darien, Illinois, has reportedly one of the country's largest religious wood carvings: a statue of St. Theresa. You can see her daily year-round from 10 a.m. to 4 p.m. The center is located at 8501 Bailey Road. A donation is suggested. For more information, call (630) 969-3311 or visit www.saint-therese.org.

• For 32 years Don Becker has been whittling a variety of creations from a 10-foot history clock to the Apostles. See his collection at the **Becker Woodcarving Museum**, located at 15426 Becker Lane (just off Highway 136), a few miles northeast of Dyersville, Iowa. The museum is open from Memorial Day through Labor Day, Monday through Friday from 9 a.m. to 5 p.m. An admission fee is charged. For more information, call (563) 875-2087.

• See page 72 for the story behind **Slim Marroushek's Woodcarving Museum** in Harmony, Minnesota.

15 National Freshwater Fishing Hall of Fame and Museum
Hayward

Everyone's got a story to tell about "the big one" caught, say, at 5 a.m. while fishing on a remote lake, miles from anyone who could verify the fact that it was a 100-pound muskie. Some of the fisherman's more gullible friends may believe the story, but there's no fooling the folks at the National Freshwater Fishing Hall of Fame and Museum who painstakingly verify every alleged world's largest fish capture. For about 40 years the Hayward-based organization has acted as a hub for freshwater fishing industry news, facts, history, and fun. Perhaps it is most famous for the four-and-a-half-story-high leaping (or appearing to leap) muskie.

Go ahead and have a photo taken of you standing below its gills or in its mouth. The 143½-foot-long muskie, made of concrete, steel, and fiberglass, is not that tough to climb; there are many photos to stop and look at while you ascend the stairs. Unlike many of the world's largest something or other, the big muskie and the museum buildings on the six acres below can occupy anglers, or anyone interested in the sport's history, for hours. After you have mounted the muskie, take your pick of five museum buildings and behold 450 antique outboard motors, 400 fish mounts, hundreds of rods, reels, lures, and photos of world-record fish catches.

A giant muskie welcomes visitors to the National Freshwater Fishing Hall of Fame and Museum, Hayward

The main hall of fame room contains biographical displays about the inductees (more on them in a bit). However, it's the looming mannequins of father and son Sasquatches—both badly in need of a body shave—that grab the attention of visitors. The fabricated Sasquatches are some examples of the many random, amusing features in the museum. After admiring the big guys' hairiness, step back and check out the tons of mounted world-record fish: a hybrid muskie weighing 51 pounds, 3 ounces, caught in 1919 in Lac Vieux Desert; a 22-pound, 4-ounce, 32½-inch-long largemouth bass caught in Montgomery, Alabama in 1932; the world's largest brown trout and largest walleye, among many others. Most of these fish are more than 50 years old, but still look shiny and tough. Ah, the wonders of taxidermy.

On to the inductees. The first ones: Dame Juliana Berners, an English nun (yes, not only a woman, but a nun) who was credited with writing the first treatise on angling in 1496; Isaak Walton, who wrote *The Complete Angler* in the 1600s; and Ole Evinrude, who produced the first marketable outboard motor in 1905 (many of his motors are on display at the museum). Other hall of fame members include legendary anglers, industry experts, and outdoor writers.

Continue on and read about the history and techniques of fly-fishing, pass by a birch-bark canoe from the 1860s, rows of spears and decoys from the 1920s, and Great Lakes fishing gear from the 1900s. Numerous display cases are stocked with antique bait holders, tackle boxes, glass minnow traps from the 1890s to 1900s, a hand spring gaff from the 1950s, fish and depth finders from the 1960s, lures, lures, and lures. You'll pass by a motor graveyard and a replica of an ice-fishing shack. And most likely you'll chuckle or groan at the occasional fishing cartoon posted on the walls: "Fishtalk: 'Benearlong?' 'Couplour.' 'Ketchaneny?' 'Goddafew.' "

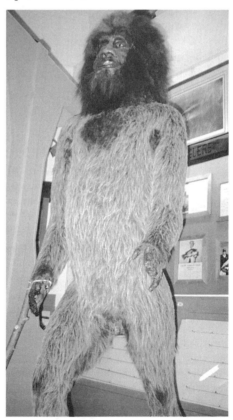

One of the Sasquatches on display at the National Freshwater Fishing Hall of Fame and Museum

This entertaining and comprehensive museum got its start when local resort owners Bob and Fannie Jutz, both fishermen, spent their winters traveling around the United States and visiting other halls of fame—basketball, hockey, you name it. They asked their friends, "Wouldn't it be great if there was a hall of fame to honor the sport of fishing?" Hayward was a logical place since many of the world record muskies were caught in the area. After convincing people it was a good thing, a group of hall of fame supporters formed a nonprofit in 1970 with the sole purpose of collecting, preserving, and displaying artifacts associated with freshwater angling. They commissioned the huge muskellunge and it opened in 1976.

"I never thought it'd be this big," Fannie Jutz says, literally of the giant muskie and the fact that thousands of people visit the museum grounds every year. "It's done a lot for Hayward and I think the muskie is a big drawing point for people." And that giant muskie is looking pretty good for being more than 25 years old. It just needs to be washed occasionally and glazed every two years, Fannie points out.

The grounds surrounding the hall of fame contain a number of fiberglass fish (in addition to the big boy muskie), and trees and shrubbery dedicated to fishermen by their families. The staff also has placed a variety of fish cribs around the grounds. These contraptions made of wood and debris are placed on the bottom of a lake to attract panfish, which ultimately attract larger fish.

Fishermen should be prepared to spend a lot of time at this museum. Don't head to the Cineplex on your next rainy day Up North. Instead, spend hours inspecting old jigs. Visitors with an average interest in fishing and fishing history have been known to spend more than an hour and a half on the museum grounds. More than 70,000 people visit every summer, most of them coming by the busload in June, July, and August. Try stopping by in May or September to avoid the crowds.

Want to see more fishing paraphernalia? Try the Minnesota Fishing Hall of Fame in Walker, Minnesota, where you'll find more lures, motors, and rods to admire. Kids can cast a line for free into the pond. For more information, call (218) 347-2000.

10360 Hall of Fame Drive (Highway 27 and County B), Hayward
(715) 634-4440
www.freshwaterfishing.org
Open daily April 15 to November from 10 a.m. to 5 p.m.
Admission charged

16 Wildlife Museum and Moccasin Bar
Hayward

Only in Wisconsin can you find a museum of stuffed animals attached to a full-service bar. Simply called Wildlife Museum, this collection of everything from a stuffed grackle to a grizzly bear arguably represents the best in taxidermy displays. Some may say the mounted beasts at Bernie Towrek's Wildlife Museum are just as cool as the ones in the Field Museum of Natural History in Chicago.

When you enter the museum from the bar you will first walk through the muskie hall of fame, which includes about 70 muskies displayed in tanklike cases. There are a few reproductions of huge fish caught, but not mounted, years ago. (They're not real, but they are certainly awesome to look at.) For example, Towrek has a reproduction of a 72-inch muskie weighing 105 pounds with a girth of 34 inches that was found dead in the Chippewa Flowage. And have a look at the world-record muskie bait—a catfish—that for some people actually is the largest fish they have ever caught. Nuzzle up to black bears, brown bears, grizzly bears, and a polar bear. Get up close to birds like the horned grebe, crow, purple grackle, and puffin. Antler animals like the caribou, moose, mule deer, and white-tailed deer also are well represented here.

Many of the animals in the museum were mounted decades ago, and in some cases, more than 100 years ago. There are snow, shore, and songbirds mounted in 1886 and a baby harp seal mounted in 1927. Although some of the animals, like the Alaskan moose shot by a man from Pardeeville, Wisconsin, met their match by hunters, most of them were killed while trying to cross highways.

Surprisingly, Towrek is not a hunter, but a fisherman. (But he's been so busy with his bar and museum he doesn't spend as much time fishing as he'd like.)

Wildlife Museum and Moccasin Bar, Hayward

He has been collecting since the late 1970s, scouring flea markets and shops and buying out other small museums or shops in Wisconsin and Minnesota. Many times he acquires his pieces by word of mouth.

"Folks usually retire and don't want their pieces anymore," he says. "Many of them will come into the bar and say to me, 'You know, I have this albino deer in my basement that I'm looking to get rid of.'"

There are plenty of rarities in the museum: an albino display case with an albino deer, peacock, mink, fox, pheasant, and skunk. An arctic snowy owl that was confiscated in 1930 has its ticket "$200 fine for removing this tag" still attached to it. Next to him perches a golden eagle with a similar tag from the 1920s. Ever seen a passenger pigeon? They were declared extinct in 1914 when the last one died in the Cincinnati Zoo. Towrek has a bona fide one on display.

Each time you think the museum exhibit is over you turn a corner and there's more to see. Many of the animals are poised in action: a bobcat chomping into a rabbit, a mountain lion snapping the neck of a mule deer (a display that garnered first prize in a national taxidermy show in 1992). See beavers at work on a fort, a fox with pups, and a deer with fawns.

Throughout the museum, elevator music chimes cheerily and water trickles from the faux stream where two fishermen mannequins have landed a fish. Towrek has constructed a desert scene complete with snake skins lying in the sand, turtles appearing to crawl into the stream, and squirrels gathering nuts. A local artist has painted wildlife murals along some of the walls. All in all, the collection contains about 400 pieces, including the 70 muskies. A taxidermist estimates the collection's worth at $1 million, although Towrek says he hasn't spent that much on the pieces.

Towrek also operates the Moccasin Bar, located at the northwest corner of Highways 27 and 63. The Wildlife Museum charges admission and is located separately from the bar but in the Moccasin you can throw back a bottle of Leinenkugel's beer and take a stroll around the bar to look at their decorations for free. The best decoration? The world's record mounted muskie—a 67½-pound, 60½-inch-long monstrosity caught in Lake Couderay in 1949. The Moccasin Bar has been around since 1900; Towrek purchased it in 1978 when he first started collecting. The Wildlife Museum opened in 1993.

15708 County B, Hayward
(715) 634-3386
Open daily year-round, from 9 a.m. until the bar closes, usually around midnight. If you've had too many drinks and are acting unruly, you won't be allowed into the museum.
Admission charged

17 | Peshtigo Fire Museum
Peshtigo

On October 8, 1871, Mrs. O'Leary's cow allegedly kicked over a lamp in her backyard barn in Chicago, setting her neighborhood and most of the city ablaze. It was a fire that would last more than three days and eventually destroyed 250 lives and four square miles of the city. Newspapers around the world carried news of the Chicago catastrophe, but not as much attention was paid to a blaze about 250 miles north of Chicago in the logging town of Peshtigo, Wisconsin, even though the Peshtigo fire claimed more lives and about $5 million in property damages.

While Chicago does not have a museum about its great fire, (although a group of residents has been lobbying for many years to start one) the little town of Peshtigo does; it is housed in the first church built in Peshtigo after the great fire. Not much was saved from the blaze, but what items the museum does have on display are quite interesting. Gape at the can of blueberries (though you'd never recognize it as such) that exploded, melted, and petrified. And see a melted dime saved by the family who owned the general store in Peshtigo at the time of the fire. Another piece that survived the fire is a white wooden tabernacle found downriver from Peshtigo. Father Joseph Perrin, a Catholic priest in town at the time, grabbed the tabernacle during the fire and slid it into the river, hoping to save it. It was found a few days later, reportedly bright white and not a bit of it charred.

"We have a nice museum but you can't expect to see a lot from the fire. Remember, the fire reduced the town to ashes," longtime museum volunteer Bob Couvillion reminds visitors.

In the 1860s and 1870s Peshtigo was a booming logging town like many other towns in the North Woods. It had a population of 1,700 people, most of whom had recently settled there to work in the sawmill as lumberjacks, farmers, or merchants. The spring and summer of 1871 were hot and dry, with river and stream levels dipping, wells drying out, and brush fires occasionally breaking out throughout northeastern Wisconsin and Michigan's Upper Peninsula.

During the day of October 8, another brush fire broke outside of town, winds kicked up out of the southwest and ashes reportedly flew into town like snowflakes. Eventually the winds died down and in the afternoon and early evening, winds were calm—eerily calm, according to some reports. Later in the evening, around 8 p.m., gusty winds kicked up again, this time much stronger, bringing in black clouds above town. The flames came quickly and flattened the town swiftly. Families dived into the Peshtigo River for safety, but the flames leaped across the river and people had to continue ducking under water. Many died of heart attacks while running for their lives. The fire died down before dawn, but when survivors crawled out from the river, there was little food, clothes, or shelter awaiting them. A thief was caught stealing from corpses, found guilty and condemned to die, but the town had no rope; all of it had burned in the fire.

Just about everything was demolished. Browse through postfire photos in the Peshtigo Fire Museum and you'll see crusty tree stumps and crumbled smokestacks. A stunning mural in the fire museum depicts the hours before the fire (with churchgoers clasping Bibles and glancing at the red sun), the hours during the fire (with a woman grabbing onto the horns of a bull in the river), and the morning after (with people stumbling onto the banks clutching corpses).

Mural in the Peshtigo Fire Museum, Peshtigo

After the fire survivors were faced with a long, cold Wisconsin winter with no clothing, employment, or shelter. But the outpouring of relief and funds was tremendous, Couvillion says. Help came from as far away as Russia. And the Peshtigo sawmill located eight miles south of town worked day and night to build shelters.

Like What You See? Fire It Up

In the **Hinckley Fire Museum**, Minnesota remembers an 1894 forest fire that wiped out nine towns in the east central part of the state. The museum is located at 106 Old Highway 61 in Hinckley. For more information, call (320) 384-7338.

A number of boards in the museum feature photos of the class of 1896, photos of the town in 1871, and photos of the rebuilt town in the early 1900s. Newspaper articles explain how the local history museum got started and describe the anniversaries and memorials held in remembrance of the great fire. A few of the articles chronicle the life stories of some survivors. For example, Augusta Bruce was two years old when she and her family got caught in the fire just outside of town. She died in 1973 at 104 years old. One baby, whose scalp was scorched and who would never grow hair, was found alone by the side of the river and ended up being raised by a childless couple.

Other fire-related items include a trunk that a family buried in the ground of their orchard, a piece of a two-by-four taken from the only home that survived the fire, a teapot, butter dish, and pie plate salvaged from the fire and a Bible found floating in the river. A charred Bible, open to the book of Psalms, was found buried beneath a parking lot in the 1990s.

Most of the museum contains household and farm items from postfire Peshtigo. Turn-of-the-century rooms—a bedroom, kitchen, and schoolroom—are reproduced and stocked with antiques such as women's beaded purses, ornate belt buckles, furs, and gloves.

After you visit the museum head to the cemetery located across the street from the church. Residents have erected a memorial to those who died in the blaze.

400 Octonto Avenue, Peshtigo
(715) 582-3244
www.peshtigochamber.com
Open daily Memorial Day weekend through early October from 9 a.m.
to 4:30 p.m.
Donation suggested

18 | Hamburger Museum and Hall of Fame
Seymour

Did you catch a glimpse of Seymour residents on the CBS morning show in the early 1990s? They were the ones belting out "Oh What a Beautiful Morning" on a Saturday morning in August. Throngs of them had gathered to celebrate the mighty burger and their favorite citizen, Charlie Nagreen, the creator (arguably) of the hamburger, and to lend a hand in building a colossal hamburger.

Seymour residents are proud of their town's heritage and its connection to the burger world. When Burger Fest arrives in early August, this town of 3,000 people located just west of Green Bay, is transformed from a peaceful Main Street community (complete with a church, school, café, bar, and hardware store) to a waggish and merry (in good fun, of course) metropolis with thousands of hungry visitors. They participate in or watch the Hamburger Olympics, events that include the ketchup slide (imagine a Slip 'N Slide doused

Plastic burgers on display at the Hamburger Museum and Hall of Fame, Seymour

While in the Area
Visit Some Way-Up-North Museums

A few miles north of Peshtigo, the **Marinette County Historical Society** runs a logging exhibit and small display devoted to Queen Marinette, who owned the trading post and was a dominant landowner from the 1800s. While there, check out a chunk of the largest known Norwegian pine. Cut in 1963 when it was 369 years old, it survived a lead bullet piercing it in 1890. The museum is located on Stephenson Island off Highway 41 in Marinette, Wisconsin. An admission fee is charged. For more information, call (715) 732-0831.

The "world's largest miniature logging camp" is on view at the **Iron County Museum** in Caspian, Michigan, about an hour and a half north of Marinette. The museum complex contains 21 buildings and includes wildlife galleries and a 1920 mining head frame (a piece that hauled up the miners and the ore from the mine). The museum is located on Museum Road in Caspian. Open June through August: Monday through Saturday from 9 a.m. to 5 p.m.; Sunday from 1 p.m. to 5 p.m. An admission fee is charged. For more information, call (906) 265-2617.

Located in what some consider the birthplace of organized skiing, the **U.S. National Ski Hall of Fame and Museum** in Ishpeming, Michigan, features a life-size display of the Birkebeiner cross-country skiing race, a chairlift exhibit, and ski clothing developments. The museum is located at 610 Palms Avenue. Open year-round, Monday through Saturday from 10 a.m. to 5 p.m. An admission fee is charged. For more information, call (906) 485-6323.

Overlooking the first iron forge in the Lake Superior region you'll find the **Michigan Iron Industry Museum**. Scope out a bevy of mining artifacts, including helmets and buckets. Kids get a shot at loading a freighter. The museum is located at 73 Forge Road in Negaunee. Open daily May through October from 9:30 a.m. to 4:30 p.m. An admission fee is charged. For more information, call (906) 475-7857.

with ketchup), a bed race, burger toss, parade (sometimes with floats honoring people with last names such as Burger and Onions), and scores of burgers hot off the giant burger grill. Burger Fest 2001 was particularly thrilling as the town's intrepid citizens built a four-ton beauty-of-a-burger on the famous "Charlie grill," beating the record for the world's largest hamburger set by folks in Rutland, North Dakota—theirs a measly 3,591 pounds.

At Burger Fest crews of more than 15 people clap thousands of pounds of beef onto the mammoth Charlie grill (steel pans welded together and supported by cement blocks). Seasoning is taken care of by a man who is armed with seasoning shakers, strapped into a harness, and dangled from a crane. The burger takes about two and half hours to cook. When it's done, pieces are cut, wrapped, and served to all festival attendees free of charge (although they have to pay a few bucks to get into the festival grounds). Any leftovers are donated to charity organizations.

If you can't make it to the annual festival, held on the first Saturday of August, stop by the town's Hamburger Museum and Hall of Fame anytime in the summer. It's the building with the mural of a radiant Charlie Nagreen holding up his creation in pure Michelangelo fashion.

Seymour's motto, painted on the banners hanging from lampposts, is "Home of the Hamburger." (Although Hamburg, New York, and Athens, Texas, and a few other towns claim that the burger originated in their towns.) Other towns can claim to be the spot where the burger was born, but "only we have documentation, solid proof," says one volunteer, rebuffing the notion that another town in America could have created it first. Newspaper reports from the summer of 1885 prove that Nagreen was out selling his hamburgers at the Seymour fair.

According to the story, back in the 1880s, in response to county fairgoers wanting a food that they could eat while browsing the grounds, 15-year-old food vendor Charlie Nagreen, a resident of nearby Hortonville, flattened two meatballs fried in butter and smothered with onions, and plopped them between two pieces of bread. He dubbed it a hamburger. He sold his burgers from an oxen-led food cart at the Seymour fair in 1885 and eventually at other county fairs. They caused quite a stir. "Hamburger Charlie" as he became known, hired staffs of local teens to help him serve his burgers. They'd chant and hawk, "Hey you skinny rascals, don't you ever eat?" All the while Nagreen would carry a guitar and harmonica and play some tunes. Nagreen continued working the fair circuit until 1950, a year before his death at 81.

Expect to see plenty of photos of Nagreen and his crew and of previous Burger Fests in the museum's front room. Souvenirs from prior fests are also on view. The back room is chock full of novelty burger items like a talking cheeseburger condiment holder. The back room is rather small, but you could entertain yourself for quite a while perusing its contents. Check out the phony burger in its original packaging and Frederick's of Hollywood's men's underwear with the saying, "Where's the Beef" embroidered on them. Did you ever want a "Barbie loves McDonald's" play set? Look on the shelf above the doorway for one. And notice the photo of "The Legend" Bob Wian, the inventor of the Big Boy double-decker hamburger, and a can of Spam with a recipe on the label for a Spamburger. Don't miss the White Castle Employees poster, "Before Going on Duty: Correct bad breath. No body odor. Be ready to make suggestions." All these popular culture items were donated to the museum courtesy of burger fan Jeffrey Tennyson, author of *Hamburger Heaven.*

Currently housed in a small storefront on Main Street, local volunteers hope the museum and hall of fame will eventually be housed in a giant hamburger-shaped building with a fries-shaped annex that will house the hall of fame and museum, a theater, and fast-food restaurants. Preliminary design plans and a model of the complex are on display in the museum. But funding has not been secured yet. Don't forget to slip a few dollars into the donation box.

126 North Main Street, Seymour
(920) 833-9522
Open Memorial Day through Labor Day, Monday through Saturday
from 10 a.m. to 4 p.m.
Donation suggested

19 Rudy Rotter's Museum of Sculpture
Manitowoc

Ah, if only we all could have had dentists as gentle and fun loving as Rudy Rotter. (We probably wouldn't be so terrified to make an appointment.) Nearly 90 years old, Rudy Rotter, a retired dentist, greets every visitor to his sculpture museum and workshop with a grin and twinkling eye. He'll often stop hammering away at his latest piece and take his visitor by the hand to lead him or her around his sprawling warehouse, sharing stories about his parents and grandchildren along the way. Maybe you'll walk away with a little gift.

Rotter is not in the art business to make money, but to create "happy, beautiful things" that keep him going, he says. He derives joy from creating original pieces of art out of teak, plywood, plastic, and sheet metal, among many other things. He will pick up a carpet remnant given to him when a local carpet business closed or metallic shavings swept up from the floor of a trophy factory and construct a sparkly, gemlike piece to which he always signs his name and his slogan for the year: "Be happy! RR, 2000."

Without relying on any preliminary sketches or preconceived notions of what he will create, Rotter "just does" his art, he says. A self-taught artist, his work has been categorized as folk art or vernacular art by academics and industry professionals. Whatever you want to call it, it's hard to take your eyes off his creations. Stroll down the aisles piled high with chunks of wood painted with faces, page through a book of sketches, kneel down before a tabernacle-like sculpture. He has stained glass productions, carpet remnant sculptures, the "purge series" of plastic molds, and "a girl's best friend is mink" installation. Considered one of Wisconsin's most prolific artists, Rotter has created more than 16,000 pieces since the 1950s.

The son of Russian immigrants, Rotter grew up in Milwaukee above a flower shop. After graduating high school he attended the University of Wisconsin–Madison, studied zoology, and played on the football and track teams. After graduation he started working at the Milwaukee Public Museum, where he had spent a lot of time on the weekends with his family while growing up. A few years into the job, after realizing it would take a long time to work his way up the museum ladder, Rotter enrolled at Marquette University's dental school. In the late 1940s, he moved to Manitowoc to open a practice and has remained there ever since.

For many years he and his family lived above his practice and Rotter tinkered in the basement with wood and stone. He started carving human figures, Rodin-like pieces such as a woman with long, flowing hair and her arms tucked under her legs. His early art consisted mainly of wood carvings of people in religious scenes, with Judaic, Christian, Greek, African, Indian, and American Indian themes. Many of these carvings are located in the front of

Offbeat Wisconsin Festivals

- Nekoosa's **Walleye Days** is a three week fishing extravaganza held from the end of March to early April. For more information, call (715) 422-4854 or (888) 554-4484.

- The **Syttende Mai** festival in Stoughton celebrates the signing of the Norwegian constitution every May 17. The festival also holds an ugliest troll wood-carving contest. For more information, call (608) 873-7912 or (888) 873-7912.

- Join Sparta residents in paying homage to that creamy, salubrious substance Wisconsinites love so much at the annual **Butter Fest,** held the second weekend in June. Step up and test your milking and churning skills. For more information, call (888) 354-BIKE.

- Thousands of plastic ducks dash down the Sheboygan River in Sheboygan Falls for the annual **Ducktona 500** on the first Sunday in July. For more information, call (920) 467-6206.

- In a similar vein, nearby Sheboygan hosts the **Great Cardboard Regatta** in early July, when all-cardboard and human-powered boats race in the harbor. For more information, call (920) 458-6144.

- Port Washington hosts the **world's largest one-day outdoor fish fry** on the third Saturday of July every year. For more information, call (262) 284-0900 or (800) 719-4881.

- Johnsonville's **Sausage Fest** boasts sausage, beer, and polka. Held in July. For more information, call (920) 893-3054.

- Black River Falls celebrates the migration of the **Karner blue butterfly** every year with a festival in mid-July. For more information, call (715) 284-2503.

- Ripon calls itself Cookie Town U.S.A. because the Rippin' Good Cookie Company is based here. Enjoy a few at **Cookie Daze** in early August. For more information, call (920) 748-6764.

- Pardeeville hosts **watermelon seed spitting** contests the first Saturday after Labor Day in Chandler Park. For more information, call (888) 742-6242 or (608) 474-2525.

the museum. You'll recognize figures like Moses and King Solomon. Head toward the rear of the museum and you'll see how Rotter branched out over the years and started working with materials like tin and plastic. Instead of images of Moses, you'll see many faces of ordinary women painted on items including old computer parts.

Rotter is truly an inventive man. While he was sculpting and filling cavities, he also happened to be whipping up his own inventions: a sugarless bubble gum, a shoeshine roller and a sterilizing autoclave (a dentist's tool). But you won't hear him bragging about these projects; he is also quite humble. "Yes, I invented a sugarless bubble gum," he may casually remark while taking a visitor through his museum.

In 1987 he retired from dentistry and transported the artwork from his office into part of a warehouse at 701 Buffalo Street. Since then he's taken over all three floors of the approximately 21,000-square-foot building. In spite of the arthritis that has plagued him for the last several years, he usually goes to his museum and workshop every day.

His collection won't disappear when he passes away, thanks to the Friends of Rudy Rotter organization whose objective is to ensure that Rotter's collection remains accessible.

If you can't make it to Rotter's museum when it's open, but still want to see his work, consider visiting the John Michael Kohler Arts Center in Sheboygan where some of his pieces are on display.

701 Buffalo Street, Manitowoc
(920) 682-6671
www.rudyrotter.com
Hours vary, although Rotter tries to be there every day, so call ahead.
Free admission

20 Houdini Historical Center and Outagamie County Historical Museum
Appleton

One of the greatest acts of deception Harry Houdini played upon the public was his claim that he was born and raised in Appleton, Wisconsin. The escape artist, aviator, author, and exposer of spiritualist frauds never wanted his own past to be revealed. He did live for a while in Appleton when he was a young child, but Houdini was not born here, even though he disputed that fact to the grave. In actuality, Harry Houdini was born as Ehrich Weiss in Budapest, Hungary, in 1874. He and his family relocated to Appleton when the town's Jewish community hired his father to be their rabbi and to help build them a temple. Appleton was, and for the most part still is, a predominately white, middle class, middle-of-America kind of town. And that white-bread image was the one Houdini wanted to project to the public.

The Houdini Historical Society, appropriately headquartered in a former Masonic temple, was organized in the 1980s when a group of community boosters wanted to bring Appleton's name into the national tourism arena. They saw Houdini's association with the town as a source of community pride and decided to play up the connection more. (Why not? Houdini did.) They formed the society and opened an exhibit in the Outagamie County Historical Museum in downtown Appleton.

Though modern-day magician David Copperfield has a large collection of Houdini artifacts (a collection that is not displayed in a public museum), many believe Sidney Radner, who was friends with Houdini's brother, Hardeen, has the largest collection of Houdini memorabilia. In fact, Radner claims that Hardeen, who gave Radner the famous cache of handcuffs and magic toys, told him shortly before he died in the 1940s that it was the largest collection of Houdini artifacts. Radner is himself a former escape artist who entertained U.S. troops overseas in the 1940s by inviting them to strap him into a straitjacket or handcuff him to a chair. ("In those days people knew how to strap on a straitjacket. You had to be young and awfully lucky to do that sort of thing back then," he says.) Radner decided to exhibit a large part of his collection in Appleton because Houdini always claimed it as his hometown, even though it was proven a few years ago that it wasn't. "He just loved the place," Radner says. His collection was added to the Appleton museum in 1988.

Though he's in his eighties, Radner still travels around the country conducting Houdini séances and making appearances in the Appleton museum and on travel and history television shows. His favorite items in his collection are Houdini's scrapbooks, which are housed in Appleton but are not on public display because they are so fragile.

But there are plenty of other fascinating Houdini artifacts on view in the museum. You'll find a number of contraptions from which Houdini broke free: handcuffs, ropes, trunks, straitjackets, a milk can, and part of a prison cell. You'll see the handcuffs that held President Garfield's assassin. And there are a number of picklocks to wonder at. Scan the posters, newspaper articles, and advertisements announcing Houdini's shows. Examine the childhood photographs and watch a video with clips from Houdini's silent film that shows him flying in a biplane. And listen to the only known recording of Houdini's voice (he's introducing his water-torture-cell act), on an Edison wax cylinder in 1914. Houdini's mahogany and glass water-torture cell, exhibited in a Niagara Falls museum years ago, will be on permanent display in Appleton following its restoration.

The museum staff has also shared details about Houdini's life in the exhibit. A few years after living in Appleton, Houdini's family relocated to Milwaukee and in 1882 he kick started his stage career as a trapeze artist in a carnival. During his reign as a master illusionist and escape artist, Houdini escaped from many sticky situations, among them Scotland Yard and a locked packing case that was dropped into a New York City harbor. In 1926 he stayed underwater for 91 minutes in an airtight case with only enough air to keep someone alive for about five minutes; the 52-year-old escape artist had been practicing breath control and made a point not to move around a lot while in the case. He survived that gig, but later in the year Houdini's appendix ruptured after a university student punched him several times in the stomach. (The student asked Houdini if it was true that he could sustain countless punches to the midsection; Houdini didn't have time to flex his muscles before the student started punching.) He died a few days later on Halloween night.

While you're in Appleton, pick up a copy of the Houdini Historical Center's walking-tour guide, which pinpoints sites such as Houdini's childhood home, a spot by the Fox River where he said he nearly drowned, and the site of the drugstore where Edna Ferber interviewed him. If you're interested in attending a magic show, occasionally held in the museum, call for a schedule.

The building also contains a small exhibit on Edna Ferber, the author of *So Big*, which won a Pulitzer Prize in 1924, and *Giant*, later made into a movie starring James Dean. Born in Kalamazoo, Michigan, she graduated from high school in Appleton and was the first female reporter at the local newspaper. She went on to write for the *Milwaukee Journal Sentinel* and the *Chicago Tribune*. She was also an accomplished short-story writer, novelist, and playwright (*Show Boat* and *Cimarron* are among her works). See some of her letters and her typewriter. Other parts of the museum are dedicated to local history, particularly the paper industry.

330 East College Avenue, Appleton
(920) 733-2033
www.foxvalleyhistory.org
Open June, July, and August: Monday through Saturday from 10 a.m.
to 5 p.m.; Sunday from noon to 5 p.m.
Closed on Monday throughout the rest of the year.
Admission charged

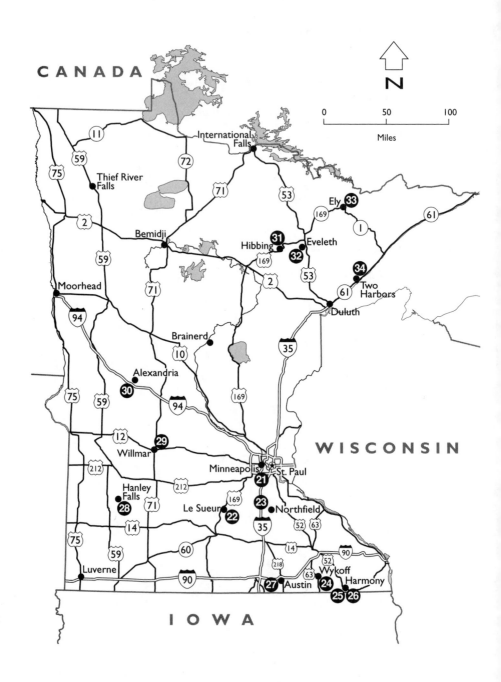

Owner Bob McKay and a visitor to his Museum of Questionable Medical Devices, Minneapolis

the 1960s, which was primarily devoted to debunking UFO sightings, and now with his ever-expanding collection of quack medical devices.

He has the country's largest display of quack medical devices from the 1790s to the 1990s, most of them on loan from the American Medical Association, Food and Drug Administration, and the National Council for Reliable Health Information. While visitors are welcome to strap themselves into devices like the Normalizer, McKay or his wife will be happy to explain and demonstrate the odd-looking gadgets they've placed in display cases. One of the McKays is always on hand at the museum to answer questions.

In the museum's "radium corner" sits a Geiger counter, another one of McKay's favorite devices. He may demonstrate how it works by wagging it over a jar of radium rocks, then exclaiming they're "hot" and diving into a spiel about radiotherapy, popular in the United States in the 1920s. People used to drop radium powder into a cup of water, mix the radioactive liquid, and take a big swig to boost their sex drive or wipe out any ailments they had. "One guy drank 1,400 bottles of this stuff [Radithor, premixed radium water]. And in two years he lost his teeth and lower jaw. Eventually it was outlawed," McKay says. He also has a box containing a scarflike piece of cloth that contained radium pads. People would tie these around their necks to alleviate any throat problems. Jazz singer Al Jolson endorsed the product and said he wore the radium tie to relax and improve his vocal chords.

McKay has photocopies of the original pamphlets that were distributed with products like the Omnipotent Oscilloclast, prostate warmers, or solar pads. Take a few minutes to read them. Here's what the manufacturer said about the Tricho System, a product that sent direct X rays onto the cheeks and upper lips

Like What You See?
The Midwest's Two-Story Outhouses

About 30 miles south of Minneapolis, attached to a Victorian house, is believed to be the only two-story outhouse in Minnesota. The outhouse is located at 410 North Cedar Street in Belle Plaine. Stop by anytime, but if you want to go inside, call ahead for hours. For more information, call (952) 873-6109.

The tiny central Illinois town of Gays is also home to a two-story outhouse. Built around 1866, it was originally attached to a general store. The store has been torn down, but the outhouse has remained. The outhouse is located on Front Street off Highway 16.

Two-story outhouse in Belle Plaine, Minnesota

of women who wanted to remove excess hair: "Everybody knows that success and happiness in life have been denied in multitudes of otherwise lovely women through growths of disfiguring hair, and that mental distress suffered in consequence has served to break the health of many." But the Tricho System didn't last long after thousands of patients' skin atrophied and began pigmenting; some women even died.

What else can you expect to see at the museum? A Relaxicisor, a tissue oscillator, and an orgone energy accumulator box from the 1950s. The orgone box is a classic quack device. According to its inventor, Dr. Wilhelm Reich, orgone was the primal force responsible for evolution; orgone energy is what made the sky blue, he said. Sit inside the compartment made with walls of galvanized steel for a little while and all your ailments, from impotence to cancer, will be cured. McKay is not impressed; he calls it "a box, just a box."

And then there's the Solarama Board whose manufacturer claimed it could regenerate organs, but it's only a piece of Formica. People were so gullible back then, you might think while at the museum. Back then? One of the museum's newer contraptions is the Stimulator, basically a gas grill igniter masquerading as a medical device. For $80 in 1996 you could purchase it and be the recipient of nothing more than a harmless electric shock. McKay says that 800,000 of these things were sold. Another relatively recent quack device on display is Acu-Stop, a gadget that you affix to your nose that helps you lose weight. The FDA banned it in 1995.

Looking for stories about the folks who invented these devices or photos and diagrams of more products? Head to McKay's comprehensive Web site or buy his book, *Quack! Tales of Medical Fraud*. For hands-on demonstrations of these testaments to human gullibility—and a chance to meet McKay—head for the museum itself.

201 Main Street Southeast (lower level of St. Anthony Main), Minneapolis
(612) 379-4046 or (763) 545-1113
www.mtn.org/quack
Open year-round Tuesday through Thursday from 5 p.m. to 9 p.m.; Friday through Saturday from noon to 9 p.m.; Sunday from noon to 5 p.m.
Free admission

22 | Jolly Green Giant Exhibit
Le Sueur

In the middle of July, the green valley around Le Sueur, Minnesota, resembles the one depicted in early advertising pictures for the Green Giant Company. Most promo shots for its canned peas, corn, or carrots featured a grinning giant standing proudly in the middle of a bucolic valley, among rolling hills and measured rows of corn near a rambling river. The company is not as prominent in the valley as it used to be, but the jolly giant still stands guard. When driving on Highway 169 toward Le Sueur, the town where Green Giant originated, look to the east just before the Le Sueur exit and you'll see the Jolly Green Giant—or at least a huge wooden replica of him—poking out from among the oak trees, welcoming you to the valley.

Since the beginning of the 20th century, the Green Giant Company has been a dominant force in the Le Sueur area. But when the Pillsbury Company purchased Green Giant in 1979, the company's headquarters moved to Minneapolis. And in 1995 the original canning factory in Le Sueur ceased production after 92 years. Le Sueur no longer has Green Giant executives running around the city's country club, but it hasn't forgotten the canning company's legacy. (And Le Sueur is still home to a Green Giant agricultural research and seed-breeding center.)

The Le Sueur City Museum opened as a local history museum in 1975 when a group of community volunteers saved an 1872 schoolhouse overlooking the Minnesota River from demolition. Their initial collections included artifacts from a schoolhouse, post office, and area farms. In the beginning Green Giant didn't plan to be part of the museum (although, ironically, the com-

Wooden replica of the character who's the focal point of the Jolly Green Giant Exhibit, Le Sueur

pany had rented the schoolhouse for a few years in the 1950s). After Pillsbury took over and Green Giant's office buildings closed, the staff thought the local museum should house the company's extensive archives. The Green Giant exhibit opened as part of the Le Sueur museum in 1987. And the staff believes the museum's Green Giant archives are the largest collection of industrial artifacts in the state, second only to the Burlington Railroad collection.

While the bulk of the archives are annual reports and financial statements (these

Like What You See? Nibble on More Giant History

Pay homage to the Jolly Green Giant by stopping at the world's only statue of him, erected in 1979. Located in green Blue Earth, Minnesota, home of a Green Giant canning facility, the big guy stands 55 feet tall, weighs 8,000 pounds, has a 48-inch smile, and wears size 78 shoes. The figure is located off Highway 169 in Blue Earth, just north of the Iowa border. Join the local folks for **Giant Days** held annually during the last full weekend in July. For more information, call (507) 526-2916.

are housed in storage), the staff has put together a nifty one-room exhibit on the Green Giant, an exhibit that details the company's history and the evolution of its famous logo. Work your way around the room by learning about the founders of the Minnesota Valley Canning Company, the Cosgroves, who started their venture back in 1903. Highlighted in displays throughout the room are miscellaneous facts about the company, like the fact that it turned out 11,750 cases of white cream-style corn in their first year of production. Surprisingly the Minnesota Valley Canning Company didn't adopt the Green Giant label until 1928, and in 1950 the name was officially changed to Green Giant. The walls are decked with photos and biographies about those responsible for concocting and plugging this image, including Chicago advertising guru Leo Burnett, who came up with the original idea.

As with most company logos, the giant's image changed over the years, and visitors can see his transformations in the many drawings and pictures on view. Early on, the giant looked like a character in a Grimm brothers' fairy tale; he didn't appear green at all. A few years later, designers added green skin and leaves, and throughout the decades they tweaked the giant's girth and stance. Check out an artist's wood carvings of all the different "spokespersons" the company has used to promote its products, including the chatty "Sprout," who was introduced in 1968 because the Jolly Green Giant only said "Ho, Ho, Ho." Another modification added to the giant's image was his red scarf, added when the company started marketing frozen food products.

Along the museum's walls staff members have hung advertising posters spanning decades and prints of artwork commissioned by Green Giant, in-

> ## While in the Area
> ## Quaff the Local Brew
>
> For more than 140 years, the **August Schell Brewing Company** has been making beers such as Schmaltz Alt, Zommerfest, and Doppel Bock along the Cottonwood River in the southern Minnesota town of New Ulm—a town where, during **Heritage Fest**, it's not uncommon to stumble upon a polka band playing at the local grocery store.
>
> August Schell, a German immigrant and machinist, founded the brewery in the 1860s because he couldn't find a decent brewskie in the area. The Schell Brewing Company now brews 37 different beers throughout the year and has organized a museum displaying antique brewing equipment and personal artifacts relating to the Schell family. It also has opened up its brewery for tours. The museum is located at 1860 Schell Road in New Ulm. Open daily Memorial Day through Labor Day from noon to 5 p.m.; hours are extended during Heritage Fest held annually in June. For more information and for brewery tour times, call (507) 354-5528.

cluding work done by N. C. Wyeth and Norman Rockwell. Don't miss the amusing Green Giant premium items, things like corn tie clips, Green Giant model trains, and candles. Also intriguing are the nostalgic and appreciative letters sent to the company. Many of the ones on view were written by former German POWs and migrants who worked on the farms decades ago.

After you've had your fill of Green Giant memories, don't forget to tour the rest of the museum. Local retired pharmacist Melvin Osborn (whose sister was the first female pharmacist in the region) donated a marvelous and humorous collection of pharmacy items to the museum in the late 1980s. The downstairs exhibit room is stocked with pill packets containing concoctions such as "Pheny-O-Caffein for sick and nervous headaches," "sexual pills for both sexes, for nervousness and dizziness," and chocolate-flavored laxatives more than 50 years old. Osborn also has donated a number of veterinary tools his father and brother used while working as local vets. Have you ever heard of pills being compared to horse pills? See the real thing here. Yes, they are huge. Upstairs you'll find rooms full of local antiques.

709 2nd Street North, Le Sueur
(507) 665-2050 or (507) 665-2087
Open daily Memorial Day through Labor Day from 1 p.m. to 4:30 p.m. During the rest of the year the museum is open Tuesday, Wednesday, and Thursday from 8 a.m. to noon and 1 p.m. to 4:30 p.m. During the winter, though, call before you come.
Donation suggested

23 First National Bank Museum
Northfield

On September 7, 1876, the James-Younger Gang tore into quiet Northfield, Minnesota, and made a daring attempt to rob the First National Bank of Northfield. And local residents have never forgotten it. Jesse James and his comrades didn't expect trouble when they jumped over the counter of the bank and demanded money. (Northfield's motto is cows, colleges, and contentment.) But the cashier, Joseph Heywood, refused and was shot and killed. Citizens took up firearms outside and shot two members of the gang. Most of the rascals escaped town, but eventually all were nabbed.

Northfield is justifiably proud of its victory and celebrates the event every year. The bank, which the town has remodeled into a modest museum, offers tours every day of the week during the summer. The visit starts with a video of a reenactment of the robbery, and includes a follow-up on what became of the members of the James-Younger gang. Follow your guide into the actual bank (no longer operating) where everything is set up as it was in 1876; all contents are original with the exception of the countertops. Make your way around and peer into a glass case containing guns left behind by the gang, photos of the gang members (three of them were dead when they had their picture taken), and a tribute to Heywood, considered a local hero. No one ever found out which gang member shot Heywood. Even before going to trial, after being asked who had killed Heywood, gang member Cole Younger wrote, "Be true to your friends if the heavens fall." After Younger served his time, he was released and toured the country, lecturing on the theme "What life has taught me."

First National Bank Museum, Northfield

Northfield also relives this event every year in September with the Defeat of Jesse James Days. Activities include a reenactment of the foiled bank robbery, a rodeo, steak fry, and square dance.

408 Division Street, Northfield
(507) 645-9268
www.defeatofjessejamesdays.org or www.northfieldhistory.org
Open during the summer: Monday through Saturday from 10 a.m. to 4 p.m.;
Thursday until 8 p.m.; and Sunday from 1 p.m. to 4 p.m. During the winter
the museum is closed on Monday.
Admission charged

Midwest Capital Claims

- Band Instrument Capital of the World: Elkhart, Indiana
- Bratwurst Capital of the World: Sheboygan, Wisconsin
- Cherry Capital of the World: Traverse City, Michigan
- Covered Bridge Capital of the World: Parke County, Indiana
- Hibiscus Capital of the World: Park Ridge, Illinois
- Horseradish Capital of the World: Collinsville, Illinois
- Ice Cream Capital of the World: Le Mars, Iowa
- Inner Tubing Capital of the World: Somerset, Wisconsin
- Jump Rope Capital of the World: Bloomer, Wisconsin
- Kolacky Capital of the World: Montgomery, Minnesota
- Limestone Capital of the World: Lawrence County, Indiana
- Loon Capital of the World: Mercer, Wisconsin
- Magic Capital of the World: Colon, Michigan
- Musky Capital of the World: Boulder Junction, Wisconsin
- Petunia Capital of the World: Dixon, Illinois
- Pumpkin Capital of the World: Anamosa, Iowa
- Round Barn Capital of the World: Fulton County, Indiana
- Swiss Cheese Capital of the World: Monroe, Wisconsin
- Snowmobile Capital of the World: Eagle River, Wisconsin
- Taconite Capital of the World: Mountain Iron, Minnesota
- Toilet Paper Capital of the World: Green Bay, Wisconsin
- Troll Capital of the World: Mount Horeb, Wisconsin
- Turkey Capital of the World: Worthington, Minnesota

24 | Ed's Museum
Wykoff

Folks in Wykoff who knew Ed Krueger share a similar image of him: "He smoked like a steam engine, and he always had this big long ash at the end of his cigarette," laughs one resident, adding that Krueger was in the habit of forgetting about things and letting them pile up. Ed Krueger was a pack rat—the town's most notorious one. But thanks to him, Wykoff (a town of less than 500 residents) has thousands of items from the early half of the 20th century that otherwise may have been thrown out.

Okay, some items could have been tossed, like his 25 gallstones—which, luckily, are sealed in a jar in the museum's front display case. And perhaps he could have buried Sammy, his cat, instead of placing him in a shoe box in the basement. The gallstones and Sammy are some of the items that have made Krueger a bit famous posthumously when the museum volunteers appeared on Comedy Central's *The Daily Show* back in the 1990s with some of the items Krueger collected during his lifetime. Yes, the gallstones and cat may make you second guess a visit to Ed's Museum (why should you care that some guy saved almost every envelope he ever received in the mail?), but he did save many other interesting items that, thank goodness, overshadow the more unsavory ones. And volunteers have kept the museum clean, compared to what it must

The exterior of Ed's Museum, Wykoff

have been like when Krueger lived there. The museum volunteers are also a joy to talk to as they share stories of Krueger and life "way back when."

Born in Columbus, Ohio, Ed Krueger and his family moved to Wykoff in 1901 when his father became the town's postmaster. Krueger attended local schools, played sports, and eventually graduated (in a class of 11). He married a local girl, Lydia, and her father purchased the building at 100 South Gold Street for the couple. It had been a saloon, brewery, and grocery store before the Kruegers opened it as a Jack Sprat. Krueger and his family lived above the store. Krueger ran the Jack Sprat grocery store from 1933 to about the late 1940s. After he shuttered the store, Krueger kept a lot of the merchandise, displayed in the same manner it was when he closed, such as a lollipop tree with lollipops that went for $.01. (Yes, the lollipop tree is still there with some lollipops from the 1930s.)

After Lydia died in 1940 of heart failure, Krueger didn't have anyone to get after him for that growing pile of Social Security check envelopes in the corner. Like most eccentric collectors, he lived with cats. But Krueger wasn't exactly a hermit. He was Wykoff's treasurer and town historian for more than 40 years, served as a firefighter, took care of the ice rink, and often invited people in to check out his vast array of stuff—not just the envelopes of all his Social Security checks, but his movie star photographs plastered to his wall and his enormous record collection. Infatuated with films and the beauties that appeared in them, Krueger also operated the projector at the town theater. He kept every single magazine he ever received—*Life, National Geographic,* you name it. They are all catalogued and stored in the basement near his enormous record collection and the infamous Sammy.

Hats off to the volunteers who cataloged and cleaned everything following Krueger's death in 1989. (He willed everything to the town.) "When they went in there, the place was full of soot," remembers a volunteer. "I don't know how they had the courage to go in there. It must have been a labor of love."

The Jack Sprat store looks very similar to what one would have looked like in the 1930s: a 1900 meat block, cigarette cartons, Jell-O boxes, and 25-year-old candy bars that you wouldn't dare open. The Wykoff Historical Society has decorated the rooms similar to the way they believe they were during the time the Kruegers lived there: son Freddy's room is filled with antique toys and a player piano is topped with numerous music rolls and piles of sheet music. The group also started a room off to the side of the store devoted to artifacts from Wykoff High School, including yearbooks, uniforms, and trophies. "Ed loved attending games and kept records of all the graduating classes, well into the 1970s," says volunteer Aleda Schwier.

You'd think the place would be creepy, but it really isn't. Most museums try to re-create a general store or storefront grocery shop like this, with the big wooden and glass display gases stocked with everything from soap to Spam. At Ed's, you walk in and don't have to imagine yourself back 50 years. It hasn't changed much (though it's probably a lot cleaner now that the historical society is running things).

"Look at his picture," says volunteer Raymond Schwier, pointing to a framed black-and-white photo of Krueger walking down Main Street with his signature ash and grin. "He was just a happy-go-lucky guy."

Want to hear some more stories about Krueger or feel like sitting down to a cup of tea? Head over to the charming Bank Gift Haus, a gift shop and tearoom located at 105 Gold Street, just across the street from Ed's Museum.

100 South Gold Street, Wykoff
(507) 352-4205
Open April through October, Saturday and Sunday from 1 p.m. to 4 p.m., or by appointment.
Donation suggested

Famous Minnesota Natives

- Poet Robert Bly, born in 1926 in Madison
- Singer Bob Dylan, born as Robert Zimmerman, in 1941 in Duluth
- Writer F. Scott Fitzgerald, born in 1896 in St. Paul
- Singer Judy Garland, born as Frances Gumm, in 1922 in Grand Rapids
- Writer Sinclair Lewis, born in 1885 in Sauk Center
- Baseball player Roger Maris, born in 1934 in Hibbing
- Doctors William J. and Charles H. Mayo, born in 1861 and 1865 in Le Sueur and Rochester, respectively
- Former Vice President Walter Mondale, born in 1928 in Ceylon
- Singer "Prince" Rogers Nelson, born in 1958 in Minneapolis
- Actress Winona Ryder, born in 1971 in Winona
- "Peanuts" creator Charles Schulz, born in 1922 in St. Paul

---

25 Harmony Toy Museum
Harmony

Above a doorway toward the back of the Harmony Toy Museum, owner Wesley Idso has fastened a giant stick of about nine feet in length and a big black comb (the kind you see in barber shops, only 100 times larger) to the wall. Below he has tacked a note: "Walking stick and comb. Found by homesteaders near Big Spring, Minnesota. Proof that Vikings were here?" Idso has a charming sense of humor, as you'll gather while strolling through his toy museum. He has hoarded about 4,000 to 5,000 items, most of them whimsical toys—pieces ranging from five years old to 100 years old—in his Main Street museum in Harmony. Open since 1994, the museum represents 20 years of collecting. And Idso has found a place for everything: teapots hang from the rafters, toy guns are stapled to the wall beams, and pictures of farm equipment pulled out from calendars are taped to the heating ducts.

The theme that runs through the museum is to honor obsolescence. Take a look at some of the plaques he's gathered over the years: "Let your heritage not be lost but bequeath it as a memory treasury and blessing" and "Gather the lost and hidden and preserve it for the children." Idso's love of words, from the pious to the silly, is evident throughout the museum. He also likes to write pretzel prose proclamations. Onto a white board stuck on another wall, he penned: "There ain't no place like this place anywhere near this place so this

Toys galore at the Harmony Toy Museum, Harmony

must be the place." But at the bottom, he takes on a Robert Frost voice: "The woods are dark and deep, but I got promises to keep."

Though it's simply called, Harmony Toy Museum, the place has much more than just toys. There's a final edition of the *Minneapolis Star* and a copy of the *Boston Globe* announcing the sinking of the *Titanic*. Are you a movie buff? Don't miss the vintage and current movie posters, mostly from comedies, or ones with plots relating to farms or gunfights. Yes, that's a framed poster of *Babe*, the film about the talking pig. "If you look, you can find anything here," Idso declares.

A retired milk bottler, Idso's six children have all grown up, so he's created a home away from home. He has set up a little living room inside the museum and included many of the toys he made, the ones his kids played with, 4-H ribbons, and "Best of Show" ribbons won at county fairs. Idso has also won prizes at fairs for his toy creations. A little more than two decades ago he started making toys, mostly steam engines and threshing machines, and also some circus wagons. Before he moved into the South Main Street building, Idso stored his collectibles in his home in nearby Chatfield. Once he had his own museum, "I went a little nuts with the big space," he admits.

Expect a mixed bag of items—like bottles of Columbia Crest Wine and buttons from Rochesterfest dating back to 1950s—but also more poignant pieces. Notice the tobacco advertisement featuring two children—one black and one white—reading a newspaper entitled *A Tale of Two Cities*, antique African American dolls, and jazz band figurines.

30 South Main Street, Harmony
(507) 867-3380
Open May through October: Monday through Saturday from 9 a.m. to 4 p.m.;
Sunday from 11 a.m. to 4 p.m.; or by appointment.
Donation suggested

26 Woodcarving Museum
Harmony

Born and raised across the street from the Bily brothers' farm in Spillville, Iowa (see page 188 for more on the famous wood-carving brothers), Stanley "Slim" Marroushek earned a few extra dollars sweeping up wood shavings from the floor and polishing carving tools for the Bilys. In fact, the first carving he ever received was given to him by the Bilys when he was eight years old. While Marroushek didn't start carving until his mid-thirties, he has been picking up wood carvings here and there since he was in his mid-twenties. Now with 1,700 pieces to his name (although that number is always growing), Marroushek believes his museum is the largest wood-carving museum run by one man in the Midwest.

Over the years, he has accumulated quite a variety of carvings. The fanciful carvings come from all over—Mexico, India, and the garage sale across town—and some of the pieces are decades old while others were carved a month ago. He bought many of the pieces because of their peculiarity or tendency to make him chuckle. There's an Austrian carving he likes to call "Mr. Naughty Bird," which grabs cigarettes with its beak. There are kissing figures, musical figures, bookmarkers, and a shelf full of letter openers. And don't miss Marroushek's own carvings, like the chess set with Viking figures.

Slim Marroushek, a tall man of Czech descent (like many from northeastern Iowa) didn't aspire to become a wood carver. Instead, he spent about 20 years building houses. Then one day he was diagnosed with multiple sclerosis, and he found himself spending more time in a wheelchair. In the early 1980s his daughter handed him a piece of wood and some carving tools and he started whittling away. His first piece was of a pair of horses on a wood relief. That was in 1982; he hasn't stopped carving since. He and his wife, Maurene, have run the Harmony wood shop and museum since 1997.

Usually Marroushek will take you around his collection so you won't miss some of the more unique carvings, such as a Japanese cork carving of a pagoda and a bridge, peach pit carvings of a teeny owl and rabbit, hand-carved roses, a bottle stopper. Arranged neatly on shelves, the little carvings (most of them you can pick up in your hand) were made from a wide variety of woods, such as staghorn sumac, desert ironwood, or parasite wood from Bali. Marroushek has a few samples of what he calls "tramp art" created by men passing through towns during the 1920s and 1930s. What's unusual about these pieces is that they contain markings (usually understood only by fellow nomads) signifying where a guy could sleep in a barn or where "a good hearted woman lives . . . and you can use the telephone."

Go ahead and gawk at the intricate two-ring caricature circus placed in the center of the room. Made from 121 pieces of basswood, the circus was created by 23 carvers from the Caricature Carvers of America. They built the circus in one year, from 1995 to 1996. Each person was assigned to carve a separate scene in the big top, be it the trapeze artists preparing for a flip or the boy trying to peek in under the tent.

In the "Woodshed" shop, Slim and Maurene sell original wood carvings, pieces of wood and tools for carvers, as well as instructional books. For budding carvers, Marroushek holds wood-carving lessons; call in advance for a private or group lesson. If you visit Harmony during the first full weekend in July for the wood-carving show, stay at Slim and Maurene's bunkhouse, where you'll sleep in a rustic pine room a stone's throw from downtown and the Harmony-Preston Valley bicycle trail.

160 1st Street Northwest, Harmony
(507) 886-3114
www.web-site.com/slimswoodshed
Open year-round: Monday through Saturday from 9 a.m. to 5 p.m.; Sunday from noon to 5 p.m. Closed Sunday, January through April.
Admission charged

27 | Spam Museum
Austin

You may not own 52 T-shirts advertising the delicacy (as one college student claims), you may not spend your evenings composing Spamkus or singing in the Spamettes touring group, but if you've ever tasted (or thought about tasting) the famous spiced ham and wondered what on earth the big hooplah is all about, stop by the new Spam Museum in Austin, Minnesota. Spam has a surprisingly loyal and far-reaching following (just visit Austin during its Spam Town U.S.A. Festival in July) and this absolute hoot of a museum does all but canonize the meat inside the little blue and yellow cans. In the fall of 2001, Hormel Foods unveiled its ambitious Spam Museum in a former shopping center next to Hormel offices. Formerly located in a tight space in a mall, the Spam Museum has exploded into an expansive, playful museum. Spam fans should be pleased: Imagine 16,500 square feet of nothing but Spam cans, Spam memorabilia, Spam recipes, Spam T-shirts. Yes, it's a Spam love fest.

When you first walk into the museum you'll notice more than 3,000 Spam cans piled against a wall. Continue on and have a seat at the 1950s-style, Googie-esque diner, where computers have been placed on top of the counters and a sign beckons you to roll the egg yolk and click on the pat of butter on a plate of plastic breakfast food. While you're waiting for the film, "Spam— A Love Story," to start, browse through the Spam and Hormel Web sites. Then head into the theater for the approximately 15-minute film. It is not an educational or historical film about the revered canned meat that you would expect to see on PBS. Instead, laugh along to clips of folks dressed up in Spam outfits at the annual festival who share stories about

Inside the Spam Museum

Welcome sign at the Spam Museum, Austin

the first time they ate Spam. Watch Austin's congressman serve up Spam at a breakfast in Washington, D.C., and Kathie Lee Gifford show off her Spam watch. The film gets you in the mood of the museum, which is a little irreverent and a lot of lighthearted fun.

So what exactly is inside that can? One of the first exhibits you'll see explains Spam's ingredients. Surprisingly, there are only a few: ham, pork, sugar, and sodium nitrate (a preservative). Spam, introduced in 1937, stands for spiced ham. (A man named Kenneth Daigneau won $100 for the name suggestion in a contest sponsored by Hormel.) Walk through an early replica of a butcher shop and have a look at wall exhibits, which brief visitors on the Hormel family's background and recount how the Austin-based Hormel Company began. Stop by an early switchboard and listen to gossip and news about the company circa 1920. The initial exhibits tend to be more educational—you will learn how meat was cured and canned 100 ago—but keep walking for some real fun.

Meet up with comedian Al Franken—or a giant-size video version of him— in the game-show studio. Franken runs the Spam Exam, which tests your knowledge of Spam trivia. (Did you know that 435 cans of Spam are produced every minute?) Have a seat in Chez Spam, where you can watch videos of famous chefs from around the world create Spam-based specialties like Spam Musubi. Stroll through the mini grocery store and check out the Hormel products in the canned-goods aisle and in the deli section. (The sausages are not real.) In the Spam Radio exhibit, listen to the Spam Girls singing Spam-related tunes and early Spam radio commercials featuring George Burns and Gracie

Allen. Remember the slogan "Cold or Hot, Spam Hits the Spot"? Have a seat in the simulated Spam factory and see if you'd survive a day on the Spam assembly line plopping pretend hunks of Spam into canisters. How fast can you pack them in?

In another corner of the museum, the staff has set up a fake army base from the mid-1940s and displays explain Hormel's involvement in World War II. Notice the letter former President Dwight D. Eisenhower sent to the company regarding his consumption of Spam during the war: "I will confess to a few unkind words about [Spam] . . . uttered during the strain of battle." Other amusing exhibits not to miss are clips of the Monty Python sketch, "Spam, Spam, Spam," and all over the walls you'll see photographs of where Spam has been spotted and who cherishes it. (You'll see mountain climbers wearing Spam T-shirts and musicians clasping cans.)

Keep in mind that the pork and ham inside Spam have to come from somewhere. Without seeming too grim, staff has arranged a modest display that explains how Spam comes to be. You're given information such as how many hogs Hormel "processes" every year to produce its products including Spam—7.8 million in 2000. And you're shown butcher tools like the "hog splitter" from the 1890s (imagine a giant cleaver) and the more innocuous ring knife used currently in plants.

Although the production tools might deter you from stocking up on all the Spam you can stomach, the museum does promise to be a great time. It's easy to get to (right off I-90 in downtown Austin) and has activities that will please the kids, mom and dad, and the grandparents. And admission is free.

1937 Spam Boulevard (off Main Street downtown), Austin
(800) LUV-SPAM
www.spam.com
Open year-round: Monday through Saturday from 10 a.m. to 5 p.m.; Sunday from noon to 4 p.m.
Free admission

28 | Minnesota's Machinery Museum
Hanley Falls

Hanley Falls is the agriculture epicenter for Yellow Medicine County, as area farmers bring their crops to town and ship them, usually to Washington, via the many trains that rumble through in a given week. Naturally, then, the town's hub is the Farmers Elevator, which rises in front of visitors driving north on Highway 23, above the cornfields and gravel roads like a statue honoring the area's agricultural roots. The super-size silo is buzzing with activity and, like the railroad that runs through town, is the lifeblood of Hanley Falls, population 250. But the grain elevator is not the only landmark emphasizing the county's ties to agriculture. About a mile away from the elevator, you'll find Minnesota's Machinery Museum, which venerates the area's agricultural past.

Hanley Falls and Yellow Medicine County residents are dedicated to preserving the past and like most other small towns that have achieved a "first" or claim the world's largest something or other, they want the world to know it. Hanley Falls's claim to fame is that America's first "Railroad Y," or transfer track, was laid here in 1901. At Minnesota's Machinery Museum you can read about the "Railroad Y," check out some big machines, and learn about the folks who work them.

Since it opened in the 1970s, the museum has burgeoned, growing from a collection of a few threshing machines to thousands of local history items. Even though the side of the former Hanley Falls school building proclaims "Farm Museum" in large letters, you'll find more than just farm machines at the mu-

A sign announcing that Minnesota's Machinery Museum is close by, in Hanley Falls

seum. Housed in a 1939 WPA–built school, the museum contains two floors of exhibits ranging from farm implements to quilts to photography. In addition to touring the two-story school building, visitors can ramble through four exterior buildings containing vintage farm machines and automobiles. You might want to set aside more than an hour to tour this sprawling museum.

The museum started when a group of Hanley Falls–area residents got to talking after a local threshing show in the late 1970s. They turned to each other and said, "People ought to see this stuff more than one weekend per year." They were referring to the numerous vintage farm implements, and automobiles that collectors brought to the show. Every year attendees would gravitate toward these machines, inquiring about their origin, horsepower, and other characteristics. At the time, the Hanley Falls school was closed. Residents convinced the county to purchase the school building and donate it to the town as a museum.

Begin your tour by roaming through the halls and classrooms of the school building. Open the door to any of the classrooms and you'll find a slightly different scene pertaining to rural life. One contains horse equipment, with a wall of vintage horseshoes. Another enlightens visitors about soy and corn byproducts like biodegradable corn golf tees. The "Hobby Room" is full of farm dioramas built by area residents, a cluster of miniature log cabins, and one area resident's collection of political campaign buttons. A classroom upstairs has been transformed into a living room circa the early 20th century; another features quilts made during threshing bees or by the group Quilters Along the Yellowstone Trail.

Look for a photograph of a man driving his tractor in his backyard on his 98th birthday. This photo is one of many the museum has on view. One room is devoted entirely to a photography exhibit that profiles Yellow Medicine County residents. Meet a retired post-office clerk who thinks at 400 MHz and a young man who works for his father's farm implement company (and who always knew that he would be in the business). A number of stunning close-ups of residents reveal their facial lines as they clasp a cup of coffee at the local café or sit in front of their fireplace.

Before heading outside, tour the gymnasium stocked with, among many other things, a fence maker and a replica of a McCormick-Deering Reaper. The stage consists of a mural of a farm scene painted by college art students and fake electricity wires attached to poles.

One exterior building contains cars, another houses tractors, and another gas engines—don't miss the awesome 18,000-pound Bessemer. Some of the automobiles on display are a 1935 Oldsmobile, 1954 copper-colored Plymouth, 1948 Chrysler Town and Country (a woody!), and a 1930 Model A Ford. Be prepared for many tractors—the oldest pieces in their collection are a 1912 Minneapolis Threshing Machine Company tractor and a 1913 Avery. The staff has tried to have every type and brand of tractor represented in the museum. All of them have been painstakingly restored by area volunteers, who researched their histories and have tried to make them look like they did on the day the farmers brought them home for the first time.

If you can, drop by Hanley Falls's annual threshing and toy show, held the second full weekend in August. The blacksmith shop in one of the exterior buildings becomes a working shop during the threshing bee.

100 North First Street, Hanley Falls
(507) 768-3522 or (507) 768-3580
www.prairiewaters.com
Open mid-May through mid-September,
every day except Tuesday from 1 p.m. to 5 p.m.
Donation suggested

While in the Area
Get Down and Dirty

Do you want to sample rural life and see how farming has evolved over the years? Then consider spending a few hours at the following nontraditional farms near Hanley Falls.

• How does community-supported agriculture work? Tour the farm and learn organic harvesting and soil-building projects, garden techniques, and discover how ducks and chickens can be used to control insects. **EarthRise** is located about 40 miles northwest of Hanley Falls in Louisburg. For more information, call (320) 752-4700.

• Have a go at spinning and weaving at the **All Natural Fiber Farm**, located about seven miles east of Montevideo, northwest of Hanley Falls. Free tours by appointment only. For more information, call (320) 269-6780.

29 | Mikkelson's Boat Museum
Willmar

Born and raised in Willmar, a town surrounded by small lakes, Paul Mikkelson spent his summers boating and waterskiing on area lakes. As soon as his family could heat up the lake house, he and his brothers were there boating and waterskiing. "We couldn't get enough," Mikkelson remembers. In 1955, while he was still in high school, Mikkelson's family purchased their first Falls Flyers boat, a boat the Minnesota-based Larson Boat Company made in honor of Charles Lindbergh, a former resident of Little Falls, Minnesota. Back then, Mikkelson spent hours boating, and he certainly loved his '55 Falls Flyer—"I dated my wife in this boat"—but he didn't foresee himself having two warehouses packed with Flyers 40 years later.

Mikkelson collects the Falls Flyers because, he says, "They mean something to me—I grew up with these boats. And they are made locally. These are Minnesota boats," he says, tapping the stern of one of his 1955 Larson DeLuxe Cabins built for Great Lakes cruising. Indeed, the bulk of the boats in his museum (officially called the Mikkelson Collection, Inc. Antique and Classic Boat Museum and Shop) are Falls Flyers. See the 1955 Falls Flyers, single and double cockpit Flyers, and Flyers with engine hoods.

Mikkelson's career choice happened to be related to the credit and collection industry, not boating. But as the years progressed, he found himself frequently traveling to conventions and with more time on his hands. He wasn't

Model boats on display at Mikkelson's Boat Museum, Willmar

very good at sitting in a hotel room and watching television. Instead, during his free time Mikkelson headed to antiques shops and auctions and started picking up toy boats.

When he retired in the 1990s he sat down and considered his next steps. "I wanted to spend my time doing something other than going down to the American Legion," he says. He purchased a 7,500-square-foot building off Benson Avenue and a 1,500-square-foot storage building down the street and started collecting boats.

While in the Area Have Something to Crow About

Yes, that's a crow off Highway 71 in Belgrade, about 20 miles north of Willmar. The 3,000-pound feathered friend was erected as part of the Belgrade Centennial Memorial project honoring veterans, mayors, pastors, and other community members. Why a crow? Because Belgrade is Crow Country, U.S.A., that's why!

"This isn't a junkyard," he declares. Mikkelson does not purchase and display boats that are beyond repair or missing many parts. Like most museums, his is a work in progress. And the number of boating-related items he has on view is always changing.

The front part of the museum contains new and used toy boats and parts for sale, as well as his toy boat collection. Mikkelson spent hours playing with toy boats as a child, but he admits none of them survived his childhood. The pieces in his museum are ones he has picked up while traveling. There's a wide variety of toy boats on display in cases: Ocean-liner boats made in Japan after World War II; Japanese tin-litho wind-up boats; battery-operated kit boats from the United States; and wooden British clockwork boats made in the 1920s and 1930s. Mikkelson also has U.S. military toy boats, rubber band–driven wooden boats, a few French Jeps that are worth about $800 each, and Orkin craft boats—the "Rolls Royces of toy boats," according to Mikkelson. You'll also find a few remote-control boats and plenty of display cases of toy outboard motors.

The people-size boats, most of them Falls Flyers, are located toward the back of the museum. Some highlights of the Flyers collection include a 1939 single cockpit 16-foot Flyer Speedster with a 90-horsepower engine and a split cockpit 17-foot Falls Flyer. Don't miss the two rare Flyers with engine hoods. "They are great collectors pieces, but aren't very practical," Mikkelson explains. Before boat engines had mufflers, some manufacturers toyed with putting hoods on the engines to hide the noise, a feature that backfired once engineers and customers realized the hoods would become extremely hot when the engine ran.

One unusual, but non–Falls Flyers boat, is a 1956 Stylemaster featuring hydrofoils. Made by Inland Marine, this boat jets 40 percent faster than other boats because of the hydrofoils. You won't find many boats with hydrofoils around, especially in Minnesota. It wasn't that this technology didn't work, but rather that Minnesotans preferred practical boats, fishing boats, Mikkelson points out. Hydrofoil and Falls Flyers boats were leisure boats, much too capricious for most Minnesotans.

Mikkelson claims to have one of the best manual-powered boat motor collections. Propellers like a 1937 Ropeller, 1960 Man-U-Trol, and an aquacycle are placed along the perimeter of the room. Along the walls he has posted boat and accessory advertising signs.

Just about everything you see in the museum has been restored by Mikkelson. If you'd like to see any "before" photos, just ask him. (The sole owner of the museum, Mikkelson, now retired, tends to spend a lot of time there.) He has filing cabinets full of binders; each one chronicles a boat's restoration and is stuffed with "before" and "after" photos of a boat, its history, and catalog descriptions.

"It's a labor of love," Mikkelson says as he surveys his room decorated with vintage propellers. "Or I should say, a hobby that blew up."

Dig toy boats? Ask Mikkelson about the two toy boat shows he organizes every year. He also sells consignment toy boats and parts in the front part of the museum.

418 Benson Avenue Southeast, Willmar
(320) 231-0384
www.FallsFlyer.com
Open most Saturdays from 9 a.m. to 4 p.m., and by appointment.
Admission charged

An Impressive Welcome Center

Open since 1995, the **Fireplace of States and Tourist Information Center** in Bemidji is a striking and inviting place, with its architectural design resembling an early-1900s boathouse and an array of Paul Bunyan artifacts. In addition, its unique Fireplace of States, built in 1937, contains stones from every state in the continental United States as well as many Canadian provinces. The center is located at 300 Paul Bunyan Drive, off Highway 197, in Bemidji. Look for the statues of Paul and Babe. Open June through August: Monday through Saturday from 9 a.m. to 6 p.m.; Sunday from noon to 5 p.m. Open September through May, Monday through Friday from 9 a.m. to 5 p.m. For more information, call (218) 751-3541 or (800) 458-2223.

30 | Runestone Museum
Alexandria

Everyone seems to have an opinion as to whether or not the Vikings—the Scandinavian voyagers, not the football team—roamed Minnesota centuries before Christopher Columbus landed in the New World. (See page 70 for Harmony Toy Museum owner Wesley Idso's take on the theory.) Ever since a stone tablet with ancient markings was found near Alexandria, residents and scholars have debated its authenticity. Some scholars dismiss it as a crude forgery and anyone associated with it only perpetuates the myth that the Vikings, or Northmen, trekked through the land of 10,000 lakes. Other folks are sure "them boys was here all right," as the narrator on a museum video declares.

"Most people in town are believers," says Runestone Museum Director LuAnn Patton. Since October 2000, the stone has undergone rigorous scientific testing by geophysicists. Preliminary test results reveal that the stone was in the ground 50 to 500 years before it was found, meaning whoever found it did not carve it, Patton says. "Yes, the runestone has been mistreated. But one day it will be appreciated the way it deserves to be," she says.

We do know for sure that many Minnesotans have Scandinavian, particularly Norwegian, ancestry, and towns such as Alexandria revel in their Scandinavian heritage by establishing museums and festivals and erecting statues of Northmen or their ships in town squares and parks. During Minnesota's centennial celebration in 1958, Alexandria built a museum to house the runestone, and in the 1960s, in preparation for the 1965 New York World's Fair, they constructed a 28-foot Viking nicknamed Ole Oppe. Ole was built to be part of an animated exhibition titled "Minnesota: Birthplace of America," an exhibition that included the display of the Kensington Runestone. After the fair, residents trucked the statue back to Alexandria and planted Ole at the edge of their downtown, a sword's width from the Runestone Museum. For more than 40 years the museum has explored the story behind the runestone. Everyone loves unsolved mysteries. You can explore one in Alexandria.

While clearing his field one day in the fall of 1898, Swedish immigrant Olaf Ohman found a stone tablet tangled in the roots of a tree. It was a 200-pound, 31-by-16-inch flat stone with many markings in it. The stone ended up in the hands of historians at several universities, linguists, and professors well versed in Norwegian culture and history. They deciphered the runic writing as reading "We are 8 Goths [Swedes], 22 Northmen on acquisition business from Vinland far to the west we had an encampment by 2 shelters one day's time north from this stone We were fishing one day. After we came home I found 10 men red with blood and dead. Hail Mary, deliver us from evil. I have 10 men by the sea to attend to our ship 14 days journey from this wealth. Year of Christ 1362."

A 28-foot Viking near the Runestone Museum, Alexandria

In a (once) secret linguistic message the runic symbols also reveal "Ivar composed me."

Not everyone took the tablet's message at face value. In fact, many ridiculed Ohman and his family, and called the runestone a hoax. (The tauntings grated on the family so much that one of Ohman's sons committed suicide and his daughter left home.) But Ohman had only a few years of schooling; how could he have written in runic? Naysayers have stated that yes, the Vikings traveled to Newfoundland, but they could never have made it as far as Minnesota. For a while in the 1940s the stone was displayed in the Smithsonian. "But after a while they changed their mind because of the 'expert's' opinion that it was a forgery. But most of those experts never saw the stone," Patton points out.

Begin your visit by watching a video about the runestone's discovery (including a reenactment), plus a history of Viking explorations and explanations of runic writing. The narrator explains that Northmen were actually a peaceful group of tribes before A.D. 800. For one reason or another (historians aren't sure why, perhaps because of overcrowding in their own lands), bands of Northmen started pillaging their neighbors to the south and west and capturing prisoners for ransom. People in Britain, France, and parts of Russia were terrified. (A common prayer of the time was, "Oh Lord deliver us from the fury of the Northmen.") Around 1000, Viking explorer Leif Ericson journeyed to what he called Vinland, or Wineland, because of all the grapevines growing there. Historians believe this region was Newfoundland and the Labrador Coast. Some believe Vikings founded settlements in Newfoundland, like they had done in Iceland and Greenland, and that it was from these camps that groups of explorers headed westward to Minnesota through Hudson Bay and the Great Lakes.

After you've been briefed on Viking history, it's time to take a look at the actual Kensington Runestone. The gray slab of stone is kept in a glass box and displayed in the center of the museum's main room. Near the runestone, the staff has arranged an "unsolved mystery" exhibit that reviews reports of other similar stones with runic writings that have been unearthed in the United States. The exhibit also discusses artifacts like iron axes that are hundreds of years old but believed not to be Native American in origin. The exhibit also has a mooring stone on view; some people believe the Vikings tied their boats to these boulders.

Want to see where Ohman allegedly dug up the stone? Investigate the scene at Runestone Park, the site of his farmstead, just west of Alexandria on Highway 27.

The rest of the museum contains a variety of local history exhibits. The museum staff has compiled a Native American exhibit with artifacts like a Sioux eagle claw necklace and early-20th-century black-and-white photographs. Notice the Anishabe saying on the wall: "What the people believe is true." Another room in the museum is reproduced to resemble a 19th-century living room, complete with a petrified (literally) dog, named Scotty. There's a wall of military artifacts—Civil War leg shackles, a 1917 trench knife, a .69 caliber U.S. Army musket from the early 1800s—and a wildlife exhibit with stuffed great gray and boreal owls, a bobcat, and a coyote. Outside, the museum staff has arranged a cluster of log-cabin buildings including a trading post, smokehouse, and washhouse from the 1890s. Another building has been stocked with tractors, plows, thresher, boat motors, and a buggy. Go ahead and climb up in the caboose before you leave.

Have some Norse blood in you? Join Alexandrians in revering their heritage at the Ole Oppe Fest held annually in Alexandria at the end of May. The town also hosts the Vikingland Band Fest in June, when Midwest high school bands compete in a marching parade.

206 Broadway, Alexandria
(320) 763-3160
www.runestonemuseum.org
Open year-round. During the summer the museum is open Monday through Friday from 9 a.m. to 5 p.m.; Saturday from 9 a.m. to 4 p.m.; Sunday from 11 a.m. to 4 p.m. During the winter the museum is open Monday through Friday from 9 a.m. to 5 p.m. and Saturday from 9 a.m. to 3 p.m.
Admission charged

31 Greyhound Bus Museum
Hibbing

The northern Minnesota town of Hibbing has some incredible claims to fame: It's the iron ore capital of the world, the place where Bob Dylan grew up, birthplace of the bookmobile, and birthplace of the bus industry. While most Minnesotans know that Dylan was raised in Hibbing and that the region is rich in iron deposits, not many people knew about the town's connection to the bus industry until recent years. But thanks to the Greyhound Bus Museum and the museum's founder (one of Greyhound's most enthusiastic cheerleaders), thousands of people have been able to learn about Hibbing's connection to the bus industry. A visit to the museum will be surprisingly delightful. Slide into the seat of a 1956 Scenic Cruiser (soak in the bus's history for as long as you like), listen to bus drivers share memories of their more humorous or frightening rides, and read about the making of the bus company and the museum.

In the early 1970s, Hibbing resident Gene Nicolelli, a self-described history buff, was looking for a local history project to work on when he started reading about the Greyhound Bus Company and its founders.

"The success story just fascinated me. The story was so American and the guys behind it were such entrepreneurs," Nicolelli recalls. "Half of them hardly spoke English. They had the guts to leave their jobs—even though they had no background in transportation—and start this company. That's what turned me on to this project." He started researching the company's early days and

A bus from the 1940s in the Greyhound Bus Museum, Hibbing

collecting memorabilia in the hope of one day opening a museum in Hibbing. In 1975, as chair of the bicentennial celebration in town, Nicolelli approached the village board about setting up a Greyhound exhibit in city hall. They gave him the green light, and a few years (and artifacts) later the display moved to a local history museum. From 1988 to 1998, he had about 1,000 square feet of space in the Memorial Building of Hibbing, but he was running out of room.

The Greyhound exhibit deserved a building of its own, Nicolelli thought. His son, an architect, drew up plans for a new museum. Nicolelli approached the Greyhound Bus Company and received some seed money, he applied for grants, sold bricks and plaques, and took advantage of a lot of in-kind services. The 10,000-square-foot museum opened in July 1999.

Located off the original bus route, the museum features everything from a garage stocked with Greyhound buses from the 1920s to 1980s (yes, you can go inside them) to toy buses and tapes of stories shared by former drivers.

Start the tour by walking through a time tunnel, listening to recordings of early 1900s buses rumbling down the streets and learning about Hibbing's unique past: It was a town that moved. Little did the village's founders know when they settled the town in 1893 they were directly above an area rich in iron—in fact, one of the largest iron ore deposits in North America. As companies flocked to the Hibbing area and began mining, and as the demand for iron skyrocketed during World War I, the town decided it should move two miles south in order to get at that valuable iron below; in 1912 they moved businesses and houses southward. As a result, residents had a greater distance to travel to their jobs in the mines, and relatives could no longer bop down the street to visit their grandparents.

Enter three Swedes. After being laid off as a blacksmith, Carl Wickman purchased the Hupmobile dealership planning to sell these large cars. But no one was interested in buying the car with many seats; they all wanted to ride in it, though. He partnered with Charles Wenberg and Andrew "Bus Andy" Anderson and they asked each other, "Why don't we charge people for rides?" and "Why don't we shuttle people back and forth between work?" They outlined a two-mile route from Hibbing to Alice and spread the word about their service. The first day they brought in $11.50 for $.15 rides. The Hup became known as the "pup," and when they expanded their service nationwide in 1932, the company officially adopted the Greyhound Motors name and the greyhound emblem.

Continue on toward the garage, past display cases of tin Greyhound buses, photos of unique buses (streamline styles, double-deckers) throughout the years, employee uniforms (with a 1930s uniform looking very much like one from the armed services), a 1930s coin collector, and an example of the buses' first heating systems (a heavy wool blanket and heated brick).

"Each one has its own story," Nicolelli says, looking at the row of buses: a 1927 White, a 1936 all-metal one with the engine in the back of the bus, and

While in the Area
Get to Know Hibbing's Rich and Famous

If you have some time, head over to the **Hibbing Historical Museum** to learn more about the town's curious past and its claims to fame. It was once known as the Richest Little Village in the World, when it was spending more money per capita (on projects such as purchasing lit lamp posts and paving streets) than any other town, thanks to the tax revenue generated from the mining companies. The town also has churned out a number of notables, among them baseball player **Roger Maris**, basketball player **Kevin McHale**, and **Vincent Bugliosi**, author of Helter Skelter and the prosecuting attorney in the Charles Manson murder case. The museum is located at 23rd Street and 5th Avenue East in Hibbing. Open during the summer, Monday through Saturday from 9 a.m. to 4:30 p.m. During the winter it's open Monday through Thursday from 10 a.m. to 3 p.m. An admission fee is charged. For more information, call (218) 263-8522.

another with a Battle of Britain design. During World War II, Greyhound transported U.S. troops in the country and England. After the war Greyhound adopted the Battle of the Britain design including a Royal Air Force bullseye, to honor the war effort. There's also a 1948 Silver and a 1967 Buffalo (called a buffalo because a driver said the double-decker shape of the bus and its hood design reminded him of a buffalo at feeding time), a 1956 Scenic Cruiser, and a 1982 Motorcoach.

While in the garage, read or listen to some of the definitely original stories from some drivers. One story tells of the day a pregnant woman wearing a large fur coat climbed onto a Greyhound bus. While a passenger was helping her up the stairs, her coat opened and a dog jumped out. She was told to leave; no pets allowed on the bus. A few days later a similar looking woman started to get on another bus; the same driver saw her and told her to leave. But she was not the same dog-owner; this woman was really pregnant. One time a ticket agent found a drunk sleeping on a station workbench, but decided to let him be until early morning. He started walking away, heard a loud noise, and turned around to discover that the drunk had thrown a hammer at him, and its handle had broken when he missed and it hit the floor. According to another story, on a crowded bus one day, the driver bends over to scratch his itchy leg only to discover he's scratched a female passenger's leg. "We could write a book with all the anecdotes we have heard," Nicolelli laughs.

Outside the museum, in front of more buses, read about how drivers have spent their retirement years. David "Hoss" Williams, a driver from 1943 to

1986, became a clown. Harlan McConnell, a driver from 1942 to 1977, drove hearses after his retirement. ("The passengers are well behaved and don't talk back," he was quoted as saying.)

1201 Greyhound Boulevard (follow signs from Highway 169), Hibbing
(218) 263-5814
Open mid-May through September: Monday through Saturday
from 9 a.m. to 5 p.m.; Sunday from 1 p.m. to 5 p.m.
Admission charged

Offbeat Minnesota Festivals

- Celebrate Scandinavian archetypes Ole and Lena at their very own festival, **Ole and Lena Days**, every February in Granite Falls. For more information, call (320) 564-4039.

- Be ready to hear a lot of complaining at the **Grumpy Old Men Days** in Wabasha. Held every February. For more information, call (800) 565-4158.

- An American classic, Spam, is revered at Austin's **Spam Town U.S.A. Festival** in early July. For more information, call (800) 444-5713.

- Montgomery has officially adored the kolacky, the Bohemian folded pastry, with its **Kolacky Days** since 1929. Held usually at the end of July. For more information, call (507) 364-5577.

- Have you ever wanted to enter a pie-eating contest? Here's your chance. **Braham's Pie Day** is held every summer, usually in early August. Braham bills itself as the Homemade Pie Capital of Minnesota. For more information, call (763) 689-4229.

- Find a bargain at the **85-mile-long garage sale** around Lake Pepin, held the first weekend in May. For more information, call (800) 369-4123.

- You can harken back to Tom Sawyer's time at Winona's **Steamboat Days**, held around the Fourth of July. For more information, call (507) 452-2272.

- Grab your ax and head to **Rochesterfest** in June for events that include the Midwest Lumberjack Championships. For more information, call (507) 285-8769.

- Waterville's annual **Bullhead Days** celebration is held the second full weekend of June. For more information, call (507) 362-4609.

32 | U.S. Hockey Hall of Fame
Eveleth

When you live in a town as far north as Eveleth, Minnesota, which is doused in cold, ice, and snow for practically six months of the year, you've got to get out and play to avoid cabin fever. Hockey has been ingrained in the hearts of Eveleth residents (there are five thousand of them) since people first started passing around a ball on the town's Fayal Pond in 1902. As the sport grew in popularity among the locals, they built the hippodrome for hockey players in 1922, hockey officials and supporters opened the U.S. Hockey Hall of Fame in the 1970s, and the town erected one big hockey stick (the world's largest) in a downtown park in 1995. Eveleth bills itself as the Capitol of American Hockey because no other city has produced more championship hockey players. And

An early Zamboni machine at the U.S. Hockey Hall of Fame

you can't go anywhere in Eveleth without being reminded that the name Eveleth is synonymous with hockey. Look up in the sky to see the watertower that announces Eveleth as "Home of the Hockey Hall of Fame." Down the street a police car drives by with the same statement painted onto its side. Whether driving through town on your way to the Boundary Waters Canoe Area or planning to whoosh down the slopes at nearby Giant's Ridge, take some time to visit the hall of fame, a virtual hockey mecca.

"Like I tell anyone involved in the sport, 'You play the game, we preserve it,'" says director Tom Sersha. "We are a shrine to American hockey."

The three-story hall of fame has lots of options for visitors, from die-hard hockey fans to occasional watchers. In the mood to watch television? Head upstairs and watch the U.S. versus U.S.S.R. 1980 Olympic match. In the mood for art? Head to the gallery full of oil and pastel paintings with portraits of players and dramatic moments in games throughout history. Want to play a video game? Belly up to the video arcade game and play Blades of Steel. Or learn about the history of hockey, how the game actually works, and which players have achieved greatness in the last 100 years.

When you enter the main exhibit room the first thing you will notice is the scoreboard used in the Walt Disney movie *The Mighty Ducks,* a story about a children's down-and-out hockey team. Also hanging from the ceiling are championship jerseys belonging to players like Wayne Gretzky and 1998 Olympic gold-medal winner Karyn Bye. Continue on and take a look at championship gloves used by enshrinee Jack Huttla and hear the inspirational story of Steven Kirkpatrick, the first wheelchair athlete to play in a pro hockey game. (Stricken with muscular dystrophy when he was two years old, the 25-year-old Michigan native rolled onto the ice in 2001 as a goalie for the Indianapolis Ice.) Walk by a giant photograph of Glen Avon and his grinning pee-wee team from Duluth, the national champs in 1951 and 1952. And there's a giant photo of Cliff "Fido" Purpor, a 1974 enshrinee (and North Dakota's first native to play in the National Hockey League), with his five sons, all dressed in hockey gear and grinning.

On the first level you'll have a chance to get close to a 1956 Zamboni machine that the company donated to the hall of fame. Learn everything you ever wanted to know about this self-propelled ice-making marvel. Frank Zamboni, who got his start in the ice business by installing refrigerators in dairies in the 1920s, noticed ice skating rising in popularity in the 1930s and 1940s, and built a rink, Iceland, in 1940. To keep the ice smooth he had workers scrape the ice, squeegee it clean, spray water, and allow it to freeze for an hour. This process took way too long. He headed into his workshop and in 1949 perfected the machine that does it all in one operation.

A makeshift ice shack with skates hanging from the walls and socks "drying" on a wood-burning stove creates an appropriate, shivery mood in the museum. Don't forget to stop by the "ice skates through time" exhibit to see how ice skates have changed in the last 100 years. A display case containing a variety of different ice skates and vintage advertisements plastered on the museum's walls entertain and inform people who have never seen the bulky skates sported decades ago.

Upstairs you can find out how hockey has evolved in the last 100 years or so. Before we played hockey, we played bandy, 11-man hockey, and ice polo. (Look for a photo of the Duluth ice polo club from the 1890s.) When people got tired of chasing a round rubber ball all over the ice and when it kept rolling off the pond, pucks where eventually developed. At the turn of the century, rinks were about twice the size they are now and without sideboards. The museum staff believes hockey was first introduced to the United States in 1895; college hockey was first played around 1898, and pro hockey began in 1903.

Exhibits explain the positions of a hockey team, define terms such as face-off, and list the skills, like stick handling, needed to play hockey.

Before you leave, read about the hall of fame inductees and their contributions to the sport. The staff has arranged photos and bios of all the inductees into the hall since it started in 1973.

With support from basically any person or organization involved with hockey, the hall of fame and its museum continues to be renovated and expanded. The gift shop and gallery opened in 1997, and more interactive exhibits will be installed in the future.

801 Hat Trick Avenue (off Highway 53), Eveleth
(218) 744-5167
www.ushockeyhall.com
Open daily year-round: Monday through Saturday from 9 a.m. to 5 p.m.; Sunday from 10 a.m. to 3 p.m. Call before visiting during the winter; hours may vary. Admission charged

While in the Area
Run with the Pack

Get in touch with your lupine side at the **International Wolf Center** in Ely. Howl to a pack at night, explore an abandoned den, and learn about the predator-prey relationship between the beaver and wolf. Watch the pack devour dinner and learn about the center's attempts to introduce and keep track of wolves in northern Minnesota. The International Wolf Center is located on the east side of Ely at 1396 Highway 169, not far from the Dorothy Molter Museum. An admission fee is charged. For more information, call (800) ELY-WOLF.

33 Dorothy Molter Museum
Ely

Dorothy Molter is considered a folk hero among residents of Ely, Minnesota, the town that acts as a launching point for visitors to the Boundary Waters Canoe Area, and among canoeists who visited her on the Isle of Pines. In 1952 the *Saturday Evening Post* called her "the loneliest women in America." She lived alone for more than 30 years in a cabin 15 miles from the nearest road in a region where winter temperatures have nose-dived to a record –60 degrees Fahrenheit.

But Molter wasn't that much of a hermit. Known as "the root beer lady" for the root beer she made with Knife Lake water, thousands of canoeists paddling through the Boundary Waters stopped by her cabin every summer. Even during the dark and bitter winters she would put on a pot of stew every day for the occasional snowmobiler that buzzed by her cabin (that is, until snowmobiles were banned in the area in 1984).

After she died in 1987—she was the last remaining resident of the Boundary Waters—the government planned to burn her buildings on the Isle of Pines. Friends, wanting to preserve her legacy, rallied to save two cabins. They dismantled them log by log and transported them via dogsled and snowmobile to Ely. In 1993 friends opened the Dorothy Molter Museum, housed in two of her restored cabins.

You can get acquainted with the root beer lady by watching a video shot of her in 1985 when she was 77 years old. Molter tosses food to ducks, boils water on her propane stove, and plants flowers. "They said nothing can grow up here, that I couldn't grow any flowers here, the ground was too rocky and full of roots," she tells the camera. But the resourceful Molter gathered soil from around the island, dumped buckets full of earth into an old canoe and planted an array of pink, white, and orange flowers. She grins on camera and says, "I had to show them I could." This is the kind of woman Molter was: capable, determined, and caring.

"She was 5'4", not a large woman, but she was very strong and had big hands," remembers museum director Linda Glass. "And for someone who lived in the wilderness for so long, she had smooth skin, and was not crusty around the edges; a soft-spoken woman. Dorothy lived in harmony with nature and believed in her own self," Glass adds.

Another video clip shows Molter strapping on snowshoes and trekking over the snowbanks with the help of a walking stick. She declares to the space around her, "It's been a good world for me."

Born in 1907, Molter grew up in Chicago and didn't visit Northern Minnesota until 1930. In 1934, while visiting a family friend and resort owner on Knife Lake, she agreed to help him run the Isle of Pines Resort. When the owner died in 1948, she assumed ownership. After Congress passed the Wilderness

Sign at the Dorothy Molter Museum, Ely

Act in 1964, she and other residents of the Boundary Waters Canoe Area were ordered out. But Molter considered the Isle of Pines home, and she wasn't going to leave. She spread the word among her friends (everyone who signed her guest book received a Christmas card) about being forced to leave and urged them to write letters. In 1975 she was told she could stay until 1980, but she couldn't run the resort or sell her root beer. (Instead, Molter set out "donation" jars so she could bring in some sort of an income.) Five years later no one came to force her out, so she kept on brewing her root beer and chatting with canoeists. Dorothy Molter died of a heart attack in 1987.

After watching the video, guests, especially children, are asked to imagine and discuss what life was like for Molter on the island. You'll talk about winter weather and the appliances Molter used, and consider how she might have passed the time during the long winters. This discussion preps you for the tour of the cabins.

The two cabins that were saved and restored are the winter and point cabins, the winter being the first one that visitors tour. Molter lived in this cabin during the winter months; during the summer, she lived for the most part in a tent. The staff has arranged her things neatly around the cabins to resemble how they looked when she was living in them. However, considering that she was quite a collector (remember, she couldn't pile up her garbage every Wednesday at the edge of a driveway), the cabins you tour are more sparse than they were in Molter's time. Back then, the cabin was wall-to-wall boxes, tools, and trinkets. As you wander through each room (the porch, kitchen, bedroom) a tour guide will share Molter's habits and hobbies. There's the radio she used to call Ely to check in or request supplies. There are her plates stacked on the shelf and her coffeepot. There are the goose-egg music boxes she made, dangling from a makeshift Christmas tree. Visitors walk through the cabin with a guide, although you're free to look around for as long as you'd like in order to

You're Not in Kansas Anymore

Dorothy and friends welcome you to the Judy Garland Gallery at the Children's Discovery Museum, Grand Rapids

Despite the happy start to her life, performing on stage to affectionate, adoring parents, Judy Garland was a tormented soul. Born in Grand Rapids in 1922 to vaudeville parents, "Baby Frances Gumm," with her radiant stage presence, rocketed to stardom in numerous films and cabaret performances. But her roller coaster personal life (she took a lot of pills, married five men, and dealt with her parents' and sister's premature deaths) took its toll on her. As Garland said in 1967, two years before she died at age 47, "When you've lived the life I've lived and suffered and been madly happy and desperately sad, well, that's when you realize that you'll never be able to set it all down. Maybe you'd rather die first."

Whether you're a Garland or Oz fan, her hometown of Grand Rapids has three options for you to visit. You can tour **Judy Garland's Birthplace**, filled with furniture and photos from the 1920s and 1930s. Go ahead, belt out a show tune on the landing where she and her sisters frequently staged shows for their parents. The home is located at 2727 Highway 169 in Grand Rapids. Open daily year-round from 9:30 a.m. to 5 p.m. An admission fee is charged. For more information, call (218) 327-9276 or (800) 664-JUDY.

You can also tour the **Children's Discovery Museum**, located in downtown Grand Rapids, which contains additional Garland material. The gallery features pastel drawings of *Wizard of Oz* characters, newspaper clippings about Garland, memorabilia like her baptismal certificate, a test dress she wore for *The Wizard of Oz*, suede shoes she wore in *Meet Me in St. Louis*, and signed sheet music. Notice the photos of Garland in a white net dress at two and a half years old and ones of her and her mother coming home to Grand Rapids in 1938. Have a seat and watch a video of Garland's show years. (There she is in all her glory, touting, "Get Happy" donning a little hat, and tugging dramatically at the microphone.) The museum is located at 19 Northeast Fourth Street (Highway 2) in Grand Rapids. Open daily year-round; 10 a.m. to 5 p.m. An admission fee is charged. For more information, call (218) 326-1900.

More Garland posters, family photos, and costume replicas are on view at the **Itasca County Historical Museum**. Located in Old Central School at 10 Northwest 5th Street in Grand Rapids. Open year-round, Monday through Saturday from 9:30 a.m. to 5 p.m. During the summer the museum is open on Sunday from 10 a.m. to 4 p.m. An admission fee is charged. For more information, call (218) 326-6431.

get a sense of what life must have been like in a little cabin on a little island near the U.S.–Canadian border.

After you've wandered through the winter cabin, follow the broken boat paddle fence and step inside the point cabin. This cabin contains a myriad of broken paddles hanging from the walls and the ceiling (most of them given to Molter from visiting canoeists) and a number of vintage snowmobiles she used to ride, including the first one she ever owned. There's also a wind-powered paddle plane that once belonged to Molter, fishing lures, boat motors, and her root beer brewing supplies.

Molter became known as the root beer lady after planes were banned from making deliveries in the Boundary Waters and she could no longer order in soda. She had to start making her own beverages. Because she had so many soda bottles left over, the resourceful Molter started brewing root beer with water from the lake, dry yeast, sugar, and root beer extract and funneled the brew into the bottles. She brewed about 10,000 to 12,000 bottles each summer, storing them in the little icehouse on the island to keep them cool. Most of the time she had relatives up to help her bottle.

Before you leave, pick up a bottle of her root beer, now brewed by James Page Company in St. Paul.

2002 East Sheridan Street (off Highway 169), Ely
(218) 365-4451
www.canoecountry.com/dorothy
Open weekends during May from 10 a.m. to 6 p.m. Open daily Memorial Day through Labor Day from 10 a.m. to 6 p.m.
Admission charged

34 3M/Dwan Museum
Two Harbors

Did you ever awaken on a Saturday morning in spring, drive to the local hardware store, and come back with armfuls of 150-grit sandpaper, feeling as if everything were right in the world? Okay all you home improvers (and anyone else interested in learning how a company evolved from developing sandpaper to Scotch tape and a host of other innovative products), the 3M/Dwan Museum is for you. You may be like some visitors who arm themselves with a video camera and spend hours videotaping the museum's walls decorated with 3M's tape and retro reflectability products. But for those of you who are not tape fanatics, the facility can be toured in 30 minutes.

Stay for 15 or 500 minutes, and you'll walk away with a nice little history lesson about the makings of the Minnesota Mining and Manufacturing Company. Located in the former office of attorney John Dwan, the company's first secretary, the museum contains three small rooms of exhibits. (Anything more would have been too much blatant self-promotion. And really, how excited can you get about Scotch tape?)

The museum is owned and operated by the Two Harbors Historical Society, but 3M is purportedly very hands-on with the museum, a volunteer says, recently help-

Sign near the entrance to the 3M/Dwan Museum, Two Harbors

ing to restore the building and always encouraging employees to swing by. Located a few blocks from the Lake Superior waterfront, the museum is housed in the company's original office, but the building, which dates back to 1898, was relocated a few blocks south of its original site.

Start your visit by opening filing cabinet–like drawers and reading about the company's early beginnings and the background behind the minerals it mined in the early days. At the turn of the 20th century, tons of companies were mining in northern Minnesota for iron, taconite, and gold. In 1901 the mineral corundum was discovered on the north shore of Lake Superior. A year later, the Minnesota Mining and Manufacturing Company incorporated in Two Harbors with the purpose of mining corundum to make grinding wheel abrasives. But the men soon found out that what they thought was corundum was really a low-grade anorthosite, not exactly right for producing heavy-duty abrasives. The men relocated to Duluth and focused on sandpaper products instead. At the museum you can see a copy of the company's articles of incorporation, the first stock certificate issued for 50 shares, and discover that 3M's first sales order was received from the South Bend Toy Company for $12 in 1906. It took a while for 3M to develop a consistent and high-quality product. More investors were solicited and the company didn't turn a profit until 10 years after they incorporated.

Major breakthroughs occurred in the 1920s. In the early 1920s, 3M invented the world's first waterproof sandpaper. (In case you haven't toured a sandpaper factory, the museum has one big roll of sandpaper for you to look at.) In 1925 a lab assistant developed masking tape to help automobile painters apply two-toned paint. He brought a sample to some auto painters and in the middle of the application, the tape fell off. The painter told him, "Take this back to those Scotch bosses of yours and tell them to put more adhesive on it." Since then, Scotch tape has been used as an anticorrosive shield on the Goodyear blimp and to stop pantyhose runs, bind a chicken's leg together before being weighed, and hang posters. Check out the museum's tape timeline and all the varieties of tapes 3M has made—there are 1,000.

As the years progressed, 3M started inventing products far beyond their initial scope of abrasives and tape. In the 1940s it made Scotchlite, which is reflective sheeting for street signs. In the 1950s it rolled out Scotchguard fabric protector and ScotchBrite cleaning pads, and it produced waterproof and flameproof ribbons. In the 1990s, 3M perfected cook-in-pouch technology with heat-sealable film. Throughout the decades, 3M has also pioneered CD-ROM, audio, and video production.

In one room, the staff has set up a simulated laboratory with former 3M equipment. In another, computers explain the company's research developments, such as on an anti-inflammatory medication for asthma sufferers. You can learn about 3M's other projects, such as making tiny adhesives used to tag monarch butterflies and a synthetic rubber for astronaut's boots. Flip through posters showing how 3M has grown into a company that sold $13.5 billion dollars' worth of products worldwide and employed about 70,000 people in 1990. (Not to mention it was named one of America's most admired companies in 1988 by *Fortune* magazine.) Staff has made even a trip to the bathroom special; notice the shelf stocked with 3M cleaning products.

201 Waterfront Drive (south of Highway 61), Two Harbors
(218) 834-4898
Open daily May through October from 9:30 a.m. to 5 p.m., and by appointment.
Admission charged

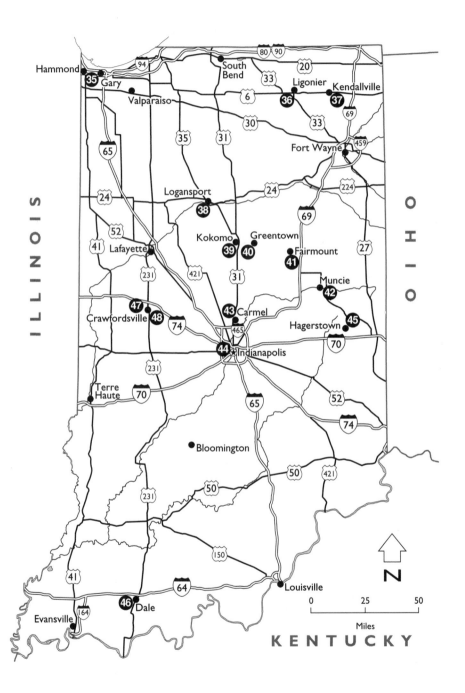

Hammond
35 Gary
Valparaiso

South Bend

80 90

20

33

Ligonier
36

Kendallville
37

94

6

69

30

35

31

33

Fort Wayne
459

65

224

24

Logansport

24

69

52

38

27

41 Lafayette

Kokomo
39 40

Greentown

Fairmount
41

231

421

Muncie
42

31

47

43 Carmel

Hagerstown
45

Crawfordsville 48

74

465

70

44 Indianapolis

Terre Haute

231

70

65

52

74

Bloomington

50

421

50

231

50

150

41

64

Louisville

46 Dale

N

Evansville

164

KENTUCKY

0   25   50

Miles

100

3 INDIANA

Cars, Clothing, and a Squirrel Cage

35 | Dillinger Museum
Hammond

For years, John Dillinger buffs, crime historians, and anyone interested in seeing the wax figure of the famous outlaw lying "bloody" on a morgue table used to trek to the Dillinger Museum in Nashville, located in southern Indiana. The owner, Joe Pinkston, a Dillinger fanatic, would talk to visitors for hours (if they had the time) about his theories of Dillinger and his death (for example, that Dillinger was actually a government pawn or that it wasn't actually Dillinger who was shot outside Chicago's Biograph Theater).

When Pinkston died in 1996, the collection was sold to the Lake County Visitors' and Convention Bureau and is now located in their visitors' center in Hammond, a clean, modern facility just off I-80/94. But Hammond-area residents objected to the museum's plan to portray Dillinger, an Indiana farm boy turned Public Enemy Number One, as a folk hero. (Area residents hadn't forgotten that Dillinger shot and killed a police officer from nearby East Chicago while robbing a bank in 1934.) Bowing to the public outcry over any glorification of a felon, the visitors' bureau opened an exhibit in 1999 with the message "Crime Doesn't Pay."

Though not as quirky as Pinkston's museum (some say the Lake County version is a bit overproduced and hides some of the best exhibits from the public, namely the wooden gun used in "The Great Escape"), the new Dillinger Museum is certainly worth a visit. Stop by if you're interested in finding out how a young crook became a big-time bank robber and how he managed to escape from a reportedly escape-proof jail. If you're into cops and robbers and criminal life in the 1930s, make sure to veer off I-80/94 the next time you're stuck in traffic and pay a visit.

The museum staff bills the Dillinger Museum as "A Hands-On Historical Adventure." It certainly is. When you walk into the Dillinger exhibit, to your right, strapped into a chair in a telephone booth–like contraption, is a dummy of Bruno Hauptmann, the man convicted of kidnapping and murdering Charles and Anne Lindbergh's infant son. (Hauptmann? Isn't this a museum on Dillinger?) You can push a button and "electrocute" the Hauptmann dummy. Though it could be a bit jarring to youngsters (and a disclaimer warns parents near the booth), visiting children have often been seen having a ball pushing the button and watching the dummy fry. Though Hauptmann was not associated with Dillinger in any way, the faux death-by-electrocution exhibit falls under the museum's message of "crime doesn't pay." After you've had your fill of zapping Hauptmann, take a few steps forward and you're presented with a bust of Patrick O'Malley, the officer shot by Dillinger, and a memorial to other area officers killed in the line of duty. Time to reflect again on the ramifications of Dillinger's and other bad guys' actions.

After what could be a somewhat jarring introduction, you will meet Dillinger as a boy and young man. Check out his baseball cleats and photos of him grinning and handsome. He joined the Navy in 1923, but it wasn't his cup of tea, and he deserted. A year later Dillinger tried to rob a grocery store with a friend and got caught. He was sentenced to 10 years in prison. While in jail he stewed, met real robbers, befriended them, learned the tricks of the trade, and promised to help them escape once he got out. Nine years into his sentence Dillinger was paroled, held true to his promise, and helped his buddies escape.

Like What You See?
On the Heels of Midwest Gangsters

- See where John Dillinger escaped from an attempted FBI raid, enraged the government, and prompted Herbert Hoover to declare him Public Enemy Number One. The **Little Bohemia** restaurant in Manitowish Waters, Wisconsin, serves up wicked Old Fashioneds and steaks in a 1930s atmosphere. Take a stroll around the restaurant and see windows shattered by the gunfire and clothes the gang left behind, plus a slew of photos and newspaper articles chronicling the Dillinger gang's activities. Open seasonally. The restaurant is located at 12575 Fallon Road. For more information, call (715) 543-8433.

- Gangster buffs visiting Chicago must hop on the black bus for the **Untouchables Tour.** Pay a visit to the site of the Valentine's Day Massacre, the Biograph Theater, and Capone's former headquarters. Tours run daily. A fee is charged. For more information, call (773) 881-1195 or visit www.gangstertour.com.

- Once Al Capone's summer retreat, **The Hideout,** in Couderay, Wisconsin, now operates as a restaurant and museum. You must tour his lavish house, the "roaring twenties museum," and grounds with a tour guide at scheduled times. You'll get a glimpse inside the lodge where Capone played poker with pals, the jail cell where disloyal associates stayed, and a view of the dark, muddy lake where Capone's dock once received seaplane shipments of Canadian booze. If you don't want to tour, order up a char-broiled steak and martini in the restaurant. Hours and tour times vary per month. The Hideout is located at 12101 West County CC in Couderay, Wisconsin. An admission fee is charged. For more information, call (715) 945-2746.

While in the Area
Check out Chesterton

When Jean Nelson opened her gift shop, **The Yellow Brick Road**, in 1978 in Chesterton, she didn't even sell *The Wizard of Oz* merchandise. In fact, she wasn't an Oz zealot. "I didn't see the movie until 1956 when it aired in black and white on television and I watched it with my kids," she confesses. Of her store's Oz-implying name, Nelson says, "I just thought it would be a neat name for a shop." Decades later, the shop is wall-to-wall Oz ephemera, with a one-room museum to the side that serves as the munchkin hub during Chesterton's annual Oz Festival. (Nelson is affectionately known as the "Mother of Munchkins" among former actors in the movie.)

Nelson sold her business in December 2000, but she still lives next door to the shop. "I live in Oz land whether I want to or not," she says with a laugh, adding, "I don't think I'll ever be able to retire from the festival." Nelson helped rebuild Ozmania in the United States, particularly in the Midwest, by starting the annual **Oz Festival**—an event that brought an estimated 80,000 to 100,000 people to Chesterton in 2000, a town of 9,000 people.

The festival is an event Nelson has worked on since shortly after she opened the doors to her shop. She wanted to bring in more visitors to Chesterton, a little town about 15 miles east of Gary, and thought, why not create a world-famous festival revolving around *The Wizard of Oz*, a movie revered by millions. Since its early years, the festival has attracted former munchkins and zillions of Oz devotees who travel to Oz-themed festivals around the country. Some annual highlights of the Chesterton festival, held in mid-September, are the Munchkin Celebrity Dinner, autograph sessions with munchkins, and more Oz memorabilia than you can imagine.

If you can't make the festival, drop by the store and museum and stock up on Dorothy dresses and Dorothy dolls. **The Oz Fantasy Museum**, located next to the shop, features a mechanical Dorothy, life-size cowardly lion, a re-creation of the Emerald City, and many items given to Nelson.

The shop is located at 109 Yellow Brick Road in Chesterton. For more information, call (219) 926-7048 or visit www.yellowbrickroad.com.

Once out, they formed a gang and robbed banks—lots of them. Many robberies, murders, incarcerations, and escapes later, Dillinger became a sort of cult hero. The public was drawn to this outlaw described in the press as a neatly groomed gentleman dressed in the latest fashions who always acted polite to those he robbed. The robberies took place during the Depression after all, and many folks didn't think too highly of banks then. (The milieu of the time is described for you in exhibits.) Many people were secretly pleased that this handsome, polite man robbed banks. The walls of the museum are plastered with photocopies of newspaper articles that describe the adventures of Dillinger and his gang. After escaping an FBI raid at the Little Bohemia restaurant in northern Wisconsin (see sidebar on page 103) in which Dillinger's gang killed FBI agents, Herbert Hoover declared John Dillinger Public Enemy Number One. Look for a picture of his warrant. Dillinger's days were numbered.

The FBI finally caught up with Dillinger in July 1934 at Chicago's Biograph Theater. Reportedly tipped off to his whereabouts by "the lady in red," officers shot and killed him in the theater's alley; there is a wax reproduction of Dillinger on that fatal night and real newspaper photos. You can also see Dillinger's original tombstone—it was replaced when so many people chipped off pieces as souvenirs—and the body basket used to carry him to the funeral home.

The museum also has quite an assemblage of weapons that once belonged to Dillinger and his gang, from a Tommy gun to a tear gas gun. (They stocked up on these guns by raiding police stations.) View a reproduction of Dillinger's fingerprints, a copy of his wanted poster, snapshots of him and his girlfriends, photos of him showing off his guns at a family picnic, and copies of newspaper articles detailing his escapes, captures, and the manhunts associated with him. There's also a replica of the wooden gun he carved in jail and thrust into the back of a jailer for "The Great Escape" from the Crown Point Jail—located a few miles south of the Lake County visitors' bureau and museum—on March 3, 1934. The real wooden gun has been placed in a safe, far away from tourists' eyes.

This museum, like most big, modern museums, has a lot of interactive displays. In fact, everywhere you turn there's an activity for you: learn the jargon of robbers, try on a bulletproof vest (though half of it is attached to a wall), peer into replicas of a crime lab and a bank. Before you exit the museum, you will pass by a wall containing photographs of each original gang member. Below each photo the criminals' fates are revealed—many died from gunshot wounds in prison—further driving home the museum's message that crime does not pay.

7770 Corinne Drive (at the Lake County Visitors' and Convention Bureau, I-80/94, exit 3A), Hammond
(800) 255-5253
www.alllake.org/jdm.php
Open year-round: Monday through Friday from 8 a.m. to 6 p.m.;
Saturday and Sunday from 9 a.m. to 6 p.m.
Admission charged

36 | Indiana Historic Radio Museum
Ligonier

As you stroll through the Indiana Historic Radio Museum you might hear "Yes, Sir, That's My Baby!" coming through a polished wooden cathedral radio or an art deco nightstand radio, and you might break into the Charleston. Blame it on the setting—a 1929 service station, built when many of the radios in the collection were manufactured. Blame it on the radios, artistically crafted music boxes, some of them designed to look like furniture. Or blame it on your white-haired host whose memory kicks in as she shows you different pieces in the collection. "Oh, I wanted to go so badly," remembers one volunteer as she passes by a radio with a scene of the 1933 Chicago World's Fair painted on it. It's easy to get wrapped up in the past in Ligonier, a town of ample lawns and aging Victorian houses, and it's especially easy to get wrapped up in the past in its radio museum.

Before the Indiana Historic Radio Museum opened, many of the radios in the collection had made appearances in the Auburn Cord Duesenberg Museum in Auburn or Union Station in Indianapolis. But the radio collection was always a guest; it never had its own space. After a string of fortunate circumstances and generous people (the service station was up for sale, the city had a ton of extra bricks for the paving of the drive-up, and residents volunteered to renovate the 60-year-old building), the folks from the Indiana Historic Radio Society were able to move the telegraph equipment, microphones, and radios into the station in 1995.

Between 1925 and 1965 about 300 million radios were built in the United States—about 40,000 different models from 1,200 companies, the museum estimates. (This number includes companies like "Joe's Shop.") The staff does its best to show a variety of these models and manufacturers: more than 400 radios are on display in the museum. You don't remember how the radio came into existence? Reacquaint yourself with its history by simply taking a walk around the museum.

All stages of the radio's development are represented here, from the telegraph to vacuum tubes to transistor radios. Learn about the Morse telegraph again and see an 1837 Morse telegraph apparatus. The museum also has a telegraph that was carried into a World War I battle on the back of a mule along with batteries, a receiver, antenna, and headphones. Did you know the "unsinkable" *Titanic* sent the first SOS signal? The museum has a telegram sent from the ship on April 14, 1912, that reads: "SOS SOS SOS WE CAN NOT LAST MUCH LONGER ENGINE ROOM FULL UP TO BOILERS SINKING FAST." A ship could have reached the *Titanic* before the other rescue boats, but it only had one telegraph operator on board and he was not on duty at the time. After the *Titanic* sunk, ships were required to have two telegraph operators on board at all times.

A number of display cases and tables are stocked with vintage vacuum tubes. Tucked into a corner of the one-room museum is a horn speaker from 1920 to 1924, believed to be the world's largest horn speaker. One wall contains radios from the 1920s, such as a Westinghouse 1921 that cost $225 when it was new, and the popular cathedral radios. A 1939 red, white, and blue Zenith stands out on the floor, as do a number of the more ingenious radios that manufacturers spun out: a 1942 radio in the shape of a stack of books; a minibar that's also a radio; a grandfather clock radio; and the Radio Lite-Tenna, a lamp that acts as an indoor radio antenna. One interesting radio is a small, plain black and white one. It's a 1938 People's Radio produced in Nazi Germany. Hitler realized the radio was a valuable way to reach the masses, but he had manufacturers produce them so people couldn't pick up signals from stations like the BBC. Continue on toward another corner of the museum and wonder at the modern novelty radios—in the shape of a Budweiser can, Alka Seltzer package, and Kraft Macaroni and Cheese box.

You'll also learn that in the 1930s the word "radio" was a magic word that stood for newness or technology, and many companies with products completely unrelated to radios sprung up: Radio Flyer wagons, Radio padlocks, and Radio perfume. Call letters are also explained for visitors and a few translated. For example, WBBM in Chicago stands for World's Best Broadcasting Medium.

Most of the museum's collection belongs to the Schultz family of Ligonier, though as more people hear about it more radios have been donated or loaned

Radio row inside the Indiana Historic Radio Museum, Ligonier

GREAT LITTLE MUSEUMS OF THE MIDWEST

The One and Only Marshmallow Fest

Although the Kidd Marshmallow Company left Ligonier in 1996, residents still put on a fete in honor of the fluff industry. Help build the world's largest marshmallow at Ligonier's annual Marshmallow Fest usually held on Labor Day weekend. For more information, call (219) 894-9000.

to the museum. The patriarch of the family and museum curator Fred Schultz has been collecting antique radios since he retired in 1981. He had no plans to disappear into the land of shuffleboard and vitamin E shakes after he retired. Instead, he wanted to hit swap meets and stockpile quality, restored radios. A former dispatcher with the Indiana State Police, he had always been fascinated with the evolution of the radio. The other main force behind the museum is the Indiana Historic Radio Society, one of the oldest radio clubs in the country. Many of its members were directly involved in the development of the radio, either inventing components or fixing radios. Fifty years ago it wasn't uncommon for men to set up little shops behind their houses to build and repair radios. Look for photos of these early shops in the museum.

Area students are also involved. They have printed and placed cards alongside many of the radios detailing events that occurred the year the particular model was manufactured: New York City installed traffic lights in 1930, the Hollywood sign was erected in 1923, the first push-button set was introduced in 1926. Not only will you learn about the history of the radio, you'll also be briefed in American history and trivia.

800 Lincolnway, Ligonier
(888) 417-3562
www.indianahistoricalradio.org
Open May through October, Tuesday, Wednesday, Thursday, and Saturday from 10 a.m. to 3 p.m. During winter the museum is open Saturday from 10 a.m. to 2 p.m.
Free admission

37 | Mid-America Windmill Museum
Kendallville

With wooden windmills creaking and turning with the wind and the warbling of birds nearby, a visit to the Mid-America Windmill Museum makes for a peaceful walk-in-the-park type of experience. Surrounded by a small subdivision, city park, and farm fields, it's quiet and rather soothing compared to a nuclear or electric power plant visit. Open since 1997, the windmill museum is located on an approximately 36-acre site, which includes a barn containing windmill artifacts, a field of windmills, and a little pond and gravel path to meander around. Since the museum's collection started in the early 1990s, staff has accumulated about 100 windmills; 40 have been restored.

The relaxing and rare museum is the brainchild of Hoosier Russ Baker, who, in 1991, nearing his retirement, found himself with a little more free time than he was used to. He began researching his family tree and discovered that his great-grandfather ran the Union Windmill Company. Wanting to learn more about the history of windmills in the United States, he picked up a copy of *The Field Guide to American Windmills* and discovered that from about 1870 to 1950, 78 wind-mill manufacturers were located within an 80-mile radius of Kendallville.

Why were so many windmill companies established in northern Indiana? Because most windmills were made out of wood and a good source of hardwood could be found in northern Indiana, southern Michigan, and western Ohio, Baker supposes. And in the first half of the 20th century, many automobile companies were popping up in the region, prompting a lot of talented skilled tradespeople to migrate to the area. Why not set up shop where there were plenty of mechanically minded people?

While Baker was learning about windmills, the town's local development committee

Mid-America Windmill Museum, Kendallville

Like What You See?
More Breezy Excursions

- If you like the look of Danish windmills, stop by the **Danish Windmill Museum and Welcome Center** in Elk Horn, Iowa. Built in the Netherlands in 1848, the windmill was shipped to Elk Horn in 1975. The museum is located at 4038 Main Street. For hours and additional information, call (712) 764-7472, (800) 451-7960 or visit www.danishwindmill.com.

- In Audubon, Iowa, area farmers have donated 18 windmills to **Nathanial Hamlin Park,** located one mile south of town on Highway 71. The park also has a pair of elks roaming around a fenced area and a local history museum with a huge collection of nails, of all things. For more information, call (712) 563-2516 or (712) 563-2764.

was researching ways to promote tourism in the area. Why not a windmill museum? Baker asked them. Windmill museums already existed in Lubbock, Texas, and Alberta, Canada, but none had popped up in the Midwest, where so many were produced and found on farms in the early part of the 20th century. The town green-lighted his project.

Start your visit inside the barn by briefing yourself about the history of windmills. Historians believe Persians were the first to harness wind around A.D. 100 to 400. They also believe windmills were introduced to Europe in the fifth or sixth century as Muslims advanced into Europe and Europeans headed to the Middle East during the Crusades. (Windmills have been documented in Spain in 912 and Crete in 1137.) In the late 1500s, Holland developed its famous smock windmill to aid grain milling and water pumping; some wheels had diameters of 120 to 160 feet. The first windmill in the United States, located about 20 miles from Jamestown, Virginia, was said to have been built by Sir George Yardley in 1620. It was a post windmill—the mill and house are located on one large post—used to grind grain. It stood 35 feet tall and had a wheel diameter of 51 feet. There are drawings of all these early windmills in the barn and scattered pieces of windmills, such as blades. While you're inside, watch a video that will refresh your memory about how wind develops and how the wind blows in Indiana.

Outside, take as long as you want to walk around the "windmill park." You'll pass by an Emertech Model E-400, a windmill with a 4,000-watt turbine and a peak output of 4,600 watts at 240 volts AC. The Emertech is equipped with a single-phase induction generator with a 100-foot tower, which means if the wind blew at 20 mph, the mill would generate about 2,800 watts of power. There's also a 10-foot Monitor L–style windmill (a wind wheel made of six sections) made by Baker manufacturing. The L style was introduced in 1915 and produced until 1940. Or how about that eight-foot-tall self-oiling Fairbanks windmill from the late 1920s? Notice its wind wheels are tilted upward in the same way as a European smock windmill. Many of the pieces in the museum's collection were donated by area residents or purchased from collectors around the country.

Baker is quick to point out that the museum came to fruition thanks to many community volunteers. Boy Scouts built a covered bridge on the site. A couple donated the barn. High school students painted the stunning mural of the wind goddess Olympia in the barn. And every week volunteers gather to help restore the windmills in the basement. Their most recent project is the restoration of a post windmill located northwest of the barn.

Drop by the museum during the end of June for the wind celebration, where antiques dealers buy, sell, and trade windmill equipment, kite flyers launch their creations into the air, and locals reenact a Civil War battle.

732 South Allen Chapel Road, Kendallville
(219) 347-2334
Open May through October: Tuesday through Friday from 10 a.m. to 4 p.m.;
Saturday from 10 a.m. to 5 p.m.; and Sunday 1 p.m. to 4 p.m.
Admission charged

38 Cole Clothing Museum
Logansport

Though it's been years since Jean Cole lived in the South, she is still a southern belle, from the casual, genuine way she calls you "honey" and escorts you through the Cole Clothing Museum to the graceful way she has decorated the Queen Anne house where her vintage clothing is on display. Cole did not grow up in a grand house like the one in which her clothing museum is located. Growing up in Tennessee without electricity, she dreamt of beautiful things like flowing dresses, lacy parasols, and tea parties. Now that she's got her very own clothing museum, she can stockpile such things. If you like fur muffs and fashion shows, then head to the Cole Clothing Museum in Logansport.

Located in a three-story Queen Anne and a carriage house, Cole's collection features clothes from approximately the late 1800s to the 1960s. Most likely you'll

begin your visit on the first floor of the house, where you'll find early-20th-century clothing, including a small hat and muff display. Go ahead and run your hand over the fur muff; Cole encourages touching. Aside from a few articles such as silver hand brushes and mirrors kept in glass cases, you can touch most items in the clothing museum. Each room on the second floor features clothing from a different decade in the 20th century. Again, feel the items to see how light white muslin dresses were in the 1910s, how heavy the "swimsuits" (they look and feel like they were made from potato sacks) were in the 1890s. Cole has accented each room with photographs and newspaper and magazine clippings

Inside the Cole Clothing Museum, Logansport

marking the major events of the years. Vintage posters from *Ladies' Home Journal* and black-and-white photographs of Logansport street scenes adorn the walls.

The collection is amazingly personal because Cole has documented the stories behind many of the clothes. Look for Miss Minnie Holman's wedding dress circa 1890s in one room on the second floor. A card pinned on it describes Minnie and her husband's wedding in Vincennes, Indiana, and the carriage ride that took them

> # *While in the Area Take a Trip Back in Time*
>
> If you're in Logansport between Memorial Day and Labor Day, take a whirl on the more than 100-year-old **Cass County Carousel** at 1208 Riverside Drive. Built by Gustav Dentzel, a leading carousel maker in his time, the hand-carved, wooden carousel has more than 40 animals to hop on. While you're riding, you're entertained with songs coming from an antique organ. For more information, call (219) 753-8725.

to her parents' home in Knox City, Indiana. In another room, admire the 50th anniversary dress of Minnie's mother, Augusta Holman, whose husband, William, opted not to attend their wedding anniversary celebration. Of all the garments in her museum, Cole's favorite is the "slip of many colors" from the 1920s or 1930s. It's a ragtag of a slip that looks like a sundress that has been left outside on the clothing line for a few decades, with a number of patches here and there. "The woman who wore it just patched and patched it. But she still had pride. I would give anything to have met that woman," Cole says.

Cole herself is an engaging and personable woman who chats freely with visitors. A native of Tennessee, she and her husband moved to Logansport in 1956. For years she acted as a bereavement coordinator and chaplain in a local hospice. In the late 1980s, after grappling with a number of distressing events—she moved her mother who suffers from Parkinson's disease to Indiana, her son was recuperating from a serious head injury, and she was diagnosed with breast cancer—Cole became burned out. "I felt I was being pointed in a new direction," the petite blonde declares.

That direction would be toward clothes—lots of clothes. She got to organizing style shows for local organizations and talking about the importance of early detection of breast cancer. She scoured clothing shows around the state, picking up a few outfits here and there. With every year that passed she got a little more intense about collecting and her collection grew. ("I can't believe what all I've got!" she may exclaim while taking someone through her museum.) Eventually Cole saw the Queen Anne house on Logansport's Broadway for sale and envisioned opening a museum. It took two years to restore the house. The clothing museum opened in November 1997.

Cole constantly adds new clothes to her collection to encourage visitors to keep coming back. One of the latest additions is a dress owned by 1950s movie star Jeanie Crane. She also recently completed renovation of the carriage house, which contains military clothing, and she has set up the basement to look like a laundry room with a number of uniforms on display. She admits she frequently adds new clothes and rearranges exhibits to satisfy her desire to buy more clothes and to decorate. "It's a disease, honey," she says with pleasure, as if her disease was an addiction to eating too many chocolate bonbons.

900 East Broadway, Logansport
(219) 753-4058
Open Tuesday, Thursday, and Friday from 1 p.m. to 4 p.m., or by
appointment. Closed in January and February.
Admission charged

Like What You See?
More Midwest Auto Museums

An early travel trailer at the RV Hall of Fame and Museum, Elkhart

- Antique Auto and Race Car Museum, Bedford, Indiana
- Auburn-Cord-Duesenberg Museum, Auburn, Indiana
- Automotive Heritage Museum, Kokomo, Indiana (see page 117)
- Door Prairie Auto Museum, LaPorte, Indiana
- Elmer's Museum, Fountain City, Wisconsin (see page 28)
- Exit 76 Antique Mall and Car Museum, Edinburgh, Indiana
- Hartford Heritage Automobile Museum, Hartford, Wisconsin
- Kruse Automotive Museum, Auburn, Indiana
- My Garage/Corvette Museum, Effingham, Illinois
- National Automotive and Truck Museum of the United States (NATMUS), Auburn, Indiana
- National Sprint Car Hall of Fame and Museum, Knoxville, Iowa
- RV Hall of Fame and Museum, Elkhart, Indiana
- S. Ray Miller Museum, Elkhart, Indiana
- Studebaker Museum, South Bend, Indiana
- Van Horn Collection of Antique Trucks, Mason City, Iowa

39 | Elwood Haynes Museum
Kokomo

In the 1890s a lot of mechanics, engineers, and guys who just liked to tinker around in the carriage house were at work assembling "horseless carriages." As a result, many men around the world claimed to have built the first car. But Kokomo's own Elwood Haynes actually went to court to be recognized as the first person to build a commercially successful, gasoline-powered automobile. (You mean Henry Ford didn't invent the automobile? By the time Ford established his auto company in 1903 to produce the first mass-marketed and affordable car, the Model T, Haynes and his buddies, Edgar and Elmer Apperson, also of Kokomo, and their Haynes-Apperson Automobile Company had already split to form their own companies.) On July 4, 1894, Elwood Haynes hauled his horseless carriage to the edge of Kokomo and drove it between 7 and 14 mph for about six miles. Imagine the horses, not to mention the neighbors, freaking out when Haynes came rolling down the road in a spidery-looking part-buggy contraption. The horseless carriage, or automobile as it was eventually called, had a one-piston engine that could get 56 mpg of gas. It remained in Haynes's possession until he donated it to the Smithsonian Institute in 1910.

If you're interested in automobile history but don't necessarily want to visit the Henry Ford Museum in Detroit (an all-day visit) and aren't in the mood to look at rows and rows of antique cars, consider a visit to the Elwood Haynes Museum in Kokomo. Located in the grand 1915 Haynes family home (built from fortunes reaped from Haynes's automobile company and his stainless-steel production company), the museum contains an early Haynes car, stories and photos about the auto industry in Kokomo, an exhibit on stainless steel, as well as early-20th-century antiques.

Although Haynes's very first car is in the Smithsonian, the museum has a 1905 Haynes Model L car displayed on the ground floor. Check out the front rumble (or mother-in-law) seat, movable steering column (because 10-year-olds could drive cars back then), the crank start, and transmission. The Model L could zip along at a speedy 35 mph. Notice the 1930 electric traffic signal near the Model L, a foot warmer, tool chest, and set of tools used by a mechanic who used to work with Haynes. And if such things excite you, you can check out family documents (Haynes and his wife's marriage certificate, a record showing his great-great-great-grandfather's crossing from England), heirlooms (Wedgwood china and glassware from Kokomo-based Jenkins Glass), and photos of the house when the Haynes family first moved in.)

On the first floor you can read all about where and how Haynes grew up in Indiana and about how he invented the car. Haynes was an inventive and precocious boy. Born in 1857, he grew up in Portland, Indiana, and spent his free time learning how to melt brass, cast iron, and carbon steel in a furnace. After undergraduate and postgraduate work in the sciences (you can see some of his books and college mementos in the museum) Haynes went on to invent a thermostat that regulated heat in homes. At the Indiana Gas Company, while trying to figure out how to prevent gas pipelines from freezing, he discovered how to dry gas by refrigeration. The process created a by-product that we now call gasoline and since no one had any use for it at the time, it was dumped. But the resourceful Haynes wanted to find some use for it. He dreamt of a horseless carriage powered by gasoline. In 1892 he purchased a one-horse-power, upright two-cycle engine that used gasoline for fuel, and hired Elmer and Edgar Apperson to help build this horseless carriage. A year later he was zipping down Pumpkinvine Pike.

After the first car's success, Haynes and the Apperson brothers formed the Haynes-Apperson Automobile Company. But in 1902 Haynes broke away and created his own car company. Check out photos of the exterior and interior of the first car, photos of the house where Haynes lived and where he developed the first car, company receipts, promotional literature about the Haynes automobile, and company photos (in 1902 he had 2,000 employees).

Ever the inventor, Haynes went on to develop stellite, which can withstand an enormous amount of heat and is used in moon-buggy production. He also developed stainless steel, reportedly at the request of his wife who was tired of always polishing the family silver. The museum's upstairs rooms are devoted to Haynes's alloy development, photos of production facilities, and examples of some products his company made. Two rooms contain products from various Kokomo-based and automobile-focused companies such as Delco car radios, Russell Glass Company paperweights, and Superior Tool Company's products.

While in the Area
Visit Kokomo's Automobile Showcase

For more on Kokomo's automotive history, stop by the **Automotive Heritage Museum.** It was the brainchild of the Pioneer Auto Club, formed in 1951 with the sole purpose of celebrating Kokomo's auto heritage by opening a museum. It took the members 40 years to do it, but they managed to open quite an impressive facility (although it's housed in an unattractive shopping center). Some cars in the collection are an 1895 Pioneer II, the second car built by Elwood Haynes, and a 1923 Apperson. The staff has also added antiques from local businesses and a re-created diner. The museum is located at 1500 North Reed Road (Highway 31) in Kokomo. Open daily year-round from 10 a.m. to 5 p.m. An admission fee is charged. For more information, call (800) 837-0971 or visit www.kokomo.org.

After Haynes died in 1925 at almost 67 years old, the house was eventually sold and became the property of General Motors Company, who used the house as their headquarters. All the while Haynes's daughter dreamt of restoring the house and preserving the memory of her father's achievements. Not long after it went on the sales block in 1965, Bernice Haynes Hillis snapped it up and donated the house to the city of Kokomo. It has been open to the public as the Elwood Haynes Museum since 1967.

1915 South Webster Street, Kokomo
(765) 456-7500
Open year-round: Tuesday through Saturday from 1 p.m. to 4 p.m.; Sunday from 1 p.m. to 5 p.m.
Donation suggested

Like What You See?
Glassy Acts

- About 45 miles southeast of Greentown, the village of Dunkirk also has honored its glass heritage with its own glass museum, with more than 5,000 pieces including hanging lamps and leaded glass from 105 factories. Located at 109 South Franklin Street, the **Dunkirk Glass Museum** is open May through November: Tuesday through Saturday from 10 a.m. to 5 p.m.; Sunday from 1 p.m. to 4 p.m. A donation is suggested. For more information, call (317) 768-6809.

- The **Woodbine Glass Museum** in Woodbine, Illinois, features work of a local glass hand-blowing artist. The museum is located at 3799 East Woodbine Street (Highway 20). For hours and additional information, call (815) 947-3904.

40 | Greentown Glass Museum
Greentown

Greentown, population 2,000, is a quiet town located off a two-lane highway east of Kokomo in the middle of Indiana. But it wasn't always so tranquil. In the late 1800s, about 50 glass factories within a 100-mile radius of Greentown were cranking out tumblers and cruets. One of those companies was the Indiana Tumbler and Goblet Company in Greentown, which produced what antiques buffs refer to as Greentown glass, from 1894 to 1903. After a fire knocked the factory to the ground in 1903, production halted and glass hasn't been produced in town since. Greentown was pretty much forgotten. But in the 1960s locals didn't think the town should be ignored any longer. As Greentown glass became increasingly popular among antiques collectors, a group of residents decided to open the Greentown Glass Museum, specifically devoted to the glass pieces manufactured in town.

Greentown glass is one of the hottest antiques on the market. Pieces that once sold out of barrels in corner stores now fetch thousands of dollars at auctions. A dolphin mustard container that sold for $.14 in the 1890s can now garner $2,000. You can admire treasures like the dolphin mustard pots in the little museum off Greentown's Main Street.

Open since the mid-1960s, the glass museum is located in a renovated city storage building, furnished with oak cabinets donated by the Hook Drugstore chain, and stocked with pieces donated or on loan from area residents. The collection represents about 1,600 pieces of Greentown or imitation Greentown glass. (One display case teaches you how to decipher genuine from fake.) Everything in the museum is at least 100 years old. View displays on patterns produced in Greentown such as cord drapery and leaf bracket (a pattern that appeared on the Hershey's

Rows and rows of glassware at the Greentown Glass Museum, Greentown

119

chocolate bar wrappers), and cases full of practical pieces like butter dishes and fanciful ones like glass hairbrushes. Tools including glass shears, turnout forks and paddles, a mold that survived the 1903 fire, and some shards discovered during an excavation of the factory site years later are all on view.

When the Indiana Tumbler and Goblet Company first started making glass, they were mostly clear ice-tea pitchers and basic tumblers. But as time went on and Jacob Rosenthal, the son of German immigrants, became the plant manager, the company produced more striking colors and patterns: Nile green vinegar cruets, golden agate paperweights, hens-on-nests mustard pots, and the thick and strong chocolate glass. Rosenthal is believed to have created the celebrated chocolate glass color by adding in burned rolled oats. Some pieces of the chocolate glass were so heavy they would explode when exposed to direct sunlight for a long time. You'll see a range of these colorful pieces in the one-room museum.

"Now my favorite, that would have to be the chocolate glass," says longtime museum volunteer Lyn Sullivan, with the word chocolate rolling off his tongue in a distinct Indiana accent (part hardy Midwest, part Southern drawl). Don't miss the 10-inch chocolate glass bowl that at one time served up Phoenix Five, a nonalcoholic fizzy drink said to calm nerves. It is the largest piece of chocolate glass Sullivan has seen, and it is worth between $2,500 and $5,000.

Sullivan, who has been with the museum for 37 years, does not seem like the stereotypical glass collector (instead, the fragile Laura Wingfield from Tennessee Williams's *The Glass Menagerie* may come to mind). A former lumberyard operator, he's used to handling pallets of two-by-fours, not dainty hens-on-nests mustard pots or picture frame toothpick holders. But he is loyal to his town and its heritage, and like many other Greentown residents, Sullivan wanted to do something to boost the town's exposure to the rest of the world and bring in more visitors.

"When we started, we knew a little bit of history about the glass and the factory. Gradually we all became pretty knowledgeable about the stuff. But I'm still learning," he says. "I enjoy trying to find pieces. They aren't as easy to find anymore. When there are auctions here, people come from all over looking for Greentown glass, but folks around here, they hold onto it."

Greentown hosts an annual antiques show around the second weekend in June, a show that usually attracts many glass collectors. Museum volunteers occasionally organize a glass festival in the town.

112 North Meridian Street, Greentown
(765) 628-6206
Open May 15 to October 31: Tuesday through Friday from 10 a.m. to noon and 1 p.m. to 4 p.m.; Saturday and Sunday from 1 p.m. to 4 p.m.
Open November, December, March, and April, Saturday and Sunday from 1 p.m. to 4 p.m., and by appointment.
Free admission

41 | James Dean Exhibit
Fairmount

For a town of about 3,500 people, Fairmount, Indiana, has turned out quite a number of notable people, among them James Dean, the ageless rebel without a cause; Jim Davis, creator of the pizza-ravaging cartoon character Garfield; television journalist Phil Jones; and author Mary Ward. (Could it be the water?) Whatever the reason for the high number of big shots from Fairmount, residents were proud of these famous folks who got their start there and wanted to pay some sort of tribute to them, as well as the many others who have passed through the halls of the local high school. Thus was born the Fairmount Historical Museum.

The real star of Fairmount is James Dean, and the bottom floor of the historical museum is devoted to him. Thousands of Dean disciples journey here every year to get a sense of where Dean grew up. (Although Dean is the big man on campus so to speak, most of the museum volunteers seem more interested in the town and school's history than in the movie star.) Without hailing Dean to an absurd degree or being overly sentimental, the museum's exhibit tells a simple and, yes, sad story about the local farm boy who became a star and died at age 24 in a car accident.

Start your visit by looking over drawings from his childhood, including a painting of an orchid Dean made for his drama teacher in high school. What? Jimmy was a sensitive artist? Girls, be prepared to swoon. He was a good artist, too. (And perhaps a vain one—see the bust he started to carve of himself before he died.) While viewing quite a few photos of him from high school, visitors learn he was a decent student, not a straight-A student, but a very active one, playing on the baseball, basketball, and track teams (see the ribbons he won at events), and landing lead roles in school plays.

The Fairmount Historical Museum, where the James Dean exhibit is housed, Fairmount

James Dean didn't live in Fairmount proper, but on a farm a few miles outside of town with his aunt and uncle. He was sent there from California after his mother died when he was nine years old. His relatives still live in town and are active with the museum, which is why there are a number of cool Dean items to salivate over. There's Dean's first motorcycle, a Czech motorcycle he bought at a Fairmount shop. There's the recorder he used to practice his lines with, letters sent to him from his girlfriend, and photographs of him on the sets of the three films that made him famous: *East of Eden, Rebel Without a Cause,* and *Giant.* And of course there are many posters to ogle over of Dean striking bad-boy poses.

It's easy to imagine Dean roaring through the streets of Fairmount on his motorcycle. It's a quiet, rural boom-and-bust town that reveres its heritage. (Fairmount recently celebrated its sesquicentennial in 2000 with beard-growing contests and horse-and-buggy rides.)

The museum was founded as a nonprofit organization in 1975 for the purpose, like most towns with local history museums, of honoring little Fairmount's big achievers and helping those that left remember what they left. After a few years in a space above a storefront downtown, they moved into a turn-of-the-century red brick home listed on the National Register of Historic Places.

Haven't had your fill of Dean-related paraphernalia? Walk a few blocks to the James Dean Memorial Gallery, a private collection of memorabilia; picnic in the James Dean Memorial Park; stroll through Park Cemetery to see his gravesite or drive by his boyhood home north of town. Free maps at the historical museum pinpoint Dean sites. Fairmount also hosts a number of Dean-related festivals: the James Dean Birthday Celebration in the beginning of February, the Fairmount Museum Days and Remembering James Dean Festival toward the end of September, and the James Dean Run Car Show also in September. A memorial service is held September 3. For more information on any of the above events, call the museum.

And don't forget that there is more to the museum than James Dean artifacts. Upstairs you'll find a room devoted to Garfield and its creator Jim Davis, an Emmy Phil Jones earned for his broadcast-journalism work, a room full of high school archives, and a mixed bag of local antiques.

203 East Washington Street, Fairmount
(765) 948-4555
Open March through November: Monday through Saturday
from 10 a.m. to 5 p.m.; Sunday from noon to 5 p.m.
Donation suggested

42 | National Model Aviation Museum
Muncie

Before they built and flew the first heavier-than-air, mechanically propelled airplane over the sand dunes near Kitty Hawk, North Carolina, Wilbur and Orville Wright tested their flying theories by building model airplanes. When they were children they tossed a model plane into the air, watching it catch wind and twirl before their eyes.

The Wright brothers weren't the first ones to pitch a small-scale plane into the big blue sky. People were probably thinking of flying ever since they saw birds sailing through the sky. How do we know this? Take a look at a replica of a wooden bird in the National Model Aviation Museum. The original, estimated to be 2,300 years old, was found in an Egyptian tomb and featured an airfoil, or a vertical tail, which is a unique characteristic of a model airplane.

After the Wright brothers' flights, more and more children took to building model airplanes. But after Charles Lindbergh flew across the Atlantic Ocean in 1927 (one of the most popular pieces in the museum is a scale model of the *Spirit of St. Louis*), the hobby "just exploded" says museum curator Michael Smith. "Everyone wanted to be a pilot."

Many people still do, which is good news for the Academy of Model Aeronautics, the organization that runs the model airplane museum. (Its members include astronaut John Glenn.) In 2001 the academy, which has been around since 1936 when the first companies started really rolling out model planes, had 160,000 members, their largest number ever. Once regarded as a youth activity, model plane building and flying has become more and more popular among adults; the average age of a model aeronaut is near 37.

Located on the outskirts of Muncie, the museum boasts about 215 model airplanes, helicopters, and several hundred related artifacts, and is believed to be the largest collection of model aircraft in the United States. It also has a wicked landing strip—1,000 acres of land and airspace for modelers—and a pond for model boaters. Originally located in Reston, Virginia, the academy relocated the collection to Indiana in 1994. The museum is just plain neat, even if you didn't grow up building and flying model airplanes.

There are three types of model airplanes featured and discussed in the museum: free-flight, ones that are not connected to the ground by a string or radio transmitter; radio-controlled, probably the most popular; and control line, which are planes flown on the ends of two steel cables or strings. Some planes, ultralights, are made to fly indoors. Some outdoor model planes have flown for 30 hours straight and some have reached speeds of more than 200 mph; for example, pylon racers can reach 180 mph in flight. And some model planes are powered by single-cylinder engines that burn an alcohol-based fuel. If you're intrigued with model plane engines, you'll be delighted to know the museum has many display cases full of turbine, rotary, multicylindric, and diesel engines.

The museum has quite a variety of planes for visitors to admire: powerful model planes, lightweight planes, and planes sporting snazzy designs. One model weighing just one gram will fly for an hour inside after you toss it into the air. (Its wings are composed of a lacquer-based paint and contain tungsten wires that are finer than a string of human hair.) You can see commercial jets and military planes, models designed in the 1940s and in the 1990s. Other finds are radio-controlled helicopters; a photon, or light-controlled plane; and a 1937 sound-controlled plane with a voice-activated rudder.

Don't forget to step inside the 1950s-era hobby shop set up in one corner of the museum. Its shelves are stocked with scale model project kits. Vintage accessories like a register and telephone also add to the nostalgic mood. After touring the shop, have a seat and watch the museum's film "All Because of Model Airplanes."

When you visit the museum during the summer you might see academy members flying their aircraft in competitions held at the flying site behind the museum, especially on weekends and during the national championships held annually in July and August. The club offers flying site assistance, an introductory pilot program, and insurance coverage. The grounds also contain a pond where model boaters can launch their boats or fisherman can engage in a little catch-and-release fishing. Visitors are also welcome to browse through the extensive video and book library.

5151 East Memorial Drive, Muncie
(765) 287-1256 or (800) 435-9262
www.modelaircraft.org
Open year-round: Monday through Friday from 8 a.m. to 4:30 p.m.; Saturday from 10 a.m. to 4 p.m.; Sunday from 10 a.m. to 4 p.m. Closed on Sunday from Thanksgiving through Easter.
Admission charged

Famous Indiana Natives

- Basketball player Larry Bird, born in 1956 in French Lick
- Songwriter Hoagy Carmichael, born in 1899 in Bloomington
- John Dillinger, Public Enemy Number One, born in 1902 or 1903 in   Indianapolis
- Pop singer Michael Jackson, born in 1958 in Gary
- Talk show host David Letterman, born in 1947 in Indianapolis
- TV anchorwoman Jane Pauley, born in 1950 in Indianapolis
- Former Vice President Dan Quayle, born in 1947 in Indianapolis
- Popcorn guru Orville Redenbacher, born in 1907 in Brazil
- Author Kurt Vonnegut, born in 1922 in Indianapolis
- Lew Wallace, Civil War general and Ben-Hur author, born in 1827 in Brookville

43 | Museum of Miniature Houses
Carmel

"Darling, could you pour me a cup of tea please," says Mrs. Tiny as she advances her rook.

"Why, certainly dear. One moment." Mr. Tiny leans back in his leather armchair, nudges his pince-nez, and pulls his knight back.

The imaginary inhabitants of the miniature worlds created by friends of Carmel's Museum of Miniature Houses are members of the upper echelon of society: Old-fashioned families who are not watching television and digging into a bag of potato chips, but instead are in the middle of a chess game or needlepoint project. They engage in conversation on the porch or over a home-cooked meal. In one miniature house someone has just poured a pitcher of ice tea—do you see the teeny, half-filled glasses on the front-porch table? And someone else just left a pot of stew simmering on the cast-iron stove. Miniature worlds depict romantic and exotic destinations (on market day in Juarez Plaza people lounge near a bubbling water fountain), they feature famous women in history (there's Catherine the Great and Marie Antoinette chatting in their respective parlors), and some re-create fairy tales (witness Cinderella's transformation from mousy maid to belle of the ball).

Essentially there are three different kind of miniatures you will see in the Museum of Miniature Houses: replications (usually of homes the builders grew up in), fantasies (Cinderella scenes), and decorative (a 1980s-era, all-pink living room). A miniature builder unable to transform her real living room into an all-pink celebration tends to act out her home décor fantasies in the miniatures. "With miniatures you can do many things you can't do normally," points out museum co-founder Suzanne Landshof, adding that miniaturists tend to redecorate their real houses quite frequently. Not surprisingly, most miniaturists tend to create decorative arts miniatures because you can only buy so many houses.

Yes, the miniatures reveal much about the women's (and in some cases, men's) fantasies, upbringings, and values. For example, in one room you will notice a miniature museum with an exhibit titled "American Women of Arts and Letters." The piece features female figurines—Louisa May Alcott, Emily Dickinson, Amelia Earhart, Margaret Mitchell—standing behind a rope. Also follow your eyes through the "Hall of Unicorns," a room of unicorns statues.

The devil is in the details, as the saying goes. And the creators of the miniature worlds that you will see in the museum must have had a devil of a time putting together these diminutive dollhouses, dioramas, and furniture. Every miniature you'll see in the museum is amazingly detailed and impressive. Many took hundreds of hours to create. Inside each room the ladies have placed a binder that explains the characteristics of each miniature on display

One of the many tiny exhibits at the Museum of Miniature Houses, Carmel

and discusses the scenes going on in the miniature world. For example, you are told that inhabitants of the Salt Box miniature house, appropriately named the Small family, are preparing for Lynn Small's wedding. (See Lynn in her bedroom in front of the mirror?) Mr. Small happens to be a miniature builder, and when his son married a few years ago, he and his wife converted his room to a workshop. Their prized possession? A replica of their house. (Yes, a miniature within a miniature.)

Miniature building is actually a great hobby for couples, says Landshof, who estimates that about 20 percent of miniaturists are men. "Very often men don't want to come in the museum. But once they do, they see it's not just about dolls, but building, putting in electricity, and carpentry."

Founders Landshof, Suzie Moffett, and Nancy Lesh, all from the Carmel area, didn't start seriously getting into building miniatures until the 1980s, even though they always liked small things, Landshof recalls. As the women continued building and collecting extravagant dollhouses, at one point they realized they couldn't store their creations in their houses any longer. (Don't most private museums begin that way?) And in talking with each other they came to the conclusion that they didn't want miniature collecting to remain unnoticed or become a lost art. They formed a miniaturist society and purchased a house on Carmel's Main Street. (And what better place than Carmel, a charming, clean suburb of Indianapolis with vintage lampposts and new sidewalks?) The museum opened in 1993 and over the years has come to feature six rooms of antique dollhouses (including one featured in the Dandy Doll House book series), recently built dollhouses, and other miniature creations.

In addition to the miniature collections, you'll discover miniature horses, a small exhibit on stamp collecting, and cases full of diminutive furniture and china. Before you leave, stock up on miniatures and industry publications in the gift shop and gather information about Midwest miniature clubs and shows.

111 East Main Street, Carmel
(317) 575-9466
www.museumofminaitures.org
Open year-round, except the first two weeks in January: Wednesday through Saturday from 11 a.m. to 4 p.m.; Sunday from 1 p.m. to 4 p.m. Special viewing hours are available for large groups and out-of-town visitors. Closed major holidays. Donation suggested

While in the Area
Honor Hoosier Hoops

The **Indiana Basketball Hall of Fame** is a monument to that in-state phenomenon known as "Hoosier Hysteria." A visit to this 14,000-square-foot building is intense: Read and hear about the history of basketball in every high school in Indiana, famous state players who have gone on to pla professional ball, and the stories behind numerous successful coaches. The hall of fame is located at One Hall of Fame Court (Highway 3 and Trojan Lane) in New Castle, 15 miles south of Muncie. In a basketball-crazy state, this area is especially passionate about the sport. (Notice the giant basketball shoe off Highway 3.) Open year-round: Tuesday through Saturday from 10 a.m. to 5 p.m.; Saturday and Sunday from 1 p.m. to 5 p.m. An admission fee is charged. For more information, call (765) 529-1891 or visit www.hoopshall.com.

44 | Indiana Medical History Museum
Indianapolis

The Old Pathology Building, where the Indiana Medical History Museum is housed on Indianapolis's west side, is quite a nightmarish place when you consider its contents: 100-year-old brains soaked in formaldehyde, glass-plate negatives of schizophrenic patients, and tissue samples dating back a century. But it's not a horror house. In fact, the Old Pathology Building contains a stunning museum. When you walk into the building, located on the grounds of the former Central Indiana Hospital for the Insane, you are transplanted into a turn-of-the-20th-century laboratory. Consider the all-white oak cabinets and doorways, and the microscopes and instruments placed in the center of copper-plated laboratory tables as if a lab technician will be back in a jiffy. When the last doctor left the building in the 1950s for a more modern one, he turned off the lights and shut the doors, leaving behind tons of tissue slides,

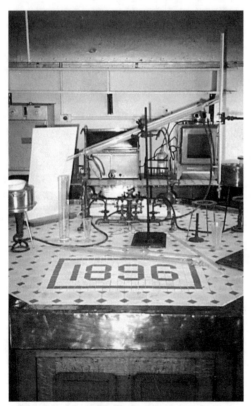

microscopes, medical journals, brains, and skeletons. Most larger museums try to recreate what the Indiana Medical History Museum just is: an authentic, practically working medical building dating back 100 years. After your tour, chances are you will thank your doctor and her latex gloves, sterilized instruments, and sterilized examining room. Or you may call your parents and thank them for not turning you over to the state mental hospital because you threw a fit in fifth grade if your mom didn't set an extra dinner plate for your imaginary friend.

Medicine, not to mention treatment toward the mentally disabled, has come a long way since the Old Pathology Building was constructed in 1896. By then, a

A laboratory from the late 19th century at the Indiana Medical History Museum, Indianapolis number of strides already had taken place in medicine: The world's first open-heart surgery was performed, X-rays were "discovered," antitoxins for tetanus and diphtheria were produced, and Sigmund Freud had just published *Studies in Hysteria*. People had enormous faith in science. In 1896 the building and its laboratories were top-notch, equipped with all the latest inventions like a photomicrograph and stocked with plenty of formaldehyde. At the time, it was the second mental hospital in the nation to have a separate building for pathology laboratories; today it is the oldest surviving pathology facility in the nation. Although the mental hospital was demolished in 1994 after a fire severely damaged the facility, the pathology building still stands.

Like What You See?
More Midwest Medical Museums

- Housed in Wishard Hospital in Indianapolis, the **Wishard Nursing Museum** covers nursing since the 1880s (particularly from the 1940s), and features a surgical amphitheater and items like antique needles. The museum is located in the Bryce Building at 1001 West 10th Street. Open year-round, Wednesday from 9 a.m. to 2 p.m. A donation is suggested. For more information, call (317) 630-6233 or (317) 630-6432.

- If you're traveling through Burlington, Iowa, chances are you plan to traipse up and down Snake Alley, the most crooked street in America. While you're there, spend about 30 minutes touring the **Phelps House**, situated at the top of Snake Alley at 512 Columbia Street. The Phelps House is a Victorian house that served as a home for a wealthy family, the town's first Protestant Hospital, and a dance hall. The School of Nursing also was housed in this building; the first class graduated in 1915 and the last class in 1973. The local nurses association runs a "Medical Memories" exhibit on the third floor. Open May through October, Saturday and Sunday from 1:30 p.m. to 4:30 p.m., or by appointment. An admission fee is charged. For more information, call (319) 753-2449.

- Chicago's **International Museum of Surgical Science** chronicles surgery advances through the years. Look out for skulls bearing the marks of skull boring (when heads were drilled to release evil spirits that caused conditions like insanity), amputation kits, and microscopes from the 19th century. The museum is located at 1524 North Lake Shore Drive in Chicago. For more information, call (312) 642-6502.

- Minneapolis's **Museum of Questionable Medical Devices** is a hoot. See page 58 for a full description.

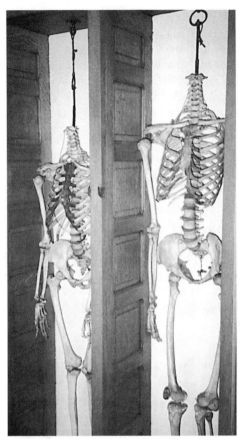

Skeletons at the Indiana Medical History Museum

The museum tour starts in the 100-seat amphitheater where medical students once listened to lectures on mental and nervous disorders (you will bypass the "anatomical museum" room, which contains the jars of brains). If you want to check out those things, you can do it at the end. Tour guide and director Virginia Terpening won't force you to look at golf ball-size tumors if you don't want to. Instead, she highlights the educational and historical features of the building. For example, while in the morgue, she breezes over the autopsy table and its pan, hose, and refrigerator (where cadavers were stored), and points out the Dictaphone on the wall. Terpening explains that during an autopsy one doctor took dictation upstairs while the other examined the body. This way, visitors don't fixate on the table where hundreds of autopsies were performed. Still, you can't help but stare at the table and items like the original 1920s sign above the refrigerator: "Funeral directors: Please be sure refrigerator door is closed after removing bodies."

Upstairs you'll find state-of-the-art turn-of-the-century laboratory rooms. The histology (study of cell structure), chemistry, and germ laboratories are bright rooms with circular tables topped with tile and copper. (Copper resists corrosion, but it is "not even remotely sterile," Terpening points out. Of course, the doctors didn't know that back then.) Cabinets are stocked with bottles of dye used to stain tissues later mounted on microscope slides. Everything is intact and authentic.

The photography room has a huge photomicrograph, which takes pictures of slides, hundreds of glass plate negatives of patients sitting and staring into the camera, and images of brains and tissues. Drop by the records room where a daily logbook from the early 1900s has been propped open on the table and meander through the library where you'll find hundreds of medical books like *How to Care for The Insane*. You might recognize the library; it was in a scene in the movie *Eight Men Out*.

Anyone in the medical profession will have a field day at this museum. Before cancer was defined and before hospitals had oncologists on staff, tumors reached frighteningly large sizes. Perhaps the goriest and yet most fascinating part of the museum is its collection of brains, some of them with tumors the size of golf balls. Because doctors now tend to catch tumors before they grow so large, medical students have often traveled far to see this tumor collection. Don't miss the skeletons behind the antique glass cabinets. And don't forget to compare the hand-crank centrifuge with the electric one.

While the museum's main focus is educating the public about how medicine was taught and practiced more than 50 years ago, you'll also hear some stories about the building's history. For example, one doctor helped cure tertiary syphilis here. He injected patients with malaria, which brought on a high fever, and with a high fever, the syphilis germs were killed off. It was the first physical treatment for a nervous disorder and earned him a Nobel Prize.

In 1969, a little more than a decade after Indiana University stopped sending its students to the Old Pathology Building, a group of local physicians and citizens established a private, not-for-profit organization with the goal of preserving the building and its medical history. Although tours were frequently given to doctors and visitors requesting visits, the pathology building wasn't officially open to the public until the late 1980s. The museum is not exactly a common tourist destination for folks visiting Indianapolis (most gravitate toward the zoo nearby), but a visit will prove to be eye-opening and rewarding.

The small staff, which includes a dedicated group of volunteer retired doctors, offers group tours and coordinates special programs regarding frontier medicine, medicine during the Civil War, and milestones in mental health.

3045 West Vermont Street, Indianapolis
(317) 635-7329
www.imhm.org
Open year-round, Wednesday through Saturday from 10 a.m. to 4 p.m.,
and by appointment.
Admission charged

While in the Area
Visit a Drugstore Museum

Drop your hotdog and pop into **Hook's American Drugstore**, a museum, drugstore, and soda fountain shop on the Indiana State Fair grounds in Indianapolis, for some divine ice cream. Open 9 a.m. to 9 p.m. during the Indiana State Fair in August, this museum and shop is an Indiana institution: Hook's Drugstores have been in Indiana since 1900.

While standing in line for that ice cream, check out the pharmacy memorabilia, turn-of-the-century soda fountain and candy counter. Admission is free, but you will have to pay to get into the fair grounds. And slide some dollar bills into the donation box: Local pharmacy devotees are raising funds to open a drugstore museum in downtown Indianapolis in future years. Hook's American Drugstore is located at 1180 East 38th Street in   Indianapolis. For more general information, call (877) 924-5886, (317) 924-1503 or visit www.americandrugstoremuseum.org for information about the future museum.

Hooks American Drugstore, Indianapolis

45 | Wilbur Wright Birthplace and Museum

Hagerstown

Surrounded by grassy fields and located off a very rural road in central Indiana, a little white farmhouse could easily be mistaken for another Indiana farmstead if viewed about a mile away from the south. Drive a little bit closer and you'll not only see a plaque in the front yard but also a 1950 F-84 bomber—announcements to passersby that a pioneering aviator once lived on the site. After Orville and Wilbur Wright achieved fame and fortune with their first flights, they eventually settled in Dayton, Ohio (where an extensive Wright-focused museum is located). But if you don't have time to drive that far east, consider stopping by Wilbur's birthplace and museum, located in the heart of Indiana farm country near Millville. It took decades for the museum to get built—it opened officially in 1996—but it is finally coming into its own with a new community room and director added in 2001.

During your tour you will visit a museum building, a reconstruction of the Wright family home, gift shop, and welcome center. The two centerpieces of the museum are a replica of the Wright's first flyer and the F-84. A photocopy of the telegram the Wright brothers sent to their father on December 17, 1903, is also an item that will thrill aviation buffs: "SUCCESS FOUR FLIGHTS THURSDAY MORNING ALL AGAINST 21 MILE WIND STARTING FROM LEVEL WITH ENGINE POWER ALONE AVERAGE SPEED 31 MILES LONGEST 57 SECONDS INFORM PRESS HOME CHRISTMAS."

Keep in mind the house you visit is not actually Wilbur's original home. The one in which Wilbur was born in 1867 was rented out for a number of years after the Wrights left, and it was eventually destroyed by fire. In 1929 the state of Indiana bought the site, constructed a replica, but reportedly didn't keep up with maintenance. With the house and grounds looking abandoned, eventually vandals ruined it. The state tried to promote the property as a historical site, but not many people came to visit. For a while officials considered moving the replica house to the popular tourist destination Summit Lake. But neighbors and distant relatives of the Wrights objected. (What was the point of having a replica birthplace house miles away from the actual birthplace? they asked each other.) Hagerstown and Millville area residents formed a historical society and convinced the state they would operate the museum. In 1995 the state deeded the property to the local society, and a welcome center and museum were built in 1996. Now in the hands of local citizens who grew up near the homestead, the museum is thriving.

While many visitors probably have read about the Wright brothers' accomplishments when they were students, a video complementing the museum ex-

Wilbur Wright Birthplace and Museum, Hagerstown

hibits shares the history of the Wright family as well as Wilbur and Orville's aviation development. Wilbur was born in the farmhouse in 1867, but because his father, Milton, was a traveling bishop in the Methodist Church, the family moved not long after settling on the homestead in the late 1860s. Most people believe the brothers received the knack for tinkering with things from their mother, the daughter of a carriage builder, who encouraged them with their projects. And at the museum you will hear the story that Wilbur and Orville's father bought them a French helicopter toy with which they were enthralled. After high school in the 1880s, the two entrepreneurs published a weekly newspaper in Ohio called the *West Side News*. You can read some of their news copy in the museum. In the 1890s the brothers switched gears and started building and selling bicycles; look for photographs of their shop. Then they got into flying kites, gliders, and eventually airplanes. After the Kitty Hawk flights, the brothers produced planes for the government and formed the Wright Company in 1909 near Dayton. A few years before being stricken with typhoid fever, Wilbur hoofed it over to France for the Michelin Cup in 1908. He won, flying 77 miles in two hours and 20 minutes.

One of the more touching displays contains excerpts from Milton's journal, passages that document the last months and days of Wilbur's life: "I slept with my clothes on. Doctors think the case very bad," Wilbur's father wrote. "Night was cool . . . he passed away . . . a short life, full of consequences. An unfailing intellect, imperturbable temper, great self-reliance and great modesty." The young aviator died of typhoid fever in 1912.

In keeping with the aviation exploration theme, the museum also contains a small exhibit on NASA space programs, including numerous badges and postcards depicting missions throughout the years.

Stop by on a Saturday and chances are you'll catch some of the Wright Flyers launching their model airplanes from the fields behind the museum.

1525 North County Road 750E, Hagerstown
(765) 332-2495
Open April through October: Monday through Saturday from 10 a.m.
to 5 p.m.; Sunday from 1 p.m. to 5 p.m.
Admission charged

While in the Area
Ride on America's First Interstate

Starting in Cumberland, Maryland, and ending in Vandalia, Illinois, the old **National Road** weaves through Indiana as Highway 40. It is now paralleled by I-70—the modern interstate that superseded it as a major east-west highway. Designated a National Scenic Byway in 1988, the National Road has developed a loyal following among road preservationists and back roads travelers because of the nostalgia it evokes: classic Cadillacs, soda fountains, and founder's day parades. In recent years the Indiana National Road Association has worked to preserve the National Road and the towns that abut it. The organization helped save a gas station in Terre Haute, erected signs directing people to and along the road, and hired consultants to promote it.

In Indiana the National Road is the Main Street of many towns—Greenfield, Knightstown, and Cambridge City, to name a few. Some have bustling downtowns on Saturday mornings and town squares with ice cream festivals. Others have one or two antiques shops, maybe a gas station. Some have excellent little museums. Here are a few of them.

- **Trump's Texaco Museum** in downtown Knightstown is located in a vintage gas station and contains service station memorabilia. For more information, call (765) 345-7135.

- **Huddleston Farmhouse Inn Museum** in downtown Cambridge City is a "Movers house" that has served National Road travelers since 1841. For more information, call (765) 478-3172.

- The **Overbeck Pottery Museum** spotlights work of Cambridge City's Overbeck family, specifically art nouveau, art deco, and figurine work. The museum is located in the basement of the public library in Cambridge City. For more information, call (765) 478-3335.

- The **Richmond Art Museum** located at 350 Hub Etchison Parkway in Richmond contains paintings by American impressionists and a pottery collection. For more information, call (765) 966-0256.

- For information on **James Whitcomb Riley Old Home and Museum** in Greenfield, see page 142.

46 Dr. Ted's Musical Marvels
Dale

Dr. Ted's Musical Marvels is not a museum to be timid in. There's an expansive cement floor out there for you to grab and twirl your partner as your finger-snapping, smiling guide pumps the player piano. The numerous music players housed in this museum located not far from I-64 induce toe tapping, hand clapping, and head bobbing; they were made to be played outside in community parks, in raucous saloons, or crowded theaters. Coming off the highway and need to stretch those legs? Don't head to the wayside, but to Dr. Ted's. Pretend you are on a merry-go-round (it's not hard to do since a number of restored carousel horses have been placed around the museum), or pretend you are in a saloon as your partner in cards winks at you from across the table.

The players are arranged in various scenes around the perimeter of a giant room, such as a Victorian household or a Western saloon. Each "room" is accented by items such as an ornate wooden music stand, an accordion catalog, or poster advertisements for cigars. Your guide will first unroll music paper (each slot or hole in the paper invokes a key sound), attach it to a Victorian piano player, pump the foot pedal, and explain that evening entertainment used to revolve around the music player. (During World War I, ships would have as many as six of them onboard to keep the troops entertained.) Luckily the museum has acquired the original rolls of sheet music to accompany each player. They are piled on top of the piano player in their original boxes.

The music players you'll see and hear belong to Dr. Ted Waflart, a doctor who practices family medicine in nearby Huntingburg. Raised in a family of engineers, Waflart has always been into springs, strings, hammers, wheels, and pumps. (Before he entered medical school, he worked as a mechanical engineer for six years.) It wasn't until the 1970s, while studying medicine, that he stumbled upon an old pump organ in an antiques shop in the Appalachian Mountains. He bought it, picked up a book on music-player history at the library, and restored the organ. A few years and organs later, while vacationing in Belgium he ran into another collector who convinced him to purchase a 24-foot-long, 12-foot-high Decap dance organ. Waflart had it shipped (in parts) back to Indiana.

Gradually he realized that these players should do what they were made to do: entertain people. And when he realized many children never got to see these magical types of instruments, he opened a museum on July 4, 1991, with his collectible organs. You won't find these instruments on display at any festivals or music shows; Waflart keeps them in the museum.

Sway to music from a gramophone, phonograph (a precursor to the record player), a Belgian Arburo organ, a Regina Music Box from the 1890s, and a pump organ. Look for the unusual little roller organ, or cob organ, from the early 1900s that cost $3.25 from the Sears, Roebuck catalog. It emits a sound almost like an accordion because of its pleated bellows. You'll hear what a Sieberg Elite, the forerunner to the jukebox, and a Cremona Nickelodeon sound like—players that will only run if you drop in a buffalo nickel.

Your indefatigable tour guide will operate a Dutch Music Wheel from 1890, for which players have to turn a 30-pound wheel to produce music. You can bee-bop to music from a vacuum-powered Celesta. Celestas were made to be played in silent-movie houses, but when the "talkies" came out they were sent to mortuaries. Waflart's particular model spent years in mortuaries, "but we only play happy

One of the many exhibits at Dr. Ted's Musical Marvels, Dale

sounds here," assures Waflart's mother-in-law and the museum's manager, Millie Schum.

Another gem is the Waflart-restored Limonaire Frères organ from Paris. The Frères model produces music not from the lightweight perforated paper sheets that most players use, but from cardboard, booklike documents the size of *War and Peace*. Take a few steps and bounce around to the Wurlitzer bandwagon once used on merry-go-rounds. Finally, your guide disappears behind a curtain and a thunderous performance on the gigantic Decap begins, with its drums beating, saxophones wailing, and its accordions singing. It has 535 pipes!

Expect to be entertained by more than just music players in Dr. Ted's. The rafters are lined with toys documenting American popular culture from the last 50 years, toys like the farm set you had when you were a kid, and gems like the "Kookie Kombo," a one-man band getup similar to what Dick Van Dyke wore in *Mary Poppins*. Other eye-grabbing items are a back bar that belonged to King Faruk of Egypt until 1956, a 150-year-old dentist chair, vats of vegetable shortening for baking, and vintage posters announcing music shows, such as "In Person—Ted Lewis with his famous band. Is everybody happy? Yes, Sir!"

Waflart is quite infatuated with the circus and this is quite apparent once you're in the museum. He has draped original circus curtains declaring "Two-headed giant. He's alive! Tattoos!" and "Sword Swallower!" And here's a rarity: A copper bathtub dating back to the 1790s. It was in that shoe-shaped tub that Jean-Paul Marat was murdered by French Revolutionary heroine Charlotte Corday, who was eventually sent to the guillotine for her crime.

On Highway 231 (located three-eighths of a mile north of I-64, exit 57), Dale (812) 937-4250
Open Memorial Day through Labor Day: Monday through Saturday from 10 a.m. to 6 p.m.; Sunday from 1 p.m. to 6 p.m. Weekends only in September and May. Admission charged

While in the Area
Shop at the General Store

You can buy everything from ice cream and deli sandwiches to cast-iron pots and paintbrushes at **Stephenson's General Store and Old Rivertown Museum** in Leavenworth, Indiana, a store that overlooks the Ohio River. The store, which has been in the same family since 1917, was originally located downriver from its present location, but the family rebuilt it on the bluffs off Highway 62 after a flood washed it away in 1937. The museum contains a variety of antiques from the early 20th century. Open mid-May through October: Monday through Saturday from 10:30 a.m. to 5:30 p.m.; Sunday from 1 p.m. to 5 p.m. For more information, call (812) 739-4242.

47 Old Jail Museum
Crawfordsville

Step right up! Take a ride on a giant merry-go-round (sans music)! Test your nerves at the world's only rotating jail!

It sounded like a good idea. A jail that minimized communication between prisoners and controlled them by preventing the guard from releasing more than one prisoner at a time. It seemed efficient, too, in a time when a jail was manned only by a sheriff and his deputy, when there wasn't enough manpower to open and close cell doors for prisoners all the time. But there's a reason (several, actually) why there were only seven rotating jails, or "squirrel cages," known to have been built in the United States. Follow your guide around the too-close-for-comfort Old Jail Museum, a still-rotating jail in Crawfordsville, and you'll soon realize why the prisoners stuck objects in the bars to prevent the jail's rotation (lots of crushed hands reported here). They also set their

mattresses on fire and carved and painted messages on the walls. It drove some people crazy. Claustrophobes beware.

Begin by touring the holding room or guard room and continue on through the processing room. You'll see photos of the jail when it was first installed and the items used to process criminals as they entered the jail. The second floor of the jail contained the women's and juveniles' rooms. The third floor housed the infirmary. As you walk around, your tour guide will share stories about the jail's mechanical characteristics and highlight the advantages and disadvantages to rotating jails.

Patented by William H. Brown and Benjamin F.

Inside the "squirrel cage" at the Old Jail Museum, Crawfordsville

Like What You See?
Calling All Jailbirds

- **The Squirrel Cage** in Council Bluffs, Iowa, is another rotating jail you can visit. But unlike the Crawfordsville jail, this one can no longer be rotated. The jail is located at 226 Pearl Street in Council Bluffs. For more information, call (712) 323-2509.

- Unwind in suites dubbed "The Jail Cottage" or "The Cave," in a bona fide lockup dating back to 1884. **The Old Jail Bed and Breakfast** in Taylors Falls, Minnesota, once housed the town's slammer, saloon, and livery before becoming a bed and breakfast. For more information, call (651) 465-3112 or visit www.oldjail.com.

- You can literally sleep behind bars at **The Jailhouse Inn** in Preston, Minnesota, which housed inmates from 1869 until 1979, and acted as a courthouse. Cuddle up in rooms with names like "The Dunk Tank" and "The Processing Room," where such events actually occurred. For more information, call (507) 765-2181 or visit www.jailhouseinn.com.

Haugh of Indianapolis in 1881, the rotating jail was hailed as a mechanical masterpiece. (This was the Industrial Age, after all.) The two-story circular structure sits on 16 equally spaced roller bearings. When you turn the hand crank (the cranks are in the basement and on the ground level) a series of gears and shafts moves the structure clockwise or counterclockwise. The Crawfordsville jail was the prototype for all other rotating jails. People aren't sure why Crawfordsville was home to the prototype, but many believe the town's favorite son, Lew Wallace, knew the inventors of the jail and when the town needed a new one, he recommended his buddies. The jail opened in 1882 and closed in 1973.

But the jail was not rotating for all of its 91 years. In 1939 the state fire marshal ordered that doors be installed in each cell, requiring the jailer to walk around the circular structure instead of rotating the jail. After a group of local citizens formed the Montgomery County Cultural Foundation to preserve the jail (they reopened it in 1975 as a museum), the foundation welded these doors shut in order to recreate the look and feel of the jail shortly after it was installed. Of the three remaining rotating jails in the United States, only the Crawfordsville jail can still be rotated.

Four years before the jail closed, James Clark, the inspector with the corrections department who recommended its closure, told the *Indianapolis News*,

"I can't think of a worse jail in Indiana." It certainly is not a place you want to stay in overnight or be inside of when there's a thunderstorm that could cause the facility to lose power. Even visitors walking through the cell on a sunny day with birds chirping outside can experience a case of the shivers. As your guide may tell you, people think the place is haunted. It's not uncommon for the jail's security system to detect motion in the jail when the staff has gone for the day.

This usually occurs sometime in October, near the anniversary of convicted murderer John Coffee's hanging. A small exhibit in the processing room tells Coffee's story. He was hanged in the yard behind the jail on October 15, 1885, for robbing and murdering a couple and setting fire to their house (it was the first hanging in Crawfordsville). (Look for the iron ring from which he was hanged.) Some think Coffee was not guilty and that it is Coffee shuffling around in the middle of the night. Others believe the ghost is the man who was sheriff at the time of Coffee's death, said to have known there were others involved in the murder but who didn't arrest anyone else. Check out the tickets to Coffee's hanging in the display case as well as newspaper articles about the event. After the town's second hanging in 1886, the gallows out back were dismantled. At any rate, if the ghost is not Coffee it could be the woman who hung herself in the women's cell upstairs or the man who set the padded cell on fire and smothered himself to death.

During your visit to the Old Jail Museum you will become well versed in local lore, most of it lighthearted (unlike Coffee's story). For example, when some residents heard that Al Capone would be passing through Crawfordsville on the way to a French Lick resort, they set up a blockade to avoid bringing trouble into town; Capone opted for another route. Another story goes that when the town's streets were first paved in the 1940s, a flock of geese landed in the tar thinking the streets were bodies of water. The geese got stuck and when nearby farmers heard about it, they came out in droves and started shooting them—until the sheriff broke things up. And in 1967 a motorcycle gang called The Outlaws rumbled into town and robbed a store. Thinking they could get away with it in Crawfordsville, they stuck around for a while terrorizing residents. Low and behold, the sheriff arrested the gang. When they stood before the Montgomery County judge, he ordered the group to get haircuts before standing trial. Take a look at the results in the newspaper articles and photos posted in the museum.

When you step inside one of the cells, notice the cast-iron commode. When the jail's plumbing was installed in 1886, the toilet was quite advanced for the time. It created much controversy since most Crawfordsville residents hadn't gotten indoor plumbing yet. ("The jailbirds are living better than us!") For the finale, head downstairs to the basement and your guide will rotate the jail for you.

In addition to showing visitors how prisoners lived in the early part of the 20th century, the Old Jail Museum provides glimpses into how a sheriff or jailer and his family lived at the turn of the 20th century. The sheriff's family lived in the front part of the jail. Oftentimes the sheriff's wife baked for the prisoners, as well as her family. (Some locals say wives used to bake birthday cakes for teenagers in jails and one woman's cuisine was so popular, a town drunkard reportedly used to make it a point to get arrested every weekend in order to taste her fare.) During the tour, you will pass through what used to be the kitchen and the pantry. While you're in the bathroom, look for the slot above the toilet where food was passed from the pantry to the north parlor, which used to be an office for jailers. The foundation runs temporary exhibits, such as one on quilting, in these front rooms.

225 North Washington Street, Crawfordsville
(765) 362-5222
Open April, May, September, and October, Wednesday through Sunday from 1 p.m. to 4:30 p.m. Open June, July, and August: Tuesday and Sunday from 1 p.m. to 4:30 p.m.; Wednesday through Saturday from 10 a.m. to 4:30 p.m. Donation suggested; a fee is charged for groups of more than fifteen.

While in the Area
Learn about a Great Reporter

About 45 miles southwest of Crawfordsville, the town of Dana honors one of the most famous American news correspondents of World War II: Ernie Pyle. Born in 1900 on a farm southwest of this tiny town just east of the Illinois border, Pyle studied journalism at Indiana University, then worked as a reporter at the LaPorte Herald and eventually at the Washington Daily News. His next stint was as a reporter-at-large for the Scripps-Howard newspaper chain, traveling across the United States and Central and South America. In the 1940s Pyle went to Europe to cover America's involvement in the war, and in the following years traveled through North Africa, Italy, and France. In 1944 he won a Pulitzer Prize for his war coverage. A year later he was killed while covering the war in the Pacific.

The **Ernie Pyle State Historic Site** was completed in 1976, and a new visitors' center made of two authentic World War II Quonset huts was added in 1995. It's located at 120 West Briarwood Avenue in Dana. Open mid-March through mid-December: Wednesday through Saturday from 9 a.m. to 5 p.m.; Sunday from 1 p.m. to 5 p.m. Admission is free. For more information, call (765) 665-3633 or visit www.state.in.us/ism. If you're in town in the beginning of August, drop by downtown Dana for the Volunteer Firemen's Ernie Pyle Festival.

48 Ben-Hur Museum and General Lew Wallace Study
Crawfordsville

After touring Lew Wallace's "study," you may be inspired to pull out a notepad and start that novel you've been meaning to write or drag out the violin you've been storing in the attic and meaning to master. Learning about Wallace's many impressive accomplishments can be a motivating and inspirational experience.

Lew Wallace was quite prolific in a variety of endeavors. In his 78 years of life, Wallace was a visionary architect, accomplished musician, best-selling author, honored army general, lawyer, governor, state senator, and ambassador. He was also adept at picking up souvenirs, receiving gifts, and keeping track of them. This means that when visitors come to his study almost 100 years after his death, they can view numerous genuine and intact items he collected—everything from books to fishing rods.

Even if you don't know Wallace or *Ben-Hur*, his book about Christians in ancient Rome, but if you're into architecture, libraries, literature, military history, or liked the movie *Ben-Hur*, check out this museum. (If you're seeking Charlton Heston paraphernalia, look elsewhere. Heston has made appearances at the study, but the museum is about Wallace, not Heston.) In the museum, walk by the enchanting portrait of a Turkish princess given to Wallace by the subject's father, the sultan of Turkey, while Wallace was a foreign minister. (Her eyes follow you around the room like the *Mona Lisa.*) Peer at a violin the staff believes Wallace was restoring shortly before he died. Shelves are stocked with his books, including first editions of *The Fair God* and *The Prince of India*, and books written by his wife, Susan.

Born in Brookville, Indiana, Wallace was 19 years old when he organized a company of men to fight in the Mexican War. Before the Civil War began, he organized a militia, which eventually became a regiment in the Union army. During the Civil War he worked his way through the ranks, as adjutant general of Indiana, colonel, and eventually major general of the Indiana Volunteer Infantry. Wallace acted as vice president of the Lincoln assassination trial, governor of the New Mexico Territory from 1878 to 1881, state senator from 1857 to 1861, and minister to Turkey from 1881 to 1885.

In his spare time he invented an aluminum fishing rod with a built-in reel—a reel that lines up on one side of the pole—and a fan operated by weights. Among many other items like his books and paintings, expect to see the rod and fan at his museum, a massive fortress of a building in the middle of Crawfordsville.

Completed in 1895, the study took three years to build. Designed by Wallace, he had it built not far behind his house (his original house currently is not open to the public) with hydraulically pressed walls, vitrified brick, steel

Like What You See?
A True Hoosier's Home

To visit the home of another famous Indiana author, check out the **James Whitcomb Riley Old Home and Museum** in the picturesque town of Greenfield, east of Indianapolis. Born in 1849, Riley is affectionately called the Hoosier Poet because he wrote verse in Indiana vernacular about characters like Raggedy Man, Little Orphan Annie, and Old Aunt Mary. His poems have been read to Indiana children for more than 100 years. Visit the house where Riley and Orphan Annie (her real name was Mary Alice Smith) were raised. Local ladies dressed in period costumes take guests through his home, share stories of Riley and his family, and explain what on earth some little things in the house are, such as an early vacuum cleaner. The house is located at 250 West Main Street in Greenfield. Open April 1 through October 31: Tuesday through Saturday from 10 a.m. to 4 p.m.; Sunday from 1 p.m. to 4 p.m. An admission fee is charged. For more

beams, and Bedford limestone. It's a tough building. Architecturally speaking, it's a mélange of Periclean Greek (front porch), Romanesque (40-foot tower), and Byzantine style. Wallace added features like the hand-carved frieze around the top of building with characters from his books (including *Ben-Hur*), frosted and stained glass, an inglenook, gas fireplace, and a 30-foot ceiling dome with a skylight. Wallace called his study "a pleasure house for my soul." He spent the last eight to 10 years of his life working in the study. (Who wouldn't? It's beautiful and cozy.)

The pleasure house was financed by *Ben-Hur*, which became a best seller shortly after it was published in 1880. In 1899 it was made into a play and ran on Broadway for 21 years—a remarkable production that featured live horses on stage during a chariot scene. In 1907 a short silent film was made based on the book, and in 1959 a feature-length film starring the indomitable Charlton Heston debuted. Included in the museum's collection are film souvenirs, including a Roman soldier's uniform.

After Wallace died in 1905, his family opened his study to the public and people came in droves. In 1941 relatives put the building up for sale and The Community House, a group of local women, purchased the building. Later they donated it to the city of Crawfordsville. When the city's parks department moved in, in preparation for turning it into a museum, they found the study not only was arranged in a similar fashion to when Wallace was spending time there, but it contained many of the original items. When they moved in, the staff cataloged 1,300 volumes of books, paintings, statues, and Wallace's original partners desk, which is still located in the center of the room. The building was placed on the National Register of Historic Places in 1976 and designated a National Historic Landmark in 1977. The carriage house will be renovated in coming years to house a separate gift shop.

200 Wallace Avenue, Crawfordsville
(765) 362-5769 for the museum or
(800) 866-3973 (visitors' bureau) during the winter
www.ben-hur.com
Open April, May, September, and October, Tuesday through Sunday from
1 p.m. to 4:30 p.m. Open June, July, and August: Wednesday through Saturday
from 10 a.m. to 4:30 p.m.; Tuesday and Sunday from 1 p.m. to 4:30 p.m.
Open March and November, Saturday and Sunday from 1 p.m. to 4:30 p.m.
Admission charged

Offbeat Indiana Festivals

- Purdue University's **Bug Bowl** in West Lafayette features cockroach races and insect cuisine—with tastings. Held every year in early April. For more information, call (800) 872-6648.

- The **Hot Luck and Fiery Foods Exhibition** in Madison brings out pepper fanatics for salsa tastings and pepper plant sales. Held every year during the first weekend in April on the grounds of the Thomas Family Winery. For more information, call (812) 273-3755.

- For seven days in mid-June, the town of North Webster celebrates its lake and resort culture with a **Mermaid Festival.** Events include a Queen of Lakes pageant for young misses, cutie parade for those under 14 years old, cutie pageant for those from four to six years old, a tractor pull, demolition derby, and the Tournament of Champions which includes tennis, basketball, golf, running, swimming, and biking events. For more information, call (219) 269-6090 or (800) 626-5353.

- Learn physics by blowing bubbles at Bloomington's **Bubblefest**, sponsored by the WonderLab Museum of Science, Health and Technology. You'll learn how to make honeycomb bubbles (when bubbles are blown between two glass plates and bubbles pack in together) and frozen bubbles (when bubbles are blown into a tank layered with dry ice), and how bubbles get their color. And you'll get to blow big bubbles. The annual one-day event features 30 bubble activities and is held in mid-July. For more information, call (812) 337-1337.

- Try your luck at Eastern Bloc Jeopardy, join the Slovac-Sing-Along, and polka, polka, polka at Whiting's **Pierogi Fest.** Usually held the last full weekend in July, Whiting has been celebrating its Eastern European heritage since many immigrants settled here decades ago to work for the Standard Oil Company. For more information, call (219) 659-0292.

- It's not Maui, but it's not bad. For some Pacific island ambience, take in the **Aloha International Hawaiian Steel Guitar Fest**, a luau and steel guitar festival in Winchester. Held annually in July, the three-day music extravaganza attracts renowned musicians. For more information, call (765) 584-6845.

- Frankfort becomes the land of the hotdog for its annual **Hot Dog Festival** at the end of July. Eat a dog with more toppings than you can ever imagine. For more information, call (765) 654-5507 or (765) 654-4081.

- Unlike the Bug Bowl, there are no mosquito delicacies served at Zoar United Methodist's **Mosquito Fest** in Stendal in early August. Instead, sample the homemade ice cream and sign up for the Wiffleball tournament. For more information, call (219) 536-2920.

- For a period of three days in late August, a ton of beans is cooked over an open fire in downtown Fontanet for the annual **Bean Dinner**. Not into beans? Find a treasure at the flea market or strap yourself in for a ride on the Tilt-A-Whirl. For more information, call (812) 877-1010 or (800) 366-3043.

- Until recently, the Orville Redenbacher company produced popcorn at a plant in Valparaiso. Though the plant has closed, every year in September, usually on the first Saturday after Labor Day, residents put on their party hats to pay homage to the late Orville and build elaborate popcorn-made floats for the town's **Popcorn Fest**. For more information, call (219) 464-8332 or visit www.popcornfest.org.

- Slip on your blue suede shoes for Portage's **Elvis FANtasy Fest**. Held annually in mid-October, impersonators flock here for the fan clubs, car show, and souvenirs. For more information, call (317) 844-7354 or (800) 283-8687.

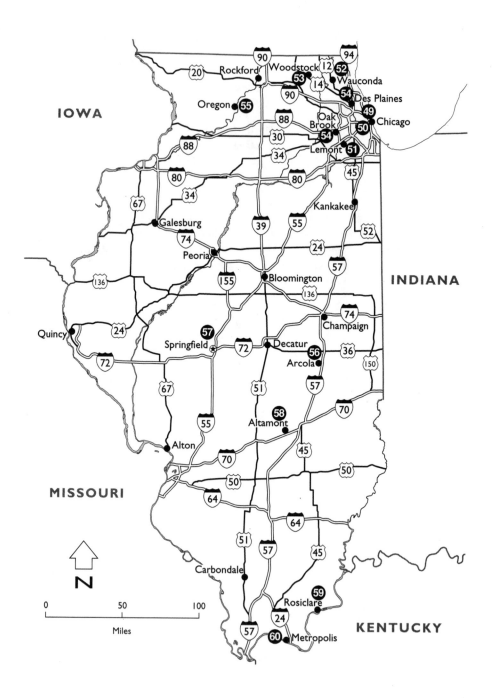

4

ILLINOIS

A Detective, a Superhero, and a Big Shoe

49 | Museum of Holography
Chicago

Stroll by an image on display in the Museum of Holography and a straight-faced woman stares out at you. Move a few inches over and the same picture shows an image of glass shattering, with the woman's face twisting angrily.

Located in Chicago's bustling and burgeoning West Loop, 11 blocks west of the Sears Tower, the Museum of Holography is a place where physics and art intertwine to form remarkable images. In modern art museums it is not uncommon to see visitors cocking their heads at the artwork in an attempt to understand the artist's vision. Here, such movement is encouraged in order for visitors to fully appreciate the holographic artwork. When you take a few steps to the right or left, many holograms appear to move, as the images and shapes morph into other forms.

As Loren Billings, a holographer and one of the museum's founders says,

Trying out the gear at the Museum of Holography, Chicago

"There's always this wonderful surprise or adventure associated with holography. After all these years, I am still excited about it." It was in the mid-1970s, when holography was still a relatively new science and art form, that Billings and a group of other holographers decided to open a museum and offer classes in holography.

From Cracker Jack toys to credit cards to a representation of the Big Bang in Chicago's Museum of Science and Industry (designed by the holography museum and staff from the School of Holography), you've probably seen holograms before, but perhaps not the kind that are as wondrous as the ones in the Museum of Holography—holograms of a woman brushing her hair or of a shark blind siding you. The main hall features extra large holograms: a larger-than-life hand with an extended palm; a portrait of Ronnie Lott, a former defensive back for the San Francisco 49ers; and a miner panning for gold. There also are images of a Medea-like woman appearing to howl, a tarantula with spindly legs, but also of flowers and things of a more genteel nature. A myriad of people—a professional artist, a nuclear engineer, and a gynecologist—created the holograms you'll see in the museum. Many of the pieces took about one week each to make. While some pieces have remained on view for quite a while, such as the miner panning for gold, the museum staff frequently adds new artwork.

Expect to see quite a variety of holograms, from the aesthetically pleasing rose hologram to finely detailed scientific ones. Don't forget to visit the room containing holograms of body parts—not just hands, but spleens, the larynx, and middle ear bones. How often do you get to admire an intricate portrait of your heart valves?

The museum displays do not offer much explanation or background information about holography, other than what is printed (in scientific jargon) on a brochure; the focus is on the artwork. But to help you understand what it is you are seeing, know that holograms are essentially three-dimensional representations, waves printed on light-sensitive material. The light waves reflect off an object when illuminated with a laser light, creating a complete and full dimensional image of the object. People may think they are looking at the real thing when they see a hologram, but it is actually a representation of the real object, Billings points out. Holography was accidentally discovered by British scientist Dennis Gabor in the late 1940s when he was researching ways to improve the resolution of electron microscopy. He produced the first "inline" transmission hologram in 1948 with a mercury arc lamp and a green filter, and went on to win a Nobel Prize for his work in holography.

Even though the advancement of holography has already aided in the development of lasers and fiber optics and the study of genetics, Billings and her colleagues believe holography is still in its embryonic stages. "That's why it's so exciting," she says.

Want to give holography a try? Upstairs from the museum, the School of Holography offers weeklong and quarter-long courses in holography for artists or scientists, from introductory holography to photochemistry and pseudocolor holography. For information on classes, call (312) 829-2292. The museum also sells plenty of items such as holographic earrings and greeting cards.

1134 West Washington Boulevard, Chicago
(312) 226-1007
Open year-round, Wednesday through Saturday from 12:30 p.m. to 5 p.m.
Admission charged

50 Feet First Exhibit–Dr. Scholl Museum
Chicago

The first thing that catches your eye as you walk into the Feet First Exhibit–Dr. Scholl Museum is the size 35 shoe once worn by the world's tallest man, Robert Wadlow of Alton, Illinois. (To put this into perspective, basketball player Shaquille O'Neal wears a size 22. The 8'11" Wadlow wore a size 44½ shoe before his death.) Marvel at the prodigious shoe for a few minutes then step inside the museum and check out a display case—almost as big as Wadlow's shoe—with the pea-size shoes (literally only a few inches in length) that belonged to Chinese women who had to bind their feet as recently as the early 1900s.

Open since 1990, the Feet First Exhibit–Dr. Scholl Museum, located in Chicago's Near North neighborhood, is part of the Scholl College of Podiatric Medicine (not affiliated with the Scholl company) and contains more than just rooms filled with big and small shoe displays. It praises the father of podiatric medicine, Dr. Scholl, and reveals fascinating information and trivia about our shoes and feet. (Did you know there was no such thing as a right or left shoe until the early 1900s and that in an average lifetime a person has walked around the world two to three times? That's more than 50,000 miles! Did you know that if you point the sole of your shoe at someone in Asia, you're essentially giving them the bird?) And since the exhibit is affiliated with a podiatry college, the exhibits remind us to treat our feet well. So don't wear your plastic red heels to this museum—or risk being scolded by the budding podiatrists you'll pass in the hall.

Back before Dr. Scholl and the advent of podiatrists, whenever people had any foot-related problems they would pay a visit to traveling medicine men called "corn cutters," who just happened to come into town when the fairs and carnivals did. If it wasn't for Scholl, we might still be saying "Well, honey, I'm off to the corn cutter" whenever we experienced any problems with our feet. Says Museum Coordinator David McKay, "Dr. Scholl brought legitimacy to the field of podiatry."

When he was 16 years old, Dr. Scholl became an apprentice at a shoemaker's shop in Indiana. After a few years there, he hopped over to Chicago to work at a shoe store and attend medical school. At the shoe store he realized how many people complained of sore feet because of improper shoes or their corns and bunions. After receiving his medical degree (he never did practice medicine), Scholl developed a gadget he called the Foot Eazer to alleviate pressure on a person's arch. At first he had a tough time selling it to shoe stores. But after persistent visits to stores, passing out samples to customers, and advertising, when people realized that it lived up to its claims, he sold quite a few. Take a look at one of the early Foot Eazers in the museum.

Dr. Scholl once said that the secret to a successful business was, "Early to bed, early to rise, work like hell, and advertise." See many of his early posters and storefront displays. Scholl was also one of the first businessmen to see the value of advertising on radio. In the 1920s and 1930s more families purchased radios for their houses and Dr. Scholl saw the radio as a way to spread the word about his company's products.

As his company grew, Scholl started a "chiropody" school in 1912 in order to teach his salespeople about the bone and muscular construction of the foot and about foot care. Scholl's school was one of few that welcomed women and minorities. "He was really a man ahead of his time," says

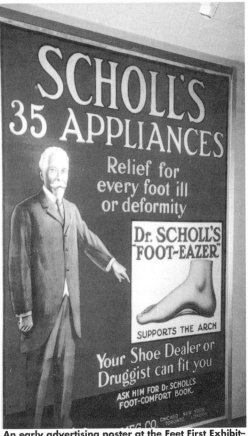

An early advertising poster at the Feet First Exhibit–Dr. Scholl Museum, Chicago

McKay. The museum contains many photographs of some of Scholl's first students and photocopies of the certificates they received. The school, still in existence, is located upstairs from the museum.

Throughout the decades, Scholl became a family name. The company developed more and more products like Zino-pads to treat corns, insoles, and hosiery. It eventually opened retail stores in Europe, a factory the size of a city block in Chicago, and ultimately factories throughout the world. Many of the products developed over the years are on view. In the 1960s, after models donned Scholl's sandals at a European fashion show, the sandals became a fashion statement and sold like gangbusters around the world.

At the museum you'll see a large, mysterious (to those born after the 1950s) wooden contraption—a fluoroscope—that was common in shoe stores until the 1950s and took X-rays of customers' feet. Don't miss the Zoetrope, the 19th-century predecessor of the film projector, which displays a person's gait

Famous Illinois Natives

- Frontiersman James Butler "Wild Bill" Hickok, born in 1837 in Troy Grove
- Actor Gary Coleman, born in 1968 in Zion
- Actors Joan and John Cusak, born in 1962 and 1966 respectively, in Evanston
- Frontier lawman Wyatt Earp, born in 1848 in Monmouth
- Writer Ernest Hemingway, born in 1899 in Oak Park
- Actor William Holden, born in 1918 in O'Fallon
- Track star Jackie Joyner-Kersee, born in 1962 in East St. Louis
- Comedian Bill Murray, born in 1950 in Wilmette
- Former President Ronald Reagan, born in 1911 in Tampico
- Writer Carl Sandburg, born in 1878 in Galesburg (visit his home)
- Actress Betty White, born in 1922 in Oak Park

cycle (if a person walks hunched over or on the balls of their feet). Have a seat before a computer that explains, layer by layer, the parts of the foot and what occurs during a bunionectomy (it's not too gross). If you want to see the real thing, call in advance, and tours through the gross anatomy and orthotics labs and surgery unit can be arranged.

The staff has also arranged a display that explains what kind of shoes can hurt your feet. For example, men's oxford shoes are too flimsy and don't allow enough air to get to the foot, which causes the foot to sweat, bacteria to breed in the shoe, and makes you have smelly feet. (Did you know your foot sweats about four to six ounces a day through 250,000 sweat glands?) You're told that the good-for-you shoes tie in the front, have thick soles, vents, and arches made of a natural fabric that allows the foot to breathe. Again, don't wear your red plastic heels to this museum.

1001 North Dearborn Street, Chicago
(312) 280-2487
www.finchcms.edu/scholl
Open year-round, Monday through Friday from 9 a.m. to 5 p.m.
Free admission

Cookie Jar Museum

Lemont

Twenty-five years ago cookie jars were easy to come by at flea markets, garage sales, and antiques shops. Now they are some of the first items to be snatched up, as there are thousands of cookie jar collectors roaming around the United States. Some of the more unusual cookie jars, or those possessed by famous people, have been known to go for thousands of dollars. (A cookie jar owned by Andy Warhol—he was a cookie jar collector, too—was said to have fetched more than $20,000 at an auction.) These days you can find cookie jar price guides and cookie jar calendars at most shops, and you can attend the national cookie jar convention, which attracts thousands of people every year. And you can visit a cookie jar museum. Who would have thought? (But then again, who would have thought that there'd be a museum of bathroom tissue or a museum of barbed wire?)

"Can you imagine the number of cookies baked, burnt, and half-done that have been in all of these cookie jars?" wonders Cookie Jar Museum owner Lucille Hodges-Bromerek as she pats "Happy," a cookie jar in the shape of a plump yellow chef, an item she received from her husband.

Categorized on shelves with labels like "pig sty" (rows of piggy cookie jars), "woodland creatures" (bunnies and bears), "Dutch colony" (windmill cookie jars), "lions and lambs," and "kitties and mice" ("They get along here," she says), Hodges-Bromerek has grouped fairy-tale and folktale characters such as Humpty Dumpty together, and transportation-related cookie jars shaped as choo-choo trains. You'll see "Puddles," a cookie jar in the shape of a duck; Howdy Doody; a few fancy, hand-painted glass cookie jars; and antique biscuit jars. The jars are showcased in a crowded and slightly dusty second-story apartment in downtown Lemont, an unpretentious canal town 20 miles southwest of Chicago (Lemont also boasts a soda fountain drugstore). This is the perfect home for Lucille Hodges-Bromerek's 2,000 or so cookie jars.

"Collectors are born, not made," declares Hodges-Bromerek, cookie jar collector extraordinaire. Some people, she says, are just more inclined than others to amass buttons, salt and pepper shakers or, in her case, cookie jars. Building a collection is more than a hobby to folks who constantly scour antiques and resale shops for mustard pots or movie posters. Collecting is therapeutic and a way of life, she says. For Hodges-Bromerek, collecting cookie jars started as a form of therapy when her counselor advised her to travel or start collecting something after she successfully completed a 12-step program for alcohol in the 1970s. (She decided on cookie jars just because they were different.) Thousands of cookie jars later, and still sober, Hodges-Bromerek has what she says is the only cookie jar museum in the world.

Inside the Cookie Jar Museum, Lemont

It is hard for her to recall which cookie jars on the shelves were among the first ones she purchased or which ones are her favorites, though she seems to have quite a few "cuties and sweeties" type of cookie jars. Manufacturers like Red Wing, American Bisque, and Treasure Craft are well represented here. And while many of her jars date from the 1970s onward, she has some pieces that date back to the late 1930s. She picked up most of the cookie jars at auctions, flea markets, and garage sales all over the United States.

Although she no longer hits the road in search of jars (she has her "elves," or network of friends, doing that for her now), she does man her museum regularly. She jokes that she's "too busy doing nothing" to travel around the United States.

But the highlight of her day is walking up the stairs to her museum off Main Street and chatting it up with her visitors. That's why she makes the three-block commute to her museum for a few hours every day. "I meet a lot of interesting people in here . . . This is what I do," she says, smiling, leaning back in her armchair, surveying a shelf of Pooh bear cookie jars, and taking a drag off her cigarette, "and this is enough."

111 Stephen Street, Lemont
(630) 257-5012
Open daily year-round from 10 a.m. to 2 p.m., or by appointment.
Admission charged

52 | Curt Teich Postcard Archives
Wauconda

Pop into any antiques shop and you're bound to come across a shoebox stuffed with vintage postcards from the early part of the 20th century. Back then, postcard collecting was enormously popular. People sent each other cards featuring photos of major news events of their town (again, this was before television); street scenes of Main Street in, for example, Peoria, Illinois; or family portraits. At the time, there were plenty of postcard companies around the country churning out cards to keep up with the demand. One of its largest, the Curt Teich Postcard Company of Chicago, produced millions of postcards, among them the popular "Greetings From" series depicting nostalgia-rich scenes of people ice skating or camping out in front of their Airstreams.

Thanks to Ralph Teich, the founder's youngest son, the Lake County Discovery Museum's Curt Teich Postcard Archives contain more than 350,000 cards relating to more than 10,000 towns and cities in North America and more than 87 foreign countries. And with one of the world's largest collections of Route 66 and Lincoln Highway images, the museum is sure to trigger the memories of blue highways travelers. Part local history museum, part shrine to the Teich Company, the Lake County Discovery Museum is a clean, modern facility that also houses excellent permanent exhibits on postcard history.

The historical exhibit, which visitors pass through first, chronicles the evolution of postcards and the artistry behind them. Expect to see jigsaw puzzle cards, New Year's cards, "hold-to-lights" postcards that glow when held up to a light, copper window postcards from the early 1900s, and postcards woven in silk. You are told that when postcards were first introduced to the public, people feared that they would forget how to write because (oh, the horror!) they only scribbled a few words or sentences onto postcards. You are also told that before the days of television, postcards were often used to send news and images of hurricanes or floods to other parts of the country. By the time Curt Teich started mass-producing postcards at the dawn of the 20th century, postcards had become standard souvenirs at roadside attractions.

Teich's cards were ubiquitous because so were the armies of photographers the company dispatched all over the world. After setting up shop in 1898 in Chicago, the German-born Teich sent photographers to countless cities across America (and eventually all over the world). The photographers snapped black-and-white photos of train depots and local monuments, all the while jotting down notes regarding colors. When they returned to Chicago, artists would draw in the color and airbrush out any unappealing tidbits like power lines or smokestacks, making the scenes look rather idealistic and fantastic. Staff would then make different sets of negatives for various colors and print

Like What You See?
A Museum Filled with Glass—and Shells

To see a huge variety of glass objects and shells collected from around the world, visit **Ward's Museum** downstate in Sullivan. Cora and Abraham Ward were antiques collectors and globe trotters who bought souvenirs at nearly every place they visited. Married at the turn of the 20th century, they accumulated more than 1,000 glass items such as glass slippers, 400 goblets, and 10,000 shells, making theirs reportedly one of the largest shell collections in the United States. When Abraham died, Cora donated their collection to the Illinois Masonic Home. The museum is located east of Sullivan on Highway 121, One Masonic Way. Open daily year-round, from 8 a.m. to 4:30 p.m. Sodas and ice cream sundaes are served daily from 1 p.m. to 4 p.m. in the old-fashioned ice cream parlor. For more information, call (217) 728-4394.

the images on heavy card stock.

Over the years the company also developed advertisements for companies like Planter's Peanuts. Many of these amusing ads are on view in the museum. During World War II, Teich halted postcard printing and produced military maps for the government. These images are also on view in the last room of the exhibit.

Teich postcards are fiercely collected—popular at postcard trading shows, antiques shows, and online. And, as one wall in the museum points out, Teich's images have appeared in thousands of newspaper and magazine articles and advertisements. Scan the wall and you'll probably come across at least one image that looks familiar—perhaps of the Rocky Mountains or the Los Angeles skyline. Luckily for us, Teich made a point of saving copies of every card his company made, building an extensive collection now housed in the museum. (Diehards are welcome to do research in a separate building containing archives, although the museum itself contains a decent little research center.) Don't forget to send electronic postcards to friends.

About half of the discovery museum is devoted to postcards, the other half contains a kid-friendly "history walk" about Lake County. Visitors are invited to saunter along a plank road, greet an 11-foot mastodon, and relax in the back of a lotus boat.

27277 Forest Preserve Drive (Highway 176 and Fairfield Road), located in the Lakewood Forest Preserve, Wauconda
(847) 968-3381
www.co.lake.il.us/forest/ctpa.htm
You can view five thousand postcards online at the museum's Web site.
Open year-round, Monday through Saturday from 11 a.m. to 4:30 p.m.
Admission charged

53 Chester Gould–Dick Tracy Museum
Woodstock

If the name Chester Gould does not ring a bell, Dick Tracy should. Gould was the creator of the comic strip featuring the yellow-fedora-wearing detective with the well-endowed jaw. Dick Tracy was the hero of the long-lasting strip (of the same name) that spurred serial movies, a cartoon show, the group Crimestoppers, and sent techno-wizards into their labs trying to create two-way wrist radios and moon mobiles like those in the strip.

And what better place to honor "Dick Tracy" and its founder than Woodstock, a bustling and almost bucolic Midwest town that also received notoriety when the movie *Groundhog Day* starring Bill Murray was filmed there. The curious Chester Gould–Dick Tracy Museum is located in a historic courthouse building in Woodstock's town square. Small towns in America love to celebrate residents who have achieved greatness, ones who were born in town or, as in Chester Gould's case, chose to spend their golden years there. Though he did not grow up in Woodstock, Gould spent the last 50 years of his life on a 60-acre estate in the area. He'd commute to the *Chicago Tribune* once a week to turn in his strips and meet with editors and artists. The rest of the time he remained in the Woodstock area.

Aside from exhibiting original Gould-designed comic strips and mementos from the 1990 *Dick Tracy* movie starring Warren Beatty, museum exhibits recount the inspirational story of the strip's creator. While growing up in Oklahoma, Gould dreamed of being a cartoonist for the *Chicago Tribune*. In 1921, at 21 years old, he left for Chicago with $50, his portfolio, and stars in his eyes. His cartoons weren't immediately accepted, but occasionally he received feedback from the *Tribune's* cartoon editor, who encouraged him to continue, saying that one day Gould would come up with the right comic strip. Gould saved these rejection slips (all 60 of them). Go ahead and read some of the editor's comments and suggestions, some of them kind, others pretty blunt. Some of the rejected strips are on display, such as "Our Gang," "Goldilocks and her three brothers," and "Money McGuire." Ten years after arriving in Chicago, Gould's perseverance paid off. The *Tribune* accepted "Dick Tracy," and it became the first detective comic strip.

Debuting in October 1931, it starred Tracy as a plainclothes detective (Gould originally wanted to call the strip "Plainclothes Tracy") who targeted criminals like the Brow, Pruneface, Mumbles, and Wormy. You can see drawings and descriptions of all these characters in the museum; a number of strips also are on view, some still in the conception phase and others printed copies. "Dick Tracy" plots revolved around classic good-guy-versus-bad-guy conflicts. The bad guys were always caught and Tracy and his fellow officers weren't afraid to use force against the criminals in order to catch them.

Dick Tracy was a hit, believes the museum's director Beth Vargo, because he was a modern Sherlock Holmes. "In the 1930s crime was a problem in big cities like Chicago, and people were concerned about it. They wanted to see the criminals apprehended, and Dick Tracy always caught the criminals."

Tracy was also a cool, tech-savvy detective, with his two-way wrist radio, two-way wrist television (actually introduced in the 1960s), two-way wrist computer (introduced in the 1980s), and magnetically powered space ship that zipped him to the moon. One display illustrates how Gould's tech-guru detective inspired people to actually invent accessories like wrist computers.

"Dick Tracy" ran for 45 consecutive years on the front page of the *New York Daily News* and appeared in 27 foreign papers. It is still produced by Tribune Media Services. If you have the time, peruse countless strips that appeared throughout the years and, with the help of one display, follow how Tracy's look has changed.

A recent addition to the museum is a side room geared toward entertaining children. Kids can play detective by piecing together a ripped letter and matching shoe prints. They can draw characters from the cartoon and movie and compare drawings of Tracy comic strip characters to photos of the movie actors with and without their makeup applied.

Open since 1991, the museum began when area residents found out about the Walt Disney film and worked to hold a premiere in Woodstock. A group of them formed a not-for-profit corporation, persuaded Hollywood to hold a little premiere in Woodstock, and partnered with Gould's family to open a museum. His relatives came aboard and donated or loaned many items to the museum, including Gould's original drawing board and chair, on view in the museum's front window.

You can stock up on "Dick Tracy" comic books, notepads, T-shirts, and movie souvenirs while you're at the museum.

Grab your yellow fedora and a water gun and visit Woodstock during Dick Tracy Days, held at the end of July or beginning of August every year.

101 North Johnson Street, located in the Woodstock Courthouse Square Arts Center, Woodstock
(815) 338-8281
www.dicktracymuseum.org
Open year-round: Thursday through Saturday from 11 a.m. to 5 p.m.;
Sunday from 1 p.m. to 5 p.m. Hours are limited in January, so call ahead.
Closed major holidays.
Group tours are welcome by appointment.
Donations suggested

54 McDonald's #1 Store Museum and Ray Kroc Museum
Des Plaines and Oak Brook

Some may blame McDonald's for the homogenization of the American roadside, allowing you to drive across the country on the interstate highway system without seeing America, as Charles Kuralt once said. But McDonald's wasn't always a corporate behemoth. Almost 50 years ago the company was a small, efficient California café run by two brothers. It wasn't until the zealous salesman Ray Kroc began franchising the quick-café concept that McDonald's turned into a billion-dollar, international company. Why not find out how it all began? During the summer you can stop by the McDonald's #1 Store Museum in Des Plaines and throughout the rest of the year you can delve into the psyche of the McDonald's "founder" at the Ray Kroc Museum in the company's headquarters in Oak Brook. Both locations are just west of Chicago.

McDonald's founder was quite a character, as you'll learn in his museum. For example, Kroc was notorious for penning letters to board members reminding them (read: scolding them) that meetings were for getting things done, not talking about getting things done. (You can read some of these letters in the mu-

Some Illinois Firsts and Facts

- **Cracker Jacks** were first introduced at the Chicago World's Fair in 1893.
- The Continental Baking Company of Schiller Park concocted **Twinkies** in 1930.
- The Weber Brothers Metal Works began to manufacture **Weber grills** in Palatine in 1951.
- In 1935 **metal beer cans** were developed by the American Can Company in Chicago.
- Comic strip character **Popeye** was created by Elzie Crisler Segar, of Chester, in 1929.
- In 1946 **corn dogs** were reportedly invented by the Cozy Dog Inn, a joint off Route 66 in Springfield.
- The **largest religious wood carving** in the United States is of St. Theresa at the Carmelite Visitors Center in Darien.
- The **world's largest ketchup bottle** stands in Collinsville. You can find this 70-foot giant off Highway 59.

McDonald's #1 Store Museum, Des Plaines

seum.) It was also not uncommon to see Kroc at a San Diego Padres games shouting about the "stupid playing" going on. (This was after he bought the team.) A trip to the Ray Kroc Museum, located on the ground floor of McDonald's corporate tower, can be amusing, or at least intriguing, even if you're not a devotee of the company or its Big Macs. Learn how Kroc went from paper cup salesman to fast-food czar.

Kroc grew up in Oak Park, an inner-ring suburb of Chicago, and was a fairly average, active boy. He may have been guided in his future career choice by the phrenolograph test he took as a child that predicted he would excel in the food and beverage business. The test is on display, along with various photos from his childhood. He would become a salesman, entertainer, and entrepreneur, but he didn't achieve success right away. For example, Kroc tried to sell square ice cream scoopers. After the ice cream stint, he donned swanky clothes and peddled paper cups for Lily. (Yes, those are genuine paper cups in the display case.) In the 1930s the smart cookie persuaded Walgreens to sell take-out sodas at their drug stores, using of course, Lily's paper cups. He gave the store 300 free cups hoping that the takeouts would be a hit and Walgreens would order more paper cups from him. They were: Eventually Kroc sold Walgreens five million paper cups.

Kroc's next job was selling Multimixers, shake mixers, to drive-ins, diners, and similar establishments in the 1940s and early 1950s on the West Coast. One of the more popular places in southern California to get a burger and shake was the McDonald brothers' restaurant, an efficient, high-volume establishment where they sold 15,000 shakes a month. (Notice photos of the original restaurant.) After Kroc toured the place and met with the brothers, the wheels started turning. He asked them if he could franchise the operation. They agreed, and Kroc opened the first franchised McDonald's store back in Des Plaines, Illinois, in 1955. All these stories, and more, about Kroc's tenacity are told for you in the museum, either through text, audiotapes, or video.

If you're interested, continue on and read or hear about McDonald's development as a corporation or admire the accolades Kroc received from former colleagues and government officials. Another display case describes the Kroc Foundation, which supported research of diabetes among other diseases.

Kroc loved his speedily produced burgers, fries, and shakes. (And there are plenty of photos in both museums that show him biting into a hamburger.) Back in the 1950s, the food was prepared quite differently than it is in the current McDonald's, as you'll learn in the McDonald's #1 Store Museum: fresh potatoes were peeled, cut, blanched, and fried on-site, and Coca-Cola and root beer were stored in kegs. But this museum is not a working restaurant; mannequins pretend to flip plastic burgers and those kegs are not stocked with root beer. The museum is actually a reproduction of the original store, built from blueprints and old photographs. From 1955 until 1984, the store underwent so many renovations that McDonald's decided to tear the building down. Head downstairs and check out the photos of the original store and watch a video about what life was like at the Des Plaines McDonald's in the 1950s, when the store didn't have air conditioning and all the roads leading to it were gravel or dirt. If you're in the mood for a burger, a modern McDonald's is located across the street.

After visiting both museums most likely you'll walk away with a good sense of Ray Kroc's frank personality. You'll see snapshots of him cheering and ranting at a Padres game, driving construction equipment for a new store, holding a broom, and carrying a tray in an Asian McDonald's. (Kroc, with his finely coiffed hair and broad smile, mastered the public relations photo.) He loved his company, but he must have driven his employees nuts, frequently popping in on his stores unannounced. Don't forget to listen to some audio clips of Kroc, or at least read some of his quotes that the staff has typed on the walls, quotes—like "Where there is no risk there is no achievement"—that capture what kind of a man Kroc was.

McDonald's #1 Store Museum
400 North Lee Street, Des Plaines
(847) 297-5022
www.mcdonalds.com
Open Memorial Day through Labor Day. Call for hours.
Free admission

Ray Kroc Museum
2715 Jorie Boulevard (just off Butterfield Road), Oak Brook
No phone number
www.mcdonalds.com
Open year-round, Monday through Friday from 8:30 a.m. to 5 p.m.
Free admission

55 | Stuka Military Museum
Oregon

At first blush, liberal Democrats, politically correct folks, or people who don't approve of lawn ornaments like a World War II cannon and a tank target, might want to drive right past the Stuka Military Museum. And they may have the same reaction when they see the Confederate flag tacked up near the museum entrance, military artifacts piled on the front porch, or the proprietor, John Coy, wearing a "Rush for President" T-shirt. (For the record, Rush is his cat, not the conservative radio talk show host.) But if you zoom past this museum located about 75 miles west of Chicago, you will miss out on one of the best collections of military items in the Midwest.

The museum is more than a repository of guns and uniforms, however. If you are able to tour the place with Coy (he's the only one that runs the museum, so this is pretty likely), you will discover there is a story behind every rifle, sweetheart pillow, and pack of Lucky Strikes—stories Coy has memorized and will share with you. And no, he won't force you to enroll in the NRA or send all 18-year-old visitors to the local armed forces recruiting office.

The displays are arranged in chronological order of each of America's military involvements—from the French and Indian War and the Revolutionary War to the Vietnam War and Desert Storm. There are also a number of military items from other countries such as Taiwan and Australia. Not only do you see regular military uniforms, but also suits that once belonged to an Afrika Corps Crewman and a Norwegian medic.

With 90 percent of the items coming from Midwest soldiers, the museum is part regional history and part familial history. Coy has collected and arranged the uniforms and medals of three generations of soldiers in one family, the Purple Hearts of twin brothers killed at the same time, and a full carton of Lucky Strikes sent by a father to his son stationed in the Philippines. The building itself is overflowing with military items. Coy just can't stop collecting pieces, he says. Everything has a story, all the stories are fascinating, and many of them take months to uncover. Not surprisingly, the museum draws plenty of veterans' family members, particularly widows who come to look at and many times shed a few tears in front of a soldier's uniform.

For every piece he acquires, Coy researches its history—not just the war and division the uniform came from, but the soldier's name, his rank, where he served, his hometown, and any other personal information he can figure out. Point to any object in the case or on a shelf—a bottle of Scotch, boots from a Union soldier—and Coy can tell you its story. A large picture frame contains high school photos of a young man and woman, their engagement photo, wedding announcement, a letter addressed to the young bride, and a telegram. The young man ended up serving in Europe during World War II, at some point wrote her

Like What You See? Drive-by Nostalgia

Cruise Highway 52, about a half mile south of Sublette, Illinois, and check out the Burma Shave–like signs. " '500 bucks for a bike!' Gramps roared. 'Paid less than that for my '39 Ford,' " they read. Boasting the only set of such signs in Illinois, Sublette, about 75 miles southwest of Chicago, was chosen by *Reminisce* magazine to post them along its two-lane highway where original Burma Shave signs were once posted.

a letter that he gave to a priest near his base, instructing him to mail it to her if he should ever become missing or killed in action; he wanted her to receive his letter before the formal government telegram. She did in fact receive the letter and never opened the telegram. Coy's eyes grow large as he tells the story, and he leans over to peer at his treasure. "This was found in the garbage. Can you believe it?!"

Coy did not serve in the armed forces, but he grew up listening to his father, a World War II veteran, trading stories with fellow vets in the garage his dad owned. (Coy decided to call his museum the Stuka Military Museum after the German dive-bomber because many of the vets spoke about those bombers.) He soaked up these military stories from his dad's pals and from his high school teachers, many of whom had also served in World War II. He was quite captivated by their patriotism and bravery, and continued reading about America's battles and conflicts. One day in 1965 he passed by an antiques shop in Warsaw, Illinois. He noticed a German military hat on the wall, was drawn to it, and just had to have it; Coy has been collecting ever since. He now has more than 450 German hats from World War II, his collection is believed to be the largest on display in a museum.

Coy's other collectibles include antique guns (such as a Civil War musket and World War I water-cooled machine gun), hundreds of military patches, wings, and flags. (That faded red and blue Korean flag was signed by POW survivors of the Korean War when they held a reunion.) A few of the contents might be unsettling to some (and did in fact ruffle a few feathers of some nearby residents). For example, Coy has one of Hitler's personal swastika flags on display as well as a knife from Hitler's youth group "Blood and Honor." Regarding his decision to collect and display these items, Coy's philosophy is that education is a pretty good hedge against repeating some of the world's more unpleasant episodes.

On the way out, don't miss Coy's collection of steins, which he has placed on view in the military museum because his wife doesn't allow them in the house.

3178 South Daysville Road, Oregon
(815) 732-2091
Open by appointment
Admission charged

55 | Johnny Gruelle–Raggedy Ann and Andy Museum
Arcola

Raggedy Ann and Andy are two tough dolls. They can be thrown across the floor, dropped under the kitchen table, hugged ten times a day, served hundreds of cups of "tea" (read: air), dragged to a tree house, and stuffed into a backpack. Unlike Barbie dolls, whose arms can be pulled apart, and army action figures, whose movements are stiff and limited, Raggedy Ann and Andy dolls are very versatile and very lovable. Creator Johnny Gruelle knew he had a good thing in 1915 when he patented the doll, but he probably didn't know the dolls would still be rocked in cradles and taken along on car rides in the 21st century.

Because the dolls' popularity endures—many collectors continue to trade them and parents all over the world still buy Raggedy books—Gruelle's descendants decided to gather his personal items and the many curios he created before, during, and after Raggedy Ann and Andy. Open since 1999, the Johnny Gruelle–Raggedy Ann and Andy Museum is tucked into a storefront in downtown Arcola, about 170 miles south of Chicago. The facility fits right in among the Amish handcrafted-furniture stores, antiques shops, and cafés. With exhibit cases framed with forest scenes (a recurring image in the Raggedy books), stocked with dolls, and containing informative, clearly written cards that fill visitors in on the Raggedys' history, the museum will be a nostalgic trip for anyone who had a Raggedy doll.

The museum contains a recreation of Johnny Gruelle's studio, with an unpublished draft of Raggedy Ann and the Queen, and a number of Gruelle's proverbs such as "Successful ones are those who see the smiles of opportunity" and "Those who go from bad to worst reach good only in a hearse." Museum owners Joni Gruelle Wannamaker (Johnny Gruelle's granddaughter) and her husband Tom Wannamaker have staged a recreation of Marcella's playroom, complete with a vintage tea set and a copy of Frank L. Baum's *The Wizard of Oz*. Raggedy Ann and Andy murals that hung on the walls of an ice cream parlor in Oregon in the 1920s decorate one wall of the museum. Discovered in a basement in Vermont, the museum had them restored in 2001.

Though Johnny Gruelle and his family lived in Arcola when he was a toddler, the Wannamakers thought the museum should be located in his birthplace. "We wanted it to be grounded in the Midwest. This is where his roots were," Joni says. Born in 1880, Gruelle moved with his family to Indianapolis in 1882. After Gruelle graduated school he eventually joined the local newspaper as a cartoonist. At the paper he befriended Hoosier poet James Whitcomb Riley, who later wrote a poem "The Raggedy Man," said to be an inspiration for Gruelle's Raggedy Ann doll. Gruelle married in 1901 and he and his

Dolls on display at the Johnny Gruelle–Raggedy Ann and Andy Museum, Arcola

wife, Myrtle, had a girl, Marcella. In 1907 he reportedly found an old rag doll in his mother's attic, painted a new face on it and gave it to Marcella. When the family relocated to the Northeast, Gruelle continued working as a cartoonist, artist, and illustrator, designing original playthings and illustrating books and magazines such as *Mr. Twee Deedle* and *Polly Puddleduck's Trip to the Fair.* You'll see examples of his early work, like the *Twee Deedle* books, as well as a copy of the "The Raggedy Man" poem in the museum. Sadly, not long after moving to the East Coast, Marcella received vaccinations for smallpox, became ill, and died in November 1915.

Devastated, Gruelle turned to his art. He further developed the Raggedy Ann doll and followed up with a book series in 1918, naming the character in the book who owned the Raggedy dolls, Marcella. "But he gave the Marcella in the book blonde hair; the real Marcella had brown hair. It was probably too painful to draw a little girl that looked like his daughter," Joni says. Early versions of the doll, as well as the book series, are in display cases.

Raggedy Ann was a soft, grinning doll with button eyes, striped stockings, red hair, and a dappling of freckles. The first dolls were said to have included candy hearts sewed inside them, with the message, "I love you" printed on the hearts. But none of these dolls with candy hearts have ever been found or documented. Though the first doll was created in 1915, Raggedy Ann and Andy were most popular in the early 1940s, when everything from Raggedy bookends to safety blocks were snatched up. You'll find many of these items in the museum. While the dolls' popularity died down after World War II, a renaissance came about from 1960 to 1974. The publisher printed new books, reprinted old ones, and introduced new dolls. With every year the dolls became more sophisticated—dolls that could talk and play music were introduced. In the 1980s the dolls became collectibles and were sought after at antiques and doll shows. The display cases are arranged chronologically so you can follow the development of the dolls.

Since their inception, Raggedy Ann and Andy dolls have been introduced to and adored by children in countries other than the United States. With a devoted Japanese following in mind, Joni and Tom opened an exhibit in the summer of 2001 on the Raggedys' Asian presence. Also proud of their family's artistic endeavors, the Wannamakers set aside one corner of the museum to display original artwork created by the family post-Johnny, from Raggedy-centric paintings to landscapes.

If you consider yourself a Raggedy aficionado, then head to Arcola in mid-May for the annual Raggedy Ann and Andy Festival. Activities include a street parade, carnival, appearances by members of the Gruelle family, doll shows, art shows, puppet shows, look-alike contests, and storytelling hours.

110 East Main Street, Arcola
(217) 268-4908
www.raggedyann-museum.org
Open year-round: Tuesday through Saturday from 10 a.m. to 5 p.m.; Sunday from 1 p.m. to 4 p.m. Call before visiting in January and February. Donation suggested

Like What You See? Bring on the Midwest Militia

- Get debriefed on America's war efforts from the War of 1812 to Desert Storm at the **Illinois Citizen Soldier Museum**, located in the Robert Dunlap Room of the Admiral James Stockdale Building at 1001 Michigan Avenue in Galesburg, Illinois. Admission is free. For more information, call (309) 342-1181.

- The **All Wars Museum**, located on the grounds of the Veterans Home in Quincy, Illinois, features a replica Revolutionary War cannon. The museum is located at 1701 North 12th Street. Admission is free. For more information, call (217) 222-8641.

- Right smack in the middle of the Mississippi River is the **Rock Island Arsenal** in Rock Island, Illinois, one of the largest arsenals in the world. As luck would have it, there's an arsenal museum in Building 60. Admission is free. For more information, call (309) 782-5021.

- The **Scouting Museum** in Ottawa, Illinois, celebrates the history of the Boy Scouts, Girl Scouts, and Camp Fire Girls. The collection includes a braille scouting book, a Pinewood Derby car, and plenty of vintage badges. The museum is located at 1100 Canal Street. An admission fee is charged. For more information, call (815) 431-9353.

- Grab your powder horn and head to the **National Muzzleloading Rifle Association**'s national competitions in Friendship, Indiana. Their museum is open during the competitions, which are held annually in June and September at Highway 62 and Maxine Moss Drive. Each year the exhibits vary because the staff invites various specialty collectors to display their pieces. Past exhibits have highlighted long-range muzzleloaders and double guns. For more information, call (812) 667-5131 or visit www.nmlra.org.

- The **Historical Military Armory Museum**'s specialty is big guns. If you're with a group tour call ahead and you can eat in the mess hall. The museum is located at 2330 Crystal Street in Anderson, Indiana. For more information, call (765) 649-TANK.

- Learn about Wisconsin's 32nd Division and the development of Camp Williams at the **National Guard Museum** in Camp Williams near Camp Douglas, Wisconsin. The museum is located in an 1896 log building on Volk Field Air National Guard Base. For more information, call (608) 427-1280.

- The nearly 40 Minnesota men who have received the Medal of Honor over the years are honored at the **Minnesota Military Museum**, located at 15000 Highway 115 in Camp Ripley near Little Falls. Look for the tanks lined up on the front yard. For more information, call (320) 632-7344 or (218) 575-2212.

- Purchased by auctioneer Dean Kruse, the military artifacts in the **World War II Victory Museum** represent the Allied struggle to free western Europe. See almost 150 military vehicles, an equal number of uniforms, and many other rare items, such as a model of the British-built Humber Hexonaut, in this Auburn, Indiana, facility. The museum, which opens late spring 2002, is located at County 11A and I-69. For more information, call (219) 927-8042 or visit www.americanheritagevillage.com. The **War Birds Museum**, run by the same folks and located in the same space, contains military aircraft exhibitions. For more information, call (219) 927-1499.

- See page 6 for information on the **Kenosha Military Museum** in Pleasant Prairie, Wisconsin.

57 | Parks Telephone Museum
Springfield

Oliver Parks's life revolved around the telephone. For 40 hours a week, for more than 40 years, he washed and repaired telephones for Illinois Bell. In his free time he collected phones, starting in 1949 with an 1898 Stromberg Carlson. When Parks retired in 1962 he donated the phones to Illinois Bell, now Ameritech.

Upon entering the two-room museum, you'll first be reacquainted with Alexander Graham Bell and then will follow the development of the telephone including technological advances (including a wall of equipment for the hearing impaired and physically challenged) and design advances (remember pastel phones from the 1980s?). The museum has 117 telephones on display, including wooden wall phones, candlestick models, early coin phones, and an early switchboard.

While in the Area
Enjoy Arcola Attractions

- After browsing through the Johnny Gruelle–Raggedy Ann and Andy Museum, walk a few blocks to the **Arcola Depot Welcome Center**, which features a large coffee cup exhibit. The personalized cups once belonged to members of the coffee club that met at a local pharmacy and soda fountain shop years ago. After a customer downed 100 cups he or she earned a cup and a place on the shelf to store the cup. The welcome center also has its own Raggedy Ann and Andy doll collection, depot exhibit, and an impressive brush and broom corn exhibit. Broom corn is no longer produced in Arcola, but three broom factories in town still manufacture them and residents celebrate broom corn every year at the **Arcola Broom Corn Festival**, usually held the weekend after Labor Day. For more information, call (217) 268-4530 or (800) 336-5456.

- And don't miss the unusual **World's Only Hippie Memorial**, an oblong structure of scrap metal and peace signs, created by the late Arcola artist Bob Moomaw. It is located just north of the Arcola Depot on Oak Street.

- Would you like a taste of Amish life in Arcola? Then sit down to a meal with them, visit one of their houses, or walk through an Amish-focused museum. For more information or to book a meal or tour, call the **Illinois Amish Interpretive Center** at (888) 45-AMISH.

Some early 20th-century phones at the Parks Telephone Museum, Springfield

Perhaps one of the most intriguing items in the museum is a 1964 Picture Phone. Believe it or not, the first television picture sent over telephone lines actually occurred in 1927 and was sent from New York to Washington, D.C. But since so many circuits were needed to initiate the service over a widespread area, not many new developments took place after that transmission. Decades later, in 1964, the Picture Phone was launched at the New York World's Fair, and the first transcontinental call was made to Disneyland in California. But because the Picture Phone cost a lot of money, not many people purchased one. Production halted in 1980.

529 South 7th Street,
Springfield
(217) 789-5303
Call for hours
Free admission

171

58 Ben Winter Museum
Altamont

Ben Winter loves anything that chugs, whistles, and puffs smoke—hulking, powerful engines that pull threshing machines, corn binders, or little children on train rides through his orchard. "I just love firing 'em up," he says with a grin and twinkling eyes as he pats a steam engine. It is one of 10 full-scale steam engines, five scale-model steam engines, and 12 stationary engines in his museum—one of many engines that Winter hauls to area threshing shows every year. About 15 minutes west of Effingham, and just outside the little town of Altamont, the Ben Winter Museum contains a hodgepodge collection of farm equipment, steam and oil engines, and local and personal collectibles like bullet pencils and Linotype machines from the 1890s. You can't miss Winter's museum from I-70: It's the big red barn with the word "Museum" painted on the roof in tree trunk–size letters.

The Ben Winter Museum also could be called "neat things according to Ben."

Winter hasn't posted many explanatory signs about the engines and machines; visitors who did not grow up in rural communities or who have not visited the American Farm Implements Heritage Museums in Iowa for an introduction to agricultural history in the Midwest (see page 207) may be baffled by the machines. Just make sure you walk around with Winter; he's got plenty of stories to share about the steam engines he's picked up over the years and can explain in detail how they work.

The ground floor is chock-full of threshing machines and engines: an 1895, 150-horsepower Buckeye steam engine from a grist mill; an oil engine used in Little Rock, Arkansas, to pull a cotton gin; and a Buffalo Springfield steamroller from 1923. Some of these pieces are worth $30,000 each; some of his engines fire at every revolution with smoke trails that run 40 feet high (not in the museum, but when Winter lugs them to threshing shows). Miscellaneous farm and factory equipment includes a turn-of-the-century corn binder and a 1910 generator from a Greenville, Illinois, milk company.

Even Winter is amazed at what he has in his barn. "I'm not sure how all this started," he says. "I bought one piece of equipment and then another one and next thing I know I needed to add on to the building."

Winter, the museum's curator, acquisitions director, cleaning crew, gardener, and model railroad engineer, is a former stonecutter. He retired from the stone business in 1980, but opened a sawmill nearby and operated that until 1998. He's been pretty busy with the museum since then, adding an extra level for his model trains, a little greenhouse where you can stand under a lemon tree and smell roses in February, and over the years he's added pecan trees around his property.

When locals found out he was into collecting old machinery and curios, many of them offered him pieces that had been gathering dust in their base-

A wall filled with pencils at the Ben Winter Museum, Altamont

ments, like an Altamont fire truck from 1889 and 105-year-old Linotype machines from the *Altamont News*. And if you're into pencils, you have to stop at the museum: Winter has devoted one section of the barn to a pencil collection he inherited from Altamont schoolteacher Richard Popp. Each one of the 4,000 pencils is different from the next—bullet pencils, carpenter pencils, some bearing company names, and some with erasers at both ends. Other stuff Winter has scattered about the museum are an approximately 200-year-old church bell from Lincoln, Nebraska (its thunderous bell still works), the headlight from an 1860 steam engine train, and a nearly 50-foot-long Oldsmobile like the one your dad might have had sitting in the garage.

The top floor of the museum contains a number of model trains Winter built or ordered from companies. In the summer, he runs one mini steam and one gasoline train on 3,300 feet of track through the fruit and nut orchard in his backyard. A woodworker, Winter also has some carvings such as turtles and puzzles for sale.

1815 East 900 Avenue, Altamont
(618) 483-6665
Open mid-April to mid-June: Monday through Saturday from 8 a.m. to
6 p.m.; Sunday from 1 p.m. to 4 p.m. Open mid-June to mid-October,
Monday through Saturday from 10 a.m. to 5 p.m. Winter recommends you call
before visiting; otherwise he may be out running errands when you stop by.
He runs the minitrains from May to November.
Donation suggested

59 American Fluorite Museum
Rosiclare

In southern Illinois, where towns are a stone's throw from Kentucky and the topography is vastly different from the flat and uniform cornfields in central Illinois, many residents earned a living spending 40 hours a week or more in mines. Stroll through the streets of Rosiclare and you can almost see the ghosts of miners with their rock picks slung over their shoulders, metal lunch boxes at their sides, and carbide hats fitted onto their heads. It wasn't too long ago that they were heading into local mine shafts to earn a living.

Rosiclare is a modest town of 1,200 people situated at the eastern edge of the Shawnee National Forest, right on the Ohio River, and not too far from Cave-in-the-Rock, which river pirates once called home. To geologists and miners, Rosiclare conjures up images of calcium fluoride, barite, and calcite. Those names don't ring a bell? Even if you don't carry around a pocket *Periodic Table of the Elements*, you'll get a kick out of Rosiclare's American Fluorite Museum.

The relatively new museum, run by former miners and volunteers, teaches southern Illinois residents and people passing through about the region's mineral heritage. It celebrates the mineral off of which many Rosiclare area resi-

---

Like What You See?
Get Your Kicks at the Route 66
Hall of Fame

One of the most famous truck stops in Illinois, or anywhere else for that matter, is the Dixie Truckers Home, featuring the **Route 66 Hall of Fame**. This is one exhibit that's true to its name: it's literally a short hall located on the way to the bathrooms and video arcade. While the hall might not warrant a separate trip, its Route 66 memorabilia and tributes to businesses like the former Pig Hip restaurant in Broadwell, Illinois, provide a touching reminder that Route 66 used to be the most famous highway in America. Run by the Route 66 Association of Illinois, the centerpieces of the exhibit relate, not surprisingly, to Illinois attractions. If you're traveling the great road for some nostalgia, this place is a must-stop. A handy map outlines the route and pinpoints possible detours. The hall of fame is located at I-55 and Highway 136 in McLean, about 10 miles south of Bloomington. Admission is free. For more information, call (309) 874-2323.

A chunk of the mineral that's the focal point of the American Fluorite Museum, Rosiclare

dents made their livelihood—the state mineral, fluorite, or fluorspar. Located in the former office building of the Rosiclare Lead and Fluorspar Mining Company, off Highway 34, the town's main drag, the American Fluorite Museum contains, as expected, a decent collection of fluorite, unique rocks, and mineral formations (barite on fluorite, calcite needles, galena, petrified wood, fossilized wood), and photos depicting mining life in Rosiclare since the late 1800s.

Before making your way around the museum, read a little about the mineral's characteristics (explained for you in the entrance hall). Fluorspar is made of calcium fluoride, and on a hardness scale from one to 10, 10 being the hardest, fluorite is a four. (A diamond is a 10.) You will be able to take a small, brittle piece and break it in half—quite a confidence-boosting exercise. Fluorite comes in shades of bright purple, yellow, blue, white, and green; you'll see all colors in the museum. In ultraviolet light, the mineral can become fluorescent. When the light outside is just right, a boulder-size piece of fluorite in the museum's first exhibit room becomes luminous. Fluorite is used in the processing of steel, glass, and aluminum, and to make hydrofluoric acid, ceramic products, and refrigeration gases.

In the 1870s, after scientists discovered that fluorite helped remove impurities from steel smelting, more and more companies mined the mineral, especially in the Southern Illinois–Western Kentucky Fluorite District. Rosiclare became the epicenter for fluorite mining. From approximately 1910 to 1945, the Rosiclare region was the largest fluorspar mining area in the United States. Area families started small mining and milling companies, with larger national companies eventually moving in. Unlike out West where miners could pan for gold in a stream and catch nuggets with their pans, fluorspar is mined in underground shafts, some as deep as 1,300 feet. You'll see plenty of photographs of these early mines and miners.

Because fluorspar was used in the manufacturing of bullets and steel for ships and armory during World War II, area mines beefed up their security by photographing all employees and requiring them to wear identification badges. The museum has a number of items from this time period on display, including original badges, photos of the chain-link fences installed for security, search lights, and warning posters, one of which read "Don't mess with us! We are here to help in a war!"

In addition to seeing mineral specimens displayed in antique glass cases donated by Rosiclare merchants, items like old miners' hats, rock picks, goggles, precision scales used to weigh the specimens, and blast boxers used to detonate dynamite can all be found in the museum. On the walls, maps trace the geologic makeup of the area and photo collages of miners at work depict life at the mine and in Rosiclare (notice pictures of former Fluorospar Festival queens). Newspaper articles describe major mining events, including the hydrogen sulfide accident in 1971 when seven miners died from poisonous gas fumes.

Over the decades, fluorspar production decreased as companies pulled out of the area and headed to Asia, especially China, where the mineral was easier to retrieve and labor was cheaper. In 1995 the last mine closed in the Rosiclare area, and all shafts were sealed. Shortly afterward, a group of local miners, geologists, and concerned residents who wanted to document the region's mineralogical history and its connection to fluorspar, got together to form a museum. Because workers were allowed to take home whatever mineral specimens they could fit into their lunch box (although when lunch box dimensions gradually grew in size, the company had to dictate lunch box sizes) many former workers donated mineral specimens to the museum. And when the Rosiclare Lead and Fluorspar Mining Company closed its office off Highway 34, the staff donated a number of rocks, which were already housed in the office building, to the group. The museum opened in 1997.

Scour through the ore piles near the museum's entrance and pick out some fluorite to take home ($1 a pound) or pick some recently polished fluorite in the gift shop. Look closely and you can find near-perfect pyramid shapes, clear, golden, or purple specimens. Consider visiting Rosiclare the first weekend in October for the town's annual Fluorspar Festival. Activities include a cheerleader dunking machine, street dance, and pageant.

Main Street and Highway 34 (located behind the car wash), Rosiclare
(618) 285-3513
Open March to December, Thursday, Friday, and Sunday from 1 p.m.
to 4 p.m.; Saturday from 10 a.m. to 4 p.m.
Admission charged

59 Super Museum
Metropolis

Located along the Ohio River, Metropolis is not unlike other downstate Illinois towns, with its town square, antiques stores, and coffee shops. Yet standing guard in this town square, in all of his brawny righteousness (in cerulean blue tights) is the town's favorite son, Superman—the super hero who has made a town of about 7,000 people a viable tourist destination. The only Metropolis in the United States, located about 330 miles south of Chicago, this place is a must-see for anyone who has any interest in Superman or comic book heroes. And a visit to the Super Museum, which boasts thousands of action figures, will make any collector's jaw drop.

The Super Museum is located a few feet from the strapping statue of Superman. It's possible to get lost in the museum for hours, but first you have to walk past tempting Superman merchandise. Owner Jim Hambrick, who has been collecting paraphernalia since 1959, has arranged his collectibles in booths that weave mazelike around the museum, creating a carnival-like atmosphere.

Like What You See?
More Rocks, Minerals, and Gems

- See the origin of Chicago's Tribune Tower by visiting Bedford, Indiana's, **Land of Limestone Exhibit** or by trekking through one of Bedford's quarries. The exhibit is located on the Bedford Campus of Oakland City University, north of Courthouse Square in Bedford, Indiana. For more information, call (800) 798-0769.

- Displays at the **Museum of Minerals and Crystals** include Mexican geodes, petrified wood, Brazilian agate, gemstone pictures, and fluorite. Open daily April 1 through November 1 from 9 a.m. to 5 p.m. Located on Highway 23 in Dodgeville, Wisconsin. For more information, call (608) 935-5205.

- Downstairs from **Dave's Down to Earth Rock Shop**, the owners have gathered and placed hundreds of fossils on display for visitors to view for free. The shop is located at 704 Main Street in Evanston, Illinois. For more information, call (847) 866-7374.

- Geologists will get a kick out of the unusual specimens at the **Reif Family Mineral and Rock Display** at the Kalona Historical Village in Kalona, Iowa (see page 202).

The Man of Steel welcoming visitors to the Super Museum, Metropolis

He has plastered renderings of Superman by DC Comics artists near the entrance to the museum as well as photos of the original Superman Kirk Alyn, the hero from 1948 to 1950, and shots of George Reeves. Don't miss the costume Reeves wore from 1951 to 1957 in the television series *Adventures of Superman.*

Of his collection of 100,000-plus items, Hambrick says, "It started as a hobby and now it's an occupation." He claims his Superman collection is the largest in the world, so be prepared to spend some time here. As you meander around the low-lit, one-floor museum, you will pass by Superman poker and canasta sets, trading cards, Kryptonite bubble gum, and a Superman cookie jar. Try not to gaze at the Superman pinball machine and six-foot inflatable Superman for too long. Props from the Superman television shows and movies—such as Christopher Reeve's harness and Clark Kent glasses—are stashed all over the museum. Original paintings, holographic artwork, and posters once tacked to bedroom walls now hang on the museum walls. Outfits that Supergirls and Superboys once strutted around in are also on display. One room is devoted to the ABC television series, *Lois and Clark,* which ran in the late 1980s and early 1990s and starred Dean Cain and Teri Hatcher. (Cain was given the key to the city a few festivals ago.) And there are plenty of souvenirs from past Super Fests.

A native Californian, Hambrick used to cart his collection to fairs around the country before moving to Metropolis. Towing a U-Haul crammed with Superman costumes, trading cards, and glasses behind him, he migrated to Metropolis because it was the perfect place to open his museum, he says. It took many trips over a period of several years to move his entire collection there. The Super Museum opened in 1993. Not long after Hambrick flew into town, he became one of the town's biggest cheerleaders, promoting the town by organizing the Super Fest and other tourist-generating events in Metropolis.

Officially declared Superman's hometown in 1972 by the Illinois House, Metropolis had big plans to capitalize on its name. (Keep in mind, Metropolis, Illinois, is nothing like the Metropolis in the comic book or movies; there are no skyscrapers here.) In the 1970s investors planned to construct a theme park, the Disneyland-esque Amazing World of Superman, but when the economy took a nosedive, the extensive plans were abandoned. Ironically, not long after the plans for the park were dropped, Christopher Reeve leaped onto the silver screen in the first Superman movie and thousands of fans flooded the chamber of commerce with calls, prompting locals to organize the Superman celebration and eventually raise funds for a bronze statue in the town's square.

The Super Fest, which usually takes place the second weekend in June, features a Superman Drama (during which actors feign a bank robbery and one lucky guy dresses up as Superman and saves the day), Little Miss Supergirl and Little Superboy contests, dog shows, and a Superman Tennis Tournament. Stars from the television shows and movies have been known to show up, and each year attendees are asked to arrive costumed according to a different theme. Attendees to the 2001 fest pretended to be their favorite DC Comics character. You may have a use for those Wonder Woman or Aquaman costumes yet.

517 Market Street, Metropolis
(618) 524-5518
www.supermuseum.com
Open daily from 9 a.m. to 5 p.m.
Admission charged.

Offbeat Illinois Festivals

- Sublette, the "Little Town with the Big Toy Show," hosts its **Toy and Antique Tractor Show** usually the third Sunday in March. Cast-iron, plastic, and metal toys, scale models of antique tractors to models of the latest farm equipment are all on display. For more information, call (815) 849-5242.

- Everything is coming up lilacs at Lombard's **Lilac Fest** held in mid-May every year. For more information, call (630) 953-6000.

- Enter the root toss or root golf contests at Collinsville's **Horseradish Festival** held the first weekend in June every year. For more information, call (618) 344-2884.

- Sample rhubarb pie, yogurt, and preserves at Aledo's **Rhubarb Festival** in the beginning of June. For more information, call (309) 582-5373.

- Danville holds its **Turtle Races** every year in June. For more information, call (217) 446-5327.

- After losing many trees to Dutch elm disease in the late 1960s, the Dixon-area men's garden club wanted to spruce up the town's barren streets. They decided to beautify their local roads with hundreds of petunias; Dixon promotes itself as the **Petunia Capital of the World**. Celebrate flowers with them around the Fourth of July. For more information, call (815) 284-3361.

- Illinois and Iowa residents meet on the banks of the Mississippi every year to test their strength in a **Tug-O-War** contest using a 2,400-foot, 680-pound rope that stretches across the great river. Held in mid-August in Port Byron, Illinois. For more information, call (309) 523-3734.

- The central Illinois town of Pekin blooms in mid-September for **Marigold Fest**. For more information, call (309) 346-2106.

- Got a yearning for some down-home comfort food? Try Clinton's **Apple and Pork Festival**, held the last weekend in September. For more information, call (217) 935-6066.

- The lovely **Honeybee Festival** in Paris is typically held on the fourth weekend in September. For more information, call (217) 465-4179.

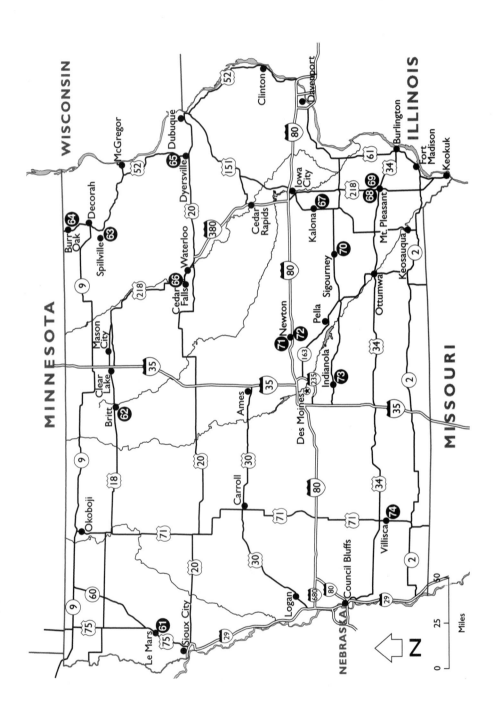

5 IOWA

The Farmer, the Hobo, and the Vaudeville Act

61 | Ice Cream Capital of the World
Le Mars

Founded in 1913 by Fred Wells with $250, a wagon, and some milk bottles, the Wells Dairy has become America's largest family-owned dairy processor. For four generations the company has churned out milk, yogurt, and ice cream products. Based in Le Mars, which bills itself as the Ice Cream Capital of the World (because more ice cream is made by one single company in Le Mars than anywhere else), Wells opened its Visitors Center, complete with an ice cream parlor and museum, in March 2000 for lactose-indulgent people.

Before ordering a banana split, work up an appetite by touring the museum. A re-created production line lights up and starts moving shortly after you walk into one room, and tubs of Blue Bunny ice cream chug along on the assembly line. See how the milk bottle, ice cream sundae, and cone evolved. And be let in on some astounding facts associated with the dairy. Every day 190,000 cows are milked to meet Wells' daily dairy needs. Every year Wells uses eight million pounds of chocolate and two million pounds of strawberries. If you line up all

the Popsicle sticks Wells Dairy has used in one year, end to end, the line would span 68,377 miles—that's three times around the equator.

Wells dips out their ice cream during Ice Cream Days, held annually around the Fourth of July.

16 5th Avenue Northwest, Le Mars
(712) 546-4090
www.wellsdairy.com
Open April through August:
Monday through Saturday
from 9 a.m. to 5 p.m.; Sunday
from 1 p.m. to 5 p.m.
Open September through
April: Monday through Friday
from 11 a.m. to 5 p.m.;
Saturday from 9 a.m. to 5 p.m.;
and Sunday from 1 p.m.
to 5 p.m.
Admission charged

Wells Dairy Museum, Le Mars

62 Hobo Museum
Britt

With names like Liberty Justice, Minneapolis Jewel, and Lord Open Road, hoboes evoke American images such as freedom, adventure, and comradeship. Novelist and short-story writer Jack London was a hobo, so were James Michner, Red Skelton, Clark Gable, and former Supreme Court Justice William O. Douglas. Though hoboes were most prevalent throughout the United States during the Depression, when many people left their homes in search of jobs, men and women still take to the hobo lifestyle today. Many more fantasize of abandoning their three-piece suit and cubicle to bound onto a boxcar heading south, prop a sleeping bag under their heads, and watch Aspen trees whir by as the sun slides beyond the horizon. Which is why about 15,000 to 20,000 people descend upon Britt, a quiet town about 125 miles north of Des Moines, for its hobo convention every summer.

Britt has been accepting of hoboes since 1900, when a group of residents traveled to Chicago to convince a group of hoboes they should hold their annual convention in Britt. Back then, Britt was a fledgling town (it still is a small town with a little more than 2,000 people) and the residents were looking for a way to promote their village. They told the hoboes that Britt could provide them with just as good a festival location as Chicago. The hoboes decided to give it a shot and ever since the early 1900s, Tourist Union 63, as the original group of hoboes called themselves, has held the National Hobo Convention in Britt. Hoboes, their friends, supporters, and those just curious or envious of hoboes and their lives on the rails flock to town for the event.

If you can't make it to the convention, the Hobo Museum, run by the same folks who put on the annual festival, provides an intimate and engaging look at hobo life. Located in the former Chief Theater—preserved with original paintings of American Indians and covered wagons, original woodwork (and gum marks on the floor)—you'll see exhibits on hoboes' crafts (necklaces and blue-jean patches) and musical instruments (guitars and harmonicas). Photographs and original writings such as poems and excerpts from short stories introduce you to hoboes like Frisco Jack and Iowa Blackie.

One exhibit explores how a hobo becomes a hobo. Why do they do it? "I think they just love to do it," supposes museum volunteer Linda Hughes. "Some of the younger hoboes were in bad situations and perhaps hopping onto the trains was a way out," she says. "Many are married and have been for years. Some will write a letter one day to say they went fishing. But then come back a few years later." After hoboes have some money in their pocket, they usually return home. When the weather turns rough, they head south and most of them travel in pairs for safety reasons.

Famous Iowa Natives

- Comedian Tom Arnold, born in 1959 in Ottumwa
- Ex-talk show host Johnny Carson, born in 1925 in Corning
- Frontiersman "Buffalo Bill" Cody, born in 1846 in Scott County
- Former President Herbert Hoover, born in 1874 in West Branch
- Columnists and advice-givers Ann Landers and Abigail Van Buren (twin sisters), born in 1918 in Sioux City
- "The Beav," Jerry Mathers, born in 1948 in Sioux City
- Big-band-leader Glenn Miller, born in 1904 in Clarinda
- Actress Donna Reed, born in 1921 in Denison (Check out the performing arts festival named in her honor in Denison in June.)
- Author Wallace Stegner, born in 1909 in Lake Mills
- Preacher Billy Sunday, born in 1862 in Ames
- Actor John Wayne, born in 1907 in Winterset
- Crooner Andy Williams, born in 1927 in Wall Lake

You will certainly learn about hoboes in the museum. First off, understand that a hobo defines himself or herself as someone who travels in search of work, whereas a tramp is usually someone who travels and doesn't work, and a bum likes to tip more than a few drinks back and doesn't travel or work. (This is all explained for you.) Learn hobo jargon: For example, if someone caught the westbound train, he or she passed away. Memorize hobo symbols painted or carved onto the walls of sheds near rail yards, such as what area is unsafe, where an officer of the law lives, or where a hobo can sleep in barn. You'll also learn that some modern hoboes aren't hoboes in the pure sense. For example, the daughters of the late hobo Connecticut Slim carry on the hobo tradition by traveling—one of them in a boxcar (Connecticut Shorty), the other in a Winnebago (New York Maggie). And when Minneapolis Jewel is not riding the rails she works as a health care provider in Minneapolis. (Where else?) Some hoboes are tech savvy and can boot up a computer as skillfully as they open a can of beans with a pocketknife. Many hoboes have been known to pop in and out of local libraries to check and send e-mails.

The museum includes much lore about American hoboes who were frequent visitors to Britt's convention: Texas Madman was born in a boxcar to hobo parents; Frisco Jack, a hobo in his nineties, still sleeps on the ground in his sleeping bag. Read their stories by looking at some of their journals and letters. As expected, there are many wonderful photographs of grinning hoboes hanging out by boxcars.

Once word got out in the late 1980s that a museum had been established and the Chief Theatre had been purchased to house the world's only hobo museum, mementos from hoboes and their families started pouring in. Their donations make the museum more personal and charming: a worn down walking stick leans against the stage wall, a guitar autographed by a number of hoboes who attended a recent convention is propped up in a display case.

The museum's foundation has been very kind to hoboes who pass through Britt. In the early 1990s they set up a shelter by the train tracks for the hoboes passing through the area. And they continue to organize a blowout convention every year.

During the National Hobo Convention, usually held the second Saturday in August, you can taste Mulligan Stew, attend a polka mass, stake out a spot at the Hobo Jungle, and maybe be in running for King or Queen Hobo. Expect about 80 hoboes and 15,000 to 20,000 spectators. While you're in Britt, take a stroll through Evergreen Cemetery to see the memorial to hoboes like Slim Jim, Charlie Tuna, and Lord Open Road. And make sure to have some eggs over easy at The Hobo House, a café across the street from the museum.

51 Main Street South, Britt
(641) 843-9104
www.hobo.com
Open May through August, Monday through Friday from 9 a.m. to 5 p.m.,
and by appointment.
Admission charged

The marquee of the Chief Theater housing the Hobo Museum, Britt

63 | Bily Clocks Museum
Spillville

Spillville is a picturesque little town that lies along the rambling Turkey River in northeastern Iowa, about 20 miles south of the Minnesota border. It was to this community, settled by Czech immigrants in the 1850s, that the Czech composer Antonín Dvořák retreated in 1893 to concentrate on his work. The house where he once lived with his family is now home to a small exhibit on his life and works as well as the astonishing handmade clocks carved by Spillville farmers Frank and Joseph Bily.

With clocks ticking away and some of them going off every 15 minutes (so the staff doesn't have to hear all 40 clocks go off at once, the clocks are not all set to the same time) and Dvořák music playing in the background, volunteer guides share information about the Bily brothers' creations by pointing out details of each of the mammoth clocks (many of them are more than eight feet tall and weigh 500 pounds) on the first floor of the small house. The Twelve Apostles appear every hour on the hour in the Gothic-style Apostle Clock, built in 1915 and 1916. (See the little gargoyles?) The History of Travel clock contains six panels that demonstrate various modes of transportation. Look for the two church models, one of the Smallest Church in the World near Festina and the Little Brown Church near Nashua. And there are memorial clocks, one to the American pioneer (complete with panels that illustrate Columbus's "discovery" of America), and another to Charles Lindbergh.

Automotive magnate Henry Ford heard about the Bilys from reading an article about them in the *Christian Science Monitor* and traveled to their farm in 1928 to look at their clocks. He was infatuated with the pioneer clock and offered them $1 million for it. But the Bilys never sold their clocks so they turned Ford down. They were modest people and carving was their hobby; they created clocks for their own satisfaction. Even when the Bilys started charging $.10 for people to see their clocks, they stored the dimes in tin cans, which were later found after their deaths under the floorboards of their younger sister's room.

Their clocks took anywhere from eight months to four years to carve; the Bilys did all their work in the wintertime, with Joseph designing the clocks and Frank handling most of the carving. Most of the woods they used were native to the area, but sometimes they shipped in rarer woods. You'll see clocks made of oak, walnut, boxwood, and rosewood. They built the clocks largely with homemade tools and installed the music boxes and figurines themselves. All except two clocks work.

In addition to learning the clocks' characteristics, hearing them chime, and seeing the figurines parade, you will learn a little about the men behind the clocks. Every summer Frank and Joseph Bily toiled on their family's farm outside of Spillville, and during the winters, despite their father's protests, they retreated into the barn, whittling away at night to build the large, intricate clocks. They farmed for 22 years before moving into town when they were in their 60s, and for the most part they stayed to themselves. The Bily brothers could be described as homebodies. Neither of them ever traveled more than 35 miles from home and no one in the family ever married. As a result, when their younger sister died (they had intended to leave the clocks to her), they donated their clock collection to the town. But only after being persuaded not to burn them, which they had at one time considered doing.

And thank goodness they were saved. The elaborate clocks will elicit many "Wows" among visitors. Although none of the clocks were stained or varnished (the Bilys hand rubbed them with linseed oil or turpentine), the majority of them have many bells and whistles. Sure, there are a few cuckoo clocks, but there's also the Parade of Nations Clock with citizens in their native dress circling a clock face, and a couple walking down the aisle of a church. They added most of these bells and whistles to entertain their older brother who was mentally and physically handicapped.

The larger clocks are displayed downstairs; upstairs you will find mantle clocks, the Bilys' fossil and money collections (including bills from places like Madagascar), and a small exhibit on Dvořák, which includes music sheets and photos of him during his stay in Spillville.

323 North Main Street, Spillville
(563) 562-3569
Open weekends March and November from 10 a.m. to 4 p.m.
Open daily in April from 10 a.m. to 4 p.m. Open daily May through October
from 8:30 a.m. to 5 p.m.
Admission charged

Like What You See?
Biographical Clocks

Instead of writing a book about his life, John McClain decided to carve clocks depicting scenes from his life. His Johnny Clock Museum, representing 30 years of carving, is located in southeastern Iowa and contains about 50 clocks ranging in size from three-by-three inches to eight-by-five feet. The museum is located at 711 West Main Street in Lockridge. Open May through August from 9 a.m. to 5 p.m., or by appointment. For more information, call (319) 696-3711.

Laura Ingalls Wilder Museums and Sites

Burr Oak and Other Locations

As chronicled in Laura Ingalls Wilder's books, the Ingalls family moved frequently throughout the Midwest—Pepin, Wisconsin; Walnut Grove, Minnesota; Burr Oak, Iowa. There's no shortage of museums dedicated to Laura. The only problem is that since there are so many of them scattered about the region, each one has a little piece of Laura, but there is not one complete Laura collection. Still, it's not uncommon for fans, young and old, to set out on Laura pilgrimages and hit all the museums and former homesteads. Here are some Laura-related sites to visit in the Midwest, excluding South Dakota and Missouri. If you'd like to attend a Laura Ingalls Wilder pageant, you have many choices. Basically any town she lived in holds an annual event. Call the respective museums for details.

Burr Oak, Iowa

When the Ingalls family lived in Burr Oak, the town was a hub for wagons journeying westward; as many as 200 would pass through every day. (It's hard to believe, because the community is currently home to about 120 people.) When Charles Ingalls was offered the opportunity to run the Masters Hotel in the bustling town, he took it and moved his family there from Walnut Grove, Minnesota, in 1876. Of all the properties the Ingalls family called home in the Midwest, the building in downtown Burr Oak is the only remaining childhood home of Laura that still exists on its original site (though it was only home to the Ingalls family for a year). Shortly after it was discovered that the former private residence was the Masters Hotel, it was designated a National Historic Site. The town opened it as the **Laura Ingalls Wilder Park and Museum** in 1976. A gift shop is now located in the part of the hotel that was once a tavern, but the rest of the building is a re-creation of what the hotel probably looked like in the late 1870s.

You can tour the facility guided by girls dressed in period garb, girls that seem to have read Laura's books numerous times. (Visitors might be surprised to discover how small the "hotel" really is; it looks more like a cozy house.) The family lived downstairs, not far from the kitchen. You'll see where Ma cooked for the guests and the girls cleaned. Step inside the cramped room that was the family of five's living quarters (Grace was born at a house kitty-corner to the hotel). Laura was nine years old while she was at this hotel, and it was here that she met her future husband, Almanzo. At the museum you'll see a handwritten letter from an aged Laura writing to a fan of her books and learn tidbits of trivia about her. Did you know she was 4'9" and Manley was 5'3"? Because of the hustle and bustle of the hotel, Ma and Pa realized the Masters did not provide a healthy environment for children (they lived beneath the tavern, which was open late at night) and they moved back to Walnut Grove a year later.

3603 236th Avenue, Burr Oak, Iowa
(319) 735-5916
www.bluffcounty.com/liwbo.htm
Open daily May 1 through October 31 from 9 a.m. to 5 p.m., or by
appointment.
Admission charged

Walnut Grove, Minnesota

Perhaps Walnut Grove, Minnesota, is one of the more famous spots for Laura lovers to visit. It is in Walnut Grove that most of the action in the popular television series starring Michael Landon and Melissa Gilbert occurred. But before visiting the real Walnut Grove, keep in mind the show was not filmed here. The real Walnut Grove is a nice little town in southwestern Minnesota, but it does not look like the idyllic one portrayed in the show; no schoolhouse or Olson family general store to stop by. You can, however, visit the spot where their dugout was once located, the site of the Ingalls farmstead, and a Laura-focused museum.

The **Laura Ingalls Wilder Museum and Tourist Center** in Walnut Grove started in 1974 when the television series debuted. Located in a depot downtown, the museum chronicles the Ingallses' many moves around the Midwest and the events that occurred in each town. After first moving to the Walnut Grove area in 1874, the family lived in a very small dugout built by Pa Ingalls along the banks of Plum Creek. Laura was around seven years old when they first arrived. Later they moved to a house one-quarter of a mile north of town. When Charles was born the following year, they moved into town. Two years after they first settled in the area, the Ingalls family relocated to South Troy, Minnesota, and to Burr Oak, Iowa, only to return to Walnut Grove in 1877 and live downtown for another two years before returning again to South Dakota. Phew! And those moves don't even include the moving back and forth that Laura and her husband, Manley, did.

Some of the items on display at the museum include a quilt Laura and her daughter Rose made in the 1930s or 1940s. As expected, there are many photos and newspaper clippings about the stars of the television show, including Karen Grassel (Ma) and Melissa Sue Anderson (Mary), and their appearances in town. Outside the depot take a walk through a little red schoolhouse replica, a chapel built by a high school shop class in the 1980s, and the "Heritage Lane" building that contains a covered-wagon display and printing equipment from the Walnut Grove newspaper's office.

330 Eight Street, Walnut Grove, Minnesota
(507) 859-2358
www.walnutgrove.com
Open daily April through October. Call for hours.
Admission charged

While in the Area
Catch Some Fly Balls

A few miles outside of Dyersville off Lansing Road (there are plenty of signs directing you to the site), you can visit the **Field of Dreams movie site**, where Ray Kinsella, aka Kevin Costner, transformed a cornfield into a baseball diamond and attracted ghost baseball players like "Shoeless Joe" Jackson. Attend a game starring the local Ghost Players or bring a ball and bat and toss a few around. The site is owned by two separate families. You can enter via either of the two driveways and you'll see the same thing: A clean little baseball diamond with a white farmhouse perched on the hill. Take your pick of two souvenir stands where you can purchase goodies to take home. For more information, call (888) 875-8404 or (800) 443-8981 or visit www.fieldofdreamsmoviesite.com.

Pepin, Wisconsin

The log house and the big woods are long gone, but the **Laura Ingalls Wilder Wayside Park** near Pepin, Wisconsin, is the site of a log cabin that is a replica of the one in which Laura was born in 1867. The park is located seven miles south of town, off County CC. In addition, the **Pepin Historical Museum** is home to interesting memorabilia from Laura's life and from the late 1800s. The museum is located on Highway 35 in Pepin, a little town near the Mississippi River. Open mid-May through mid-October from 10 a.m. to 5 p.m. A donation is suggested. For more information, call (715) 442-3011. Pepin's annual **Laura Ingalls Wilder Days** in September include Laura look-alike contests and fun, non-Laura festivities like vegetable and pumpkin contests and tomahawk throws.

Sanborn, Minnesota

Ever since he was boy, Stan McCone dreamed of building a sod house. In 1988 the dream was realized when he hauled sod from a farm in southwestern Minnesota and constructed the 36-by-21-foot **Sod House on the Prairie** with two-foot-thick walls. He laid the sod like brick, compacted the dirt floor (so tight that it could be swept) and made the roof with peeled cottonwood, poles, and brush. Voilà! A shelter that stayed cool in summer and warm in winter. It took McCone a few months to build the main sod house and a few weeks to build the smaller ones. Stay overnight in the sod house in pure Laura Ingalls Wilder style—no electricity, so you read by oil lamp light and cozy up to a wood-burning stove. Expect air conditioners to be humming away during the summer; they're needed to keep the place from getting too mildewed. And you don't have to fetch your own breakfast. McCone's wife, Virginia, will deliver it to your door. After breakfast, stroll through restored prairie grasses and dance through fields of purple cone flowers just like Laura. Head to Virginia McCone's trailer and tie on a bonnet or put on some spurs. Look, ma—just like the 1870s.

If you don't want to stay overnight, you can still visit the sod house, dugout house, teeny log cabin, and outhouses. The grounds are open to visitors during the day. Look for the sod house signs off Highway 14 near Sanborn, Minnesota, about 20 miles east of Walnut Grove. For rates and more information, call (507) 723-5138.

The Sod House on the Prairie, Sanborn, Minnesota

65 National Farm Toy Museum
Dyersville

If you stop by the National Farm Toy Museum early in the morning, you might be treated to the sounds of Jazzercize music and a chorus of "One, and a, two, and a three" coming through the walls. It's a bit odd, considering that the museum is agriculturally focused—what about Conway Twitty tunes? The explanation is that the museum shares its warehouse location in Dyersville with the town's recreation center. But this odd arrangement means the museum is open when most others aren't. Folks who like to visit places before their morning coffee or tour museums after sunset will be pleased. And because this one is next to a workout center, go ahead and gobble down some ice cream at the restaurant next door, buy a pass to the gym, run around the track, and then step over to the museum to learn about where that ice cream came from.

"We try to make the visit educational, too," says Dave Bell, one of the museum's founders. "A city person can walk into the grocery store, get a gallon of milk, and understand little about where it came from." With dioramas of working farms from the early 1900s to present time and shelf after shelf of toys you wish you could take out to the sandbox and play with for hours, the National Farm Toy Museum is both educational and fun—for kids and adults, rural and city folks.

Dubbed the Farm Toy Capital of the World, Dyersville, about 25 miles west of Dubuque, has been home to a number of farm toy manufacturers since the 1950s, so it's only natural that the National Farm Toy Museum be located here. Most of these companies, along with the farmers who collected them, are responsible for creating the extensive museum commemorating farm toys and the farming industry. Open since 1986 with a collection about 30,000 toys, including pedal tractors, and every farm machine you can think of—corn pickers, hay balers, delivery rakes—the National Farm Toy Museum is one of the largest museums profiled in this book.

On the first floor of the museum, watch a 10-minute film about how toy companies started production in Dyersville and listen to die-hard farm toy collectors talking about their toys. "If I can teach a kid the values of farming, maybe I've accomplished something," one collector reveals on the screen. The first toy you will see in the museum is a Kelly green toy tractor, the first one ever made by the Ertl Company. Ertl has set up a 1960s-era assembly line—complete with women dressed in denim and scarves—to give you an idea about what goes on inside a toy factory. (If you want to tour an actual toy factory, call Scale Models, 301 5th Street in Dyersville, at (319) 875-2436.) Drop off your child at the brilliant "Li'l farmers" play area and have a look at the dioramas depicting farm homesteads throughout the decades; each one pointing out details, such as how close the farmhouse was to the barn at different time periods. Of course, the toys are the main attraction (and there are plenty of toy models made by various toy makers to look at), but the museum has also added a few small exhibits explaining scale and how toys are made.

The second floor contains even more farm toys—tractors, tractors, tractors—displayed in cases, some from Canada and Germany. It also has cases upon cases of semitrailer trucks, most of them built recently, some sports cars, and one case with a collection of cowboy and American Indian dolls. Like toy money banks? The museum has quite a few of these, too. Before leaving, make sure you review the corn and grain harvesting diorama that chronicles harvesting techniques from A.D. 1 to present time, depicting the progress from when a farmer could harvest one bundle of corn per day to 10,000 per day now. For the nonagriculturally proficient person, this exhibit is extremely helpful and not overly scientific, as the dioramas clearly demonstrate the procedures.

The enormously popular museum got its start when Bell, a former vice president with the Ertl Company, and the late farm toy collector extraordinaire Claire Scheibe, started the National Farm Toy Show in Dyersville in 1977 in order to promote farm toy collecting. They held the show at the local high school and about 2,500 people showed up. Every year, the crowd got larger and larger and eventually they needed a building to accommodate all the people coming to the show. And they needed a place to store the toys when they weren't being shown. So the town built a museum. The Ertl Company, the granddaddy of farm toy manufacturers in Dyersville, donated various machines from the 1950s and it produced (and continues to produce) collectible toys for the annual shows. Eventually other companies and collectors loaned or donated toys to the museum. New toys are added frequently to the museum and a new wing was added in 2000 to accommodate the growing collection.

The museum is involved in a number of annual toy shows in April, June, July, and November. The Railroad Memorabilia and Model Show typically occurs the last weekend in April. A construction and truck show and NASCAR racing show are occasionally held in Dyersville, too. Call the museum for more information about the shows.

1110 16th Avenue Southeast, Dyersville
(563) 875-2727
www.dyersville.org
Open daily year-round from 8 a.m. to 7 p.m.
Admission charged

Like What You See?
More Midwest Doll Museums

You'll find plenty of dolls in the museums profiled in this book, among them Elmer's Auto and Toy Museum in Fountain City, Wisconsin; The Angel Museum in Beloit, Wisconsin; and the Dumont Museum in Sigourney, Iowa. Haven't seen enough dolls? Here are a few more options.

With an 1880-era stove and a Cher doll, the **Dyer-Botsford Historical House and Doll Museum** is part local history museum and part doll museum, an amusing and quick museum to tour while in the Dyersville area. Like most local history museums, the Dyer-Botsford house contains turn-of-the-20th-century antiques displayed throughout the house's first floor and basement. You'll find the usual china collections and period furniture accented with dolls, appropriately dressed in Victorian garb.

Find yourself bombarded with dolls on the second floor—about 1,000 dolls, from a Shirley Temple to a Cher doll. We have the Barbie room, we have the Christmas room, and we have dolls hosting tea parties and lying in buggies and cradles. Most of the dolls are owned by Mr. and Mrs. Charles Schemmel of Cascade, Iowa, who have been collecting for 40 years.

The house itself has been restored thanks to the Dyersville Historical Society, the group that saved the building from demolition more than a decade ago. A noble endeavor considering that the town's founding father, James Dyer, and the Botsfords, a prominent Dyersville family, lived in the house before it became apartments decades ago. The Dyer-Botsford house is located at 331 First Avenue East in Dyersville. Open mid-April through November; call for hours. An admission fee is charged. For more information, call (563) 875-2414.

A private doll collection to tour while you're in the Newton, Iowa, area is Dollyville, not to be confused with the Dolly Parton theme park **Dollywood**. Norma and Bruce Conover have been making dolls for more than 20 years. You can admire 600 of them, all outfitted in handmade ensembles, by calling the Conovers at (641) 594-3449 for an appointment. They are located in Lynnville, Iowa.

Another great all-doll and toy museum is the **Fennimore Doll and Toy Museum** located in downtown Fennimore, Wisconsin. You'll find everything from 1830s-era china head dolls to popular culture dolls from movies such as Star Wars and a number of Walt Disney movies. Most of the collectibles were donated by local residents Dorothy White and Mildred Rudersdorf and California cartoonist Jeff Pidgeon.

The museum is located at 1140 Lincoln Avenue in Fennimore. Open May through December; call for hours. An admission fee is charged. For more information, call (888) 867-7935 or visit www.fennimore.com/dolltoy.

66 Ice House Museum
Cedar Falls

First off: Miller's Icehouse beer is not made in Cedar Falls. (It's made in Milwaukee.) And the Cedar Falls Ice House Museum is not devoted to the beer. The ice house is an immense and architecturally intriguing building where big blocks of ice were stored in the early 20th century.

Remember when there weren't double-sided refrigerators and freezers with automatic ice crushers? Or when milk was kept cool in iceboxes—contraptions holding actual blocks of ice? One hundred years ago, ice harvesting was a lucrative business, especially in northern towns where frigid temperatures were good for business. And especially in Cedar Falls, a town that grew in leaps in bounds in the late 1800s and early 1900s.

The Ice House Museum tells the story of how ice was harvested in the region, the role of the round ice house building in town, and the evolution of the refrigerator and freezer. (The museum has a decent collection of them from throughout the decades.) The building itself is awesome. (Practice neck-stretching exercises before visiting; you'll be looking up and around a lot.) Start your visit by reading about the building. It could hold 6,000 to 8,000 tons of ice at a time, with each block averaging about 22 inches wide by 32 inches long. (And these blocks weren't transported by forklifts, but by men and horses.) Ice wasn't stored here just in the wintertime; the building was also functional during summer. Workers packed straw between each ice block and the ice house walls in order to keep them from melting into one giant block of ice during warm weather. If the blocks melted at all, usually that occurred when they were being delivered to houses around town. Notice photos of men packing the blocks in the wagons and delivering them to customers.

Ice was harvested in Cedar Falls from about 1858 to 1934. And the first Cedar Falls ice house, a rectangular one, was built in 1858 for the purpose of storing all those blocks of ice harvested from the Cedar River by the Cedar Falls Ice Company. Years later that ice house was destroyed by fire and rebuilt in 1921 as the current round ice house. (The one you visit is not a replica.) When electric refrigeration developed and refrigerators became affordable, the ice company closed up shop. The city of Cedar Falls kept the ice house and over the years it was used to sell livestock in the spring and summer; in the winter it was flooded to make an ice skating rink. From about 1938 to 1974 it was used as a boathouse. Volunteers will share the building's history with you; if it wasn't for them, the house would have been torn down in the 1970s.

In 1975 city staff discovered the roof was caving in and declared the building unsafe. City hall didn't have the funds to replace the roof and officials planned to raze it. A year later as residents were preparing to celebrate the bicentennial, the Cedar Falls Historical Society decided they wanted to save the

While in the Area
Visit More Cedar Falls Museums

- The **Victorian Home and Carriage House Museum** is an 1863 Italianate home furnished with period décor. Head downstairs to visit the exceptional Lenoir Model Railroad exhibit. Chicago native William Lenoir pioneered model railroad building; his work was always in high demand. Look for the precise, hand-lettered train cars and little details—like the teeny pigeons perched on roofs—that add a homey feel to his creations. The museum is located at 308 West Third Street. Open year-round: Wednesday through Saturday from 10 a.m. to 4 p.m.; Sunday from 1 p.m. to 4 p.m. For more information, call (319) 266-5149.

- Harken back to 1909 by taking a seat in a one-room schoolhouse. The **Little Red Schoolhouse Museum** is located at First and Clay Streets. Open May through October 31, Wednesday, Saturday, and Sunday from 2 p.m. to 4:30 p.m. For more information, call (319) 266-5149.

- **George Wyth House and Viking Pump Museum.** Located at 303 Franklin Street, this house, once owned by the Wyth family, founders of the Viking Pump Company is designed in art deco style. The third floor contains an exhibit on the pump company, started in 1911. Learn about gear-within-a-gear rotary pump technology and the company's history. Open April through December, Sunday from 2 p.m. to 4 p.m., or by appointment. For more information, call (319) 277-8817.

- The **Behrens-Rapp Gas Station** became a tourist center when the historical society moved the 1925 brick filling station to Sturgis Park by the Cedar River (and Ice House Museum) in 1990. You'll pass it on your way to the Ice House. For more information, call (319) 266-3593 or (800) 845-1955.

building and worked to get it placed on the National Register of Historic Places. In 1976 you could still find people who not only remembered the days when ice was harvested, but who pitched in during the winter to stack the blocks in the building. In 1979 they raised enough money and collected enough ice tools and local artifacts to open the ice house as a museum.

While there are many local history displays in the museum, the main one tells the story of how ice was harvested. Blown-up photographs of horses pulling ice plows serve as a backdrop to the exhibit and an assortment of ice harvesting tools—pike poles, ice tongs, and an auger—are on view. On the ground floor rests a wagon that was used to deliver ice to homes in the Cedar Falls area.

Faux storefronts along the ice house perimeter recreate a walk through town in the late 1800s and early 1900s. Take a look at the diorama of Cedar Falls around 1893 to 1895 to situate yourself. There's the doctor's office, barber shop, gas station, and broom-making shop. (Iowa manufactured more brooms than any other state in America, though Illinois produced more broom corn.) Climb to the loft upstairs that looks like grandma's attic. It's packed with antique sleighs, a 1903 receipt register, a 1909 Lungmotor resuscitator, a potato shaker from 1900 to 1910 that shakes the dirt off potatoes, and a radio collection spanning 80 years.

303 Franklin Street, Cedar Falls
(319) 266-5149
Open May 1 through October 31, Wednesday, Saturday, and Sunday from
2 p.m. to 4:30 p.m., or by appointment.
Donation suggested

67 | Kalona Historical Village
Kalona

While many visitors flock to the Amana Colonies in search of homemade goodies and a glimpse into communal, peaceful living, Kalona, about 30 miles to the southeast, can provide a similar type of experience (and a less crowded one). Dubbed the Quilt Capital of Iowa, Kalona is a small community of apple butter, Bibles, thimbles, and bulls. (It was originally called Bulltown because of successful shorthorn breeding in the area: Kalona was actually the name of one of the prolific sires.) The town has a rich Amish and Mennonite heritage. In fact, Kalona is the largest Amish-Mennonite settlement west of the Mississippi, with about 1,000 Old Order Amish and 1,800 Mennonites.

Kalona is also the home of the Kalona Historical Village, a complex of structures that re-create the Amish and Mennonite experience. Located just off Highway 22, the village contains the Mennonite Museum and Archives, the Kalona Quilt and Textile Museum, a local history museum (featuring an extensive padlock collection), and a mineral and rock museum. And like most historical villages, it contains the standard antique log cabins, churches, depot and post office buildings that were transported to the village when faced with demolition.

Most likely you will tour the grounds with a guide, first walking through a Methodist church from the late 1800s and a home of one of the earliest settlers in the area. The next stop is the Wahl Museum, which contains many items relating to Kalona's history (many of the antiques you see were at one time owned by the Wahls). The museum is sectioned off into rooms set up to look like they did at the turn of the century. In here you'll find antique tools (alligator to monkey wrenches) and collections of fruit jars, salt and pepper shakers, and rare padlocks. You can expect some farm equipment, too, like a dog or goat treadmill once used to operate a butter churn.

On to the Mennonite Museum. This spacious, one-room museum tells visitors what the Mennonites and Amish are all about (aside from handcrafted furniture) and how they differ from each other. There are exhibits that explain how the Old Order Amish is a conservative segment of the Mennonite church and pamphlets that list tenets of belief. For example, the Amish believe in nonresistance and nonconformity and they help each other out voluntarily when the need arises, such as in a barn building. Amish women always cover their heads, don't cut their hair, and don't wear jewelry. Men remain clean shaven until they get married; after that they wear a beard but no mustache. The Amish drive a horse and buggy, while the Mennonites will drive a car. You can read all about the genealogy of area families (notice the extensive family trees on display) and see artifacts like German Bibles and prayer books, wedding outfits, a foot washing bucket, and many antique (but working) looms and

While in the Area
Marvel at Captain Kirk's
Future Birthplace

The USS *Riverside* announcing the town's annual Trek Fest, Riverside

He hasn't yet arrived, but that's no reason the little town of Riverside, seven miles east of Kalona, can't celebrate the coming birth of Star Trek's Captain James T. Kirk. Prompted by Riverside councilman and Trekkie Steve Miller, Kirk and other Star Trek–related characters and missions are honored at Riverside's annual **Trek Fest** held usually the last Saturday in June. After reading Gene Roddenberry and Steve Whitefield's *The Making of Star Trek* and discovering that Kirk would be born in 2228 in a small Iowa town, Whitefield wondered, Why can't Riverside be that town? It's been Kirk's official future birthplace since 1985. Can't make it to the Trek Fest? Stop by the city park located off Highway 218 in downtown Riverside and kneel before the spaceship model USS Riverside (similar to the Enterprise). For more information, call (319) 648-KIRK or visit www.trek-fest.com.

A collection of antique padlocks on display at the Kalona Historical Village, Kalona

spinning wheels. On some weekdays you'll catch local Mennonites spinning or knitting in the museum.

The Kalona Historical Village came into being around 1970 when the Rock Island Depot, which dates back to 1879, was about to be torn down to make room for a lumber company. Kalona residents Marilyn Woodin and her neighbor Glenn Wahl, among other residents, rallied to save it. They moved the depot to a few vacant lots behind Wahl's house. Someone donated red paint for it and a log cabin and schoolhouse were offered to the group. "From there it just snowballed," Woodin says.

While the historical village continued growing, Woodin, the part-time curator, ran the Woodin Wheel in town, an antiques, quilting, and all-occasion gift shop. Over the years she had accumulated about 200 quilts dating from 1843 to 1946 and started displaying them in a little museum in the back of her shop. After talking with Logan Reif, who owned an extensive mineral and gem collection, Woodin and Reif agreed to help raise funds for a new center to house their respective collections and a gift shop; the new building opened in April 2000. Woodin frequently changes the quilts on view, but you can always see a few permanent pieces like antique spool cabinets.

In the Reif Family Mineral and Rock Display, Logan and Helen Reif showcase the finest gems and minerals they've discovered all over the world; some are well known like agate, jade, and copper and others, such as marcasite, which looks similar to a peacock's tail, are a bit rare. Don't miss a portrait of Mary, Joseph, and Jesus made of gemstones.

By the time your visit has ended you will have toured 13 buildings, including a schoolhouse called "Straw College" (because straw bales were tucked along the exterior of the building to keep children warm in winter), general store, post office, and a Grandpa House, which offers a look into how the Amish care for their elderly.

The historical village is bustling with activity during the last weekend in September for the fall festival. Marvel at demonstrations of old-fashioned tools and machines like the dog or goat treadmill. Feast on homemade apple butter, pretzels, and bread cooked outside in the brick stove. A quilt show and sale is held annually on the last weekend in April.

If you'd like to visit the Kalona area on a mini bus tour organized by the historical society, call them at (319) 656-2519.

Highway 22 East and Ninth Street, Kalona
(319) 656-3232
Open in summer, Monday through Saturday from 10 a.m. to 4 p.m.; in winter,
Monday through Saturday from 11 a.m. to 3 p.m.
Admission charged

68 Theatre Museum of Repertoire Americana
Mount Pleasant

"Toby and Susie are coming! Toby and Susie are coming!" Such were the exclamations heard throughout various small Iowa towns in the 1920s. The misadventures of Toby, the country bumpkin, and his girlfriend Susie in what people called "The Toby Plays" were wildly popular. When children heard the vaudeville troupes that staged the plays were coming to town, they ran through the streets cheering. Created by Neil and Caroline Shaffner, "The Toby Plays" were one of more than 100 plays written by Neil and performed by his vaudeville troupe. The original character of Toby spawned at least 138 other Tobys, and was even said to have inspired the television show *Hee Haw*.

Early in the 19th century, before television and movies, residents of rural communities in the Midwest relied on touring theatre troupes like the Shaffner Players for entertainment. And at the Theatre Museum of Repertoire Americana in Mount Pleasant, you can learn all about the era when troupes staked out regions, erected tents that could hold more than 1,000 people, or set up shop in a downtown opera house, enthralling and delighting small town residents.

Inside the Theatre Museum of Repertoire Americana, Mount Pleasant

Members of the troupes, who considered themselves to be in show business, are revered in the quintessential small Iowa town of Mount Pleasant. Thanks to the late Caroline Shaffner, who moved there in 1969 after Neil died, and the Midwest Old Settlers and Threshers Association, which operates the nearby American Farm Implements Heritage Museum and Threshers Reunion, the theatre museum has become a destination for repertoire enthusiasts. Some of these people pilgrimage to Mount Pleasant for the theatre museum's annual seminar and to comb through its extensive collection of memorabilia from the Shaffner Players and similar troupes that performed from about 1900 to 1950.

Most of the items in the museum—tickets from 25 different theatre companies, portable makeup kits, and costume trunks—have been well preserved. The canvas curtains hanging in the front room are more than 90 years old and are still bright. (Twenty-three other curtains are stored downstairs.) One of Caroline's dresses, a floor-length flowery gown, is also more than 90 years old and yet almost iridescent.

"Caroline was proper and very ladylike," remembers museum volunteer Grace Davis, adding, "Neil was a true showman, a real go-getter." Most of the museum's contents belonged to the Shaffners. When Caroline and Neil retired in 1963, they often dreamt of setting up a museum to showcase the repertoire theatre era. It wasn't until after Neil passed away and Caroline met with members of the Midwest Old Settlers and Threshers Association, that the Shaffners' dream of a museum became a reality. The Midwest Old Threshers built the museum in 1972 to be part of the Heritage Museums campus and it opened shortly thereafter. Before she died at age 96, Caroline visited the museum every day, greeting visitors, or helping to catalog items.

The Shaffner Players group, which frequented southeast Iowa, western Illinois, and northwest Missouri, was one of about 400 similar theatre companies operating in the United States from around 1910 to the 1930s. The troupe would perform six different plays in six nights—all of them "clean, suitable for the whole family," says Martha Hayes, the museum's collections manager, never mind the misleading titles like *Natalie Needs a New Nightie*. You will see a few scripts in the museum exhibits, along with a script trunk, but know there are more than 1,000 additional original scripts archived in the rear of the museum. A few original posters and newspaper advertisements for plays hang on the walls.

Because a troupe usually consisted of six to eight people, most actors would play multiple roles in one play (and most certainly during the week). One museum exhibit highlights what insiders dub the "G-string" character. When an actor would play a younger role in a play, he occasionally played an old man later in the play, due to the limited number of actors in the troupe. This actor didn't have time to tape or glue a beard onto his face. Instead, he strapped a white goatee-type beard onto his face fastened with two strings tied behind his head. Another museum exhibit spotlights the additional talents of many of the actors. Many played instruments in pre-show or postshow parades down Main Street. On display are a ventriloquist's dolls, magician's accessories, an antique accordion, and a tuba.

The museum association members strive to continue to preserve and highlight this era of theatre history. Each April they invite former troupers and any repertoire buffs to a seminar about repertoire theatre. And if you're in the area in the summer, try to catch a Shaffner play produced on the museum's stage downstairs.

405 East Threshers Road, Mount Pleasant
(319) 385-9432 or (319) 385-8937
www.oldthreshers.org
Open Memorial Day through Labor Day, Tuesday through Sunday from 10 a.m. to noon and 12:30 p.m. to 4:30 p.m. During the remainder of year the museum is open Monday through Friday from 1 p.m. to 4 p.m., and by appointment.
Admission charged

69 American Farm Implements Heritage Museums
Mount Pleasant

In 1949 a group of four men from Mount Pleasant traveled to Pontiac, Illinois, for a threshers reunion, an outdoor event where owners of antique farm equipment strut their huge, loud, and powerful machines for each other. While driving back to their hometown they looked at each other and said, "We can do that." Mount Pleasant, a southeastern Iowa town grounded in agriculture, had plenty of area farmers with vintage machines they could show. A year later a local park was crowded with antique steam engines, separators, and threshers. A church group had set up a tent and sold homemade food; another group offered hayrides. Over the years the reunion grew way beyond the organizers' expectations as the town rallied behind it. It was only natural, then, for the reunion organizers and the town of Mount Pleasant to build a museum to complement the reunion.

A gravel driveway leads you to a rail yard at the edge of town to two modern corrugated metal warehouses where the contents are anything but. The American Farm Implements Heritage Museums, commonly called the Heritage or Threshers Museums, houses giant steam engines, pumps, and threshers. The multibuilding complex has farm machines run by hand, horse, steam, or gas; organizers claim to have the biggest steam engine collection around.

The first warehouse is largely devoted to antique threshing machines and the steam engines that hauled them. Old-time threshers or anyone who grew up on a farm will be entranced by these mammoth machines, while nonfarmers and city folk may be a bit overwhelmed by the rows upon rows of these hefty machines. Most of them were built from 1900 to 1930 and operated in the Midwest. While the second of the two museum buildings explains what threshers actually did (separate wheat from the chaff), the first one has display cards detailing information such as the engine's manufacturer, operation dates, the name of the family that owned it, horsepower, weight, and other power specifications. (For some threshers you have to look for the age of the machine and its function on handwritten cards tacked on the side of the machine.) This building also contains massive engines and pumps. For example, in its heyday, a 1922 Allis-Chalmers water pump from Marshalltown, Iowa, pumped from one to two million gallons of filtered water reservoirs into the city's water main. When it was donated to the museum in the 1970s, it took cranes and eight Coonrod trucks to transport it.

Since the museum's early years, organizers have asked themselves, Who wants to just look at row after row of dusty tractors? So they have not only

Mail box for the American Farm Implements Heritage Museums, Mount Pleasant

restored the equipment, but explained what each one is and added interpretive exhibits. The other heritage museum building adjacent to the threshing machines and engines features more antique farm equipment, horse-drawn buggies and wagons, electric cable cars, and interpretive exhibits. "Women: Partners on the Land" and "Water: Too little, Too Much" have been in the museum since the late 1980s and curators have added more exhibits over the years. A barn exhibit includes a scale model of a barn, tools used to build a barn, and information about round barns. An electricity exhibit chronicles the excitement of electricity coming to a remote farm in Iowa. The staff also has set up a scene of a flour mill's interior with implements from Marvin Mills, a former Iowa company that operated from the 1800s through 1947. Notice the corn sheller, separator, generator, and scale.

There are a number of easy-to-miss exhibits that add personality to what could be described as a large museum: A button collection from the late Maye Werner of Winfield, Iowa, and a short history of barbed wire collection with samples like buckthorn, brink twist, and sawtooth ribbon—compliments of private collector Lester Schuerman.

To see and hear these engines and the equipment in their full glory, visit Mount Pleasant during the Threshers Reunion. Held since 1950, the Threshers Reunion is a five-day event that usually ends on Labor Day. Enter a plowing match, tractor pull, or just unfold your lawn chair and listen to some music.

The reunion draws more than 50,000 people, so book your room early or plan to camp out near the museums.

405 East Threshers Road, Mount Pleasant
(319) 385-8937
www.oldthreshers.org
Open daily Memorial Day through Labor Day from 9 a.m. to 4 p.m. Open mid-April to mid-October, Monday through Friday from 9 a.m. to 4 p.m. Admission charged

---

Side Trips
Birthplaces of Famous Iowans

- You can visit crooner **Andy Williams's birthplace** in Wall Lake, where he lived until he was eight years old. Located at 102 East First Street. Open Memorial Day through Labor Day, Saturday, and Sunday from 2 p.m. to 4 p.m. An admission fee is charged. For more information, call (712) 664-2119.

- Visit **John Wayne's birthplace** in Winterset and you can check out such items as the eye patch he donned in True Grit and some of his personal letters. Open daily year-round from 10 a.m. to 4:30 p.m. An admission fee is charged. For more information, call (515) 462-1044.

- The **"Buffalo Bill" Cody Homestead** features the renovated house built in 1847 by Cody's father, a stagecoach, and live buffalo. The homestead is located north of Le Claire at 28050 230th Avenue in Princeton. Open daily April through October from 9 a.m. to 5 p.m. For more information, call (563) 225-2981. Also, the **Buffalo Bill Museum**, at 200 North River Drive in Le Claire, features Buffalo Bill memorabilia and local history artifacts. Open mid-May through mid-October: Monday through Saturday from 9 a.m. to 5 p.m.; Sunday from noon to 5 p.m. Open mid-October through mid-May, Saturday and Sunday from noon to 5 p.m. For more information, call (563) 289-5580 or (563) 289-4989.

70 | Dumont Museum
Sigourney

When you walk into the Dumont Museum, you may think it is a country music star museum because of the life-size cardboard cutouts of entertainers such as Shania Twain lining the front room and flanking the doors. Step inside and turn around: There's Reba McEntire grinning, almost holding the door open for you. The museum is rural in nature, with a slew of tractors and a room dedicated to the singing lasso handlers Roy Rogers and Dale Evans, but there are quite a few items in the collection that are definitely not country, like the *Beverly Hills, 90210* dolls. Simply put, the Dumont Museum contains a hodgepodge of recent American cultural and agricultural history.

After collecting Oliver tractors and Roy Rogers and Dale Evans records, among many other objects since his high school years, Lyle Dumont decided he wanted to open a museum. That was 30 years ago. In the early 1990s, approaching retirement, he decided, "well, it was now or never." He constructed a modern, barnlike building south of the little Iowa town of Sigourney and gradually he and his wife, Helen, also a collector, transferred their many tractors, bicycles, and dolls from their house and garage into the museum building. Considering how expansive the museum is, it's amazing that they kept most of their stuff in their house prior to the museum's opening in 1996. Their collection (they've never counted all their pieces) spans five vast and fully stocked rooms and includes Roy Rogers memorabilia, rows upon rows of full-size tractors, minipedal cars, covered wagons, carnival glass, teapots, and the occasional beer sign.

The first room you'll tour contains dolls, dishes, and other little things that fit on shelves and in cases. A look at Helen's popular culture doll collection (all of them in their original packages) is sure to bring back memories, especially for those who grew up in the 1970s, 1980s, and 1990s. Poised on the shelf is a Vanilla Ice doll, Brenda and Brandon dolls from the television show *Beverly Hills 90210*, and the Osmond family dolls. Another cabinet is stocked with fruit-shaped salt and pepper shakers (for example, watermelon), and vegetable-shaped shakers (like zucchini). There are shelves of china, political buttons ("Ted Kennedy for President"), a small barbed wire display (if you can't get to the barbed wire museum in LaCrosse, Kansas), farm toys (if you can't get to the National Farm Toy Museum in Dyersville, Iowa), and a few antique cameras.

The back two rooms contain clean, polished, and clearly labeled farm equipment, most of it manufactured in Iowa. Many of the tractors are Olivers, a company with whom Lyle's father worked. You'll see a 1948 Oliver 88 Standard Old Style grill, one of 1,150 built; a 1936 corn binder; and rows of boat motors. The walls are decorated with American license plates, American flags, belt buckles, and minicars (also on shelves). Meanwhile, antique bicycles are suspended from the ceiling. Since Lyle makes his living buying, restoring, and reselling antique farm equipment, he has restored a majority of the items on view. There are tons of restored tractors and minicars and engines to look at.

As a youngster he collected coins, cars, tractors, wagons, and eventually anything else that captured his fancy or made him want to restore it. It wasn't much later on in his collecting career that he seriously got into compiling Roy Rogers paraphernalia—perhaps the most impressive and entertaining collection in the museum.

Lyle had always liked Roy (who can not like the guy?) and had a few Roy collectibles. About 15 years ago the Dumonts traveled to California where they met up with Roy. They struck up a friendship and saw each other about once a year after that, Lyle says.

The Dumont's amigo hooked them up with a bounty of Roy Rogers memorabilia; their collection includes numerous autographed items and personal photographs. Can't make it out to the Roy Rogers and Dale Evans museum in Victorville, California? Then the Dumont Museum is the next best thing. The Roy room consists of wall upon wall of records, signed autograph pictures, trick lassos, Rogers and Evans cowboy band sets, dinner sets, paint sets, darts, movie poster after movie poster, and newspaper clippings about Roy and Dale. Thought you'd seen it all? Check out the "RR" insignia chenille bath set and the "Chow Wagon" Roy Rogers lunch box. Take it all in as Rogers's and Evans's voices resonate through the speakers with their signature song "Happy Trails."

Though the admission price is steep compared to other private museums profiled in this book, (the Dumonts charged $8 at press

Part of the shrine dedicated to Roy Rogers and Dale Evans at the Dumont Museum, Sigourney

time), you can spend an afternoon there. Heck, even a snapshot of you in front of Trigger is worth the admission fee. Before you go, call and ask about the Roy Rogers Jr. concerts held occasionally in the summer.

20545 255th Street (right off Highway 149), about three miles south of Sigourney
(641) 622-2592
Open May through October, Saturday and Sunday from 10 a.m. to 5 p.m., or
by appointment.
Admission charged

Like What You See?
More of Iowa's Musical Memories

• Believed to have been formed in 1857, the Cedar Falls community band is one of the oldest community bands in Iowa. **The Iowa Band Museum** in Cedar Falls is a small museum located in a vintage downtown building where the Cedar Falls community band practices. The museum harks back to a time when community bands were all the rage in American towns, when families hoofed it over to the band shell on Saturday night, and when town bands competed against each other at national contests. (Cedar Falls earned a first prize at the 1935 Chicagoland Music Fest.) Take a look at their rehearsal space, band photos from 1902, and a few instruments such as a late-1890s double B-flat sousaphone or "rain-catcher." Despite its name, the museum focuses more on the Cedar Falls community band than on Iowa bands in general.

203 Main Street, Cedar Falls (319) 266-1253
Open year-round: Wednesday through Sunday from 2 p.m. to 4 p.m.;
Monday from 7 p.m. to 9 p.m.
Donation suggested

• Since 1976 the town of Clarinda has hosted the **International Glenn Miller Festival** every year in June. Everywhere you stroll, Glenn Miller music can be heard wafting from theaters and parks. Strut your stuff at the big-band dance and meet musicians who played with Miller. Why Clarinda? The founder of the Glenn Miller Orchestra, a popular big band from the late 1930s and 1940s, was born in this southwestern Iowa town in 1904. His family moved two years later, but the town still holds Miller dear to its heart. While in Clarinda, tour the house he lived in the first two years of his life. To preserve her father's memory, daughter Jonnie Dee purchased **Glenn Miller's childhood home** in 1989, restored it, filled the house with memorabilia, and opened it to the public. The Glenn

Miller Historical Society sells Miller's music, mugs, key chains, and other goodies.

Glenn Miller's Birthplace
On the corner of Clark and Glenn Miller Avenues, Clarinda
(712) 542-2461
Open year-round, Monday through Friday from 9 a.m. to 5 p.m.
Donation suggested

Glenn Miller Historical Society
107 East Main Street, Clarinda(712) 542-2461
Open year-round, Tuesday through Sunday from 1 p.m. to 5 p.m.
Donation suggested

• For another tour of the state's musical past, visit **Meredith Willson's Boyhood Home** in Mason City. Willson wrote the musicals *The Music Man, The Unsinkable Molly Brown*, and songs like "It's Beginning to Look a Lot Like Christmas." The home is part of **Mason City's Music Man Square**, a large complex that also features a River City indoor streetscape, gift shop, and theater. A museum and conservatory are slated to open in 2002.

314 and 308 South Pennsylvania Avenue, Mason City
(641) 423-3534 or (641) 424-0700
www.themusicmansquare.org
Open May through October, Thursday through Sunday
from 1 p.m. to 4 p.m.
Admission charged

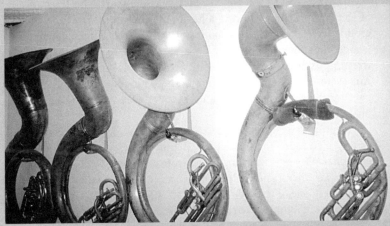

Tubas galore at the Iowa Band Museum, Cedar Falls

71 | International Wrestling Institute and Museum

Newton

It might come as a bit of a surprise to learn that Abraham Lincoln did some wrestling in his youth. Although he didn't have the typical physique of a wrestler (stout with thick legs and arms), Lincoln reportedly wrestled a fellow from a New Salem, Illinois, gang in 1831 and won. The match was said to have occurred because other boys were harassing Lincoln for being a bit different from them and for having his nose in a book. Supposedly, after the future president trounced his opponent, no one ever bothered him again.

Located in a former restaurant next to a Holiday Inn off I-80, the International Wrestling Institute and Museum is a treasure trove of information about the sport's history and its greatest heroes, from Hercules to Jesse "The Body" Ventura. The museum is the work of Mike Chapman, who has collected the paraphernalia over a period of about 20 years, and his wife, Bev. (She created the large decoupage of Jacob wrestling with an angel—another significant event in wrestling history.) Though he wasn't a professional wrestler, Chapman wrestled in the service and grew up idolizing Frank Gotch, the heavyweight champ from the early 1900s. Chapman, publisher of the *Newton Daily News* and former publisher of *WIN*, the Wrestling International Newsletter, started the museum to keep the memory of the sport's heroes, like Frank Gotch, alive. Open since 1998, the museum is located in Newton, a small town 25 miles east of Des Moines. Newton is a town where residents are sports fanatics, with everyone dressing up in high school colors the day of a match.

Start your visit by learning the history of the sport. Check out the drawings of Hercules putting a lion in a headlock, Orlando throwing Charles to the ground in Shakespeare's *As You Like It*, of American Indians wrestling in the woods, and Lincoln's match. Read about and see examples of the many wrestling styles around the world: Scottish belt wrestling, sumo wrestling, American freestyle, Greco-Roman, and Mongolian "bokh" wrestling. Yes, wrestlers face-off on more than just mats; they meet on the grass, in mud pits—you name it.

Chapman has compiled video clips of famous movie wrestling scenes. Drop by the video room and watch clips of Tom Cruise wrestling in the movie *Born on the Fourth of July*; wrestling scenes from the movie *Vision Quest*; the TV show *The Wonder Years*; and a film of a wrestling match that took place in 1920 in New York—one of the oldest-known wrestling films. In another corner of the museum, you'll find a "Wrestling in the Comics" exhibit featuring Alley-Oop, the time-traveling caveman who wrestles, as well as "Tarzan" and "Goofy" strips.

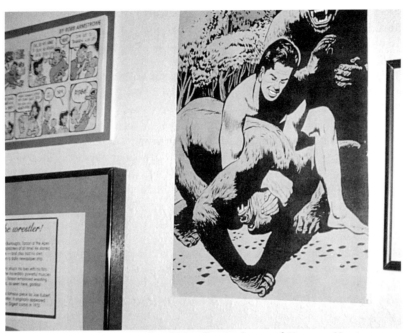

A Tarzan poster in the International Wrestling Institute and Museum, Newton

Along the museum walls are advertisements and competition posters: "Train like an Iron Man! Wrestling is a selfish sport! Give 'em nothing! Dominate!" You'll also find displays on popular WWF champs like Andre the Giant, Hulk Hogan, and Jesse "The Body" Ventura. And you'll discover wrestlers' forays into totally different careers. For example one record album cover shows a man suited up in wrestling garb, and the words "In this corner the musical world of Antonio Rocca."

The museum has plenty of collectibles and statistics for hard-core wrestling and sports fans. One aisle features the history of the Olympics from 1896 in Athens to 1996 in Atlanta. A display on the NCAA tournament includes the names of all the NCAA champs since the first Division I tourney in 1928: Another case contains wrestling cards—from William Muldoon's 1887 card to Tom Brands and Kurt Angle's 1996 cards. Take a stroll down one aisle and browse through the wrestling guides dating from 1942 to 1978.

Having grown up in the same Iowa town of Waterloo as Olympic and NCAA champ Dan Gable, Chapman has compiled a comprehensive exhibit on Gable. The shrine to Gable includes two walls and display cases containing his 1972 Olympic uniform and 1971 World Championship gold medal as well as memories from his time coaching at the University of Iowa. And there's plenty of memorabilia related to Frank Gotch, the world heavyweight champion from

1908 through 1915, such as his wrestling shoes, derby hat, and Mason's sword. And don't miss the tribute to the ladies of wrestling: Tricia Saunders was the first woman to win a gold medal for America at the Olympics two times—in 1992 and 1996.

Don't forget to visit the museum's most recent addition, a room downstairs called the Glen Brand Iowa Wrestling Hall of Fame. Four new professional wrestlers are inducted into the hall of fame every year.

And if you're looking for a smaller, Iowa-specific wrestling museum, try the **Iowa Wrestling Hall of Fame** in the northern Iowa town of Cresco. This hall honors the wrestling achievements of the state's amateur wrestlers. The hall is housed in the chamber of commerce building at 101 Second Avenue Southwest (Highway 9). For more information, call (800) 373-6293.

1690 West 19th Street South, Newton
(641) 791-1517
www.wrestlingmuseum.org
Open year-round, Tuesday through Saturday from 10 a.m. to 5 p.m., and by appointment.
Admission charged

72 | Maytag Washing Machine Exhibit
Newton

In the mid-1990s, Maytag, a company based in Newton since it started in 1893, considered moving some of its washing machine production out of town. Residents immediately launched a campaign to "Keep Maytag in Newton," mailing company executives letters and valentines, beseeching them to keep production in town in order to ensure that it remained the Washing Machine Capital of the World. The town earned this informal moniker because, since the early 1900s, numerous washing machine companies have called Newton home: Newton Washing Machine Company, Automatic, One Minute, Woodrow, Newdisco, and Maytag.

Maytag ended up staying in town, much to the relief of its residents. To honor the event, the **Jasper County Museum** expanded its washing machine exhibit to have a special focus on the company. The museum staff has also cataloged the histories of those other companies (and their washing machines), but Maytag is clearly the star of the show.

Displays introduce you to "the Dependability People" and highlight their achievements: Maytag created the first motor washer, the first all-aluminum cast tub, the first automatic safe bleach injector, the first cold water and wool wash cycles. The company, which made threshing equipment before delving into the washing machine business, produced their first washing machine in 1907. You'll see the first round porcelain tub Maytag made and the 25-millionth Maytag. Models from the late 1900s all the way to Maytag's latest—the high-tech, water-saving Neptune model —are showcased on the museum's second floor. Take a look at a 1920 Maytag model 73 double tub, a 1930 model Minute

Early washing machines at the Maytag Washing Machine Exhibit, Newton

Washer, and the last wringer washer made by Maytag on November 22, 1983. (Yes, people keep track of such things.) In the museum, you'll find every model washing machine the company ever made.

In addition to Maytag washers, look for a 1929 Frederick, the first round metal tub washer, many of the valentines and letters sent to Maytag executives, Maytag motors, a Maytag toy racer, vacuum cleaner, lawn mower, electric generator set, and aircraft parts that Maytag manufactured during World War II. Review washing machine company photographs—don't miss those depicting industry leaders chumming with Thomas Edison and Harvey Firestone—and a display on *"Smiling Through,"* the first company-owned aircraft in the United States, operated by the for Automatic Washing Machine Company.

For kicks, read over some of the old advertisements and company literature. For example, a 1929 issue of the "Gossiper" has this to say about its advertising campaign to introduce the Automatic Duo-Disc Washer: "All women dread washday . . . Through this happy advertising appeal, a flood of cheerfulness will be thrown upon the task of this dreadful day . . . Most women do not understand mechanical principles, but they do respond to emotional appeals."

Did you know Maytag makes blue cheese, too? While you're in Newton, pay a visit to the **Maytag Dairy Farms**. You can tour the cheese plant and farm and watch a video about the history of the Maytag Blue Cheese. Enjoy free cheese samples after your tour; if you don't have time for a tour, there's always the cheese shop. The farm is located at 2282 East 8th Street North in Newton. Open Monday through Friday from 8 a.m. to 5 p.m. and Saturday from 9 a.m. to 1 p.m. The tours are free. For more information, call (641) 792-1133.

Don't forget to tour the rest of the Jasper County Museum. Not far from the Maytag exhibit you'll find a little display about another booming business in Newton: specialty advertising companies. (Newton, in fact, also claims to be the world capital of specialty advertising.) Check out plates, hangers, ashtrays, and pens with companies' names printed on them. What else can you expect to see in the museum? Upstairs you'll find a reproduction of a Victorian home and a 1930s-era replica house. The lower level contains an agricultural exhibit with a quilt and sewing area and an extensive tool exhibit. There's also a display about the history of coal mining in the region. Outside by the parking lot you'll find an 1875 barn, windmill, and watering tank. Volunteers moved this barn, board by board, from a farm north of Newton.

1700 South 15th Avenue West, Newton
(641) 792-9118
www.jaspercountymuseum.org
Open daily May through October from 1 p.m. to 4:30 p.m., and by appointment.
Admission charged

73 National Balloon Museum
Indianola

"You're with the wind up there. Other than the burner heating the air inside the envelope of the balloon, it's very quiet. The trees are beautiful from the top down and the patterns of crops are amazing." So says Gene Smith, historian, balloon crewman, and longtime volunteer with the National Balloon Museum, about drifting along in a hot air balloon over Iowa's corn fields on a summer evening. With its rolling hills and expansive cornfields, Iowa has, not surprisingly, become a popular destination for ballooning enthusiasts.

While ballooning has been around for centuries, it didn't become a hobby for many people until about 30 years ago. In 1971, when a group of Indianola-area residents decided to hold the first National Balloon Championships in the area, few hot air balloons, and balloonists, existed in the world. Ten balloonists registered for the first competition. Three years later, they had 86. "It just exploded," Smith remembers. "Balloonists fell in love with Indianola."

Though the U.S. National Hot Air Balloon Championships are no longer held in Indianola, balloonists still gravitate toward this town less than 25 miles south of Des Moines for the National Balloon Classic held there every summer and for its National Ballooning Museum. After being housed in several temporary locations around Indianola throughout the 1970s (a few buildings on the Simpson College campus and in a former train depot), the balloon museum opened in its current building (shaped like two inverted balloons) on Jefferson Street in 1988. Representing more than 200 years of ballooning history, the museum is stocked with balloon envelopes (the nylon part of the balloon), wicker and metal gondolas, about 800 pins (pilots and balloonists have one for every balloon they work on), trophies, and other artifacts belonging to the Balloon Federation of America.

Begin your visit by learning about the history of ballooning and major milestones in the sport. In 1783 J. A. C. Charles was the first to ascend in a hydrogen balloon in order to conduct research on temperature and barometric pressure. The first woman to ever ride in a balloon was Elisabeth Thible from France, Andre Jacques Garnerin was the first man to pilot a balloon by himself, and Ben Franklin suggested balloons be used for military reconnaissance and for signaling sieges. You'll read about world record flights; for example, Ed Chapman carried 50 gallons of propane, a 720-channel radio transporter, and a parachute with him on *Stormy Weather,* his balloon with which he achieved the world record altitude flight of 38,900 feet.

Exhibits also explain how balloons work—they rise when the air inside the envelope becomes hotter than the air outside, which is why it is better to ride in a balloon in the early morning or evening than during the day when the sun can warm the balloon—and who is involved in launching a balloon. In addi-

Wicker gondolas inside the National Balloon Museum, Indianola

tion to the pilot, the crew consists of a crew chief and four crew members who are responsible for inflating the balloon, following the balloon's route on the ground and receiving permission to land on someone's property, and an observer. See plenty of photographs of crews inflating and deflating balloons.

As Smith says, "People involved in launching a balloon tend to develop a family type of relationship. Ballooning brings a lot of different types of people together. Some balloonists are wealthy and this is their hobby. For others the only thing they own is a balloon. But everyone communicates with nature up there and faces the elements together."

Take some time to read the touching story about *Serena's Song*, the first balloon manufactured specifically for disabled people. Gary Waldman commissioned it for his handicapped daughter, Serena, who dreamed of flying in a balloon. The balloon debuted in Indianola in 1992. Photos of this balloon also are included in one exhibit.

And don't miss photos of novelty balloons, tucked back in the corner of the museum by the conference table. Just imagine riding in a balloon shaped like an ear of corn, the Engergizer Bunny, Jesus, a space shuttle, or a whopper topped with a sesame seed bun.

Much of what you see in the museum has been donated by balloonists and balloon collectors. Volunteers are currently raising funds to expand the museum. Plans include a theater, a larger space to exhibit larger gondolas, and library and meeting space.

If you'd like to take a ride in a hot air balloon, the museum staff can refer you to area pilots.

1601 North Jefferson Street, Indianola
(515) 961-3714
www.balloon.weather.net
Open year-round (except January): Monday through Friday from 9 a.m.
to 4 p.m.; Saturday from 10 a.m. to 4 p.m.; Sunday from 1 p.m. to 4 p.m.
Donation suggested

Some Iowa Firsts and Facts

- West Bend's **Grotto of the Redemption** is the largest grotto in the world as well as the largest collection of minerals and petrification concentrated in one spot.

- According to Ripley's Believe It or Not!, **Snake Alley** in Burlington is the Crookedest Street in the World.

- Stanton's two water towers have been converted to a **Swedish coffeepot** (in 1971) and a **coffee cup and saucer** (in 2001), reminding the town of 700 of its Swedish roots. Look toward the heavens when you drive into town from Highway 34. You can't miss the towers.

- The **world's largest bull statue** is located in Audubon, off Highway 71. His name is Albert, and he's a 30-foot, 45-ton concrete Hereford.

- The **Santa Fe Swing Span Bridge** in Fort Madison is the longest double-decker swing span bridge in the world.

- Cresco native Ellen Church became the **world's first flight attendant** on May 15, 1930.

- Billed as the smallest church in the world (although many other churches make the same claim), the **St. Anthony of Padua chapel** was built in 1886 and seats eight people. The chapel is located west of Festina at Highways 150 and 24.

- Howard Snyder built the **first Maytag washing machine** in Newton in 1907.

- **Winnebago motor homes** were first made by Winnebago Industries in Forest City in 1958.

- **Schaeffer Fountain Pens** were developed in Fort Madison in 1908.

- **Eskimo Pies** were invented by Christian Nelson in Onawa in 1920.

- The **4-H** was founded by Jessie Field Shambaugh, who started it in Goldenrod in 1901.

74 | Olson-Linn Museum and Axe Murder House
Villisca

One of the worst mass homicides in Iowa's history occurred on a hot, sticky night in June 1912 in the then-bustling railroad town of Villisca in southwestern Iowa. Mr. and Mrs. Joe B. Moore, prominent citizens thought to have no enemies, along with their four children and two visiting children, Ina and Lena Stillinger, were murdered by an axe-wielding killer in their house. No one was ever convicted of the crime and it remains one of the state's biggest unsolved crimes.

Everyone—paranormal researchers, historians, filmmakers, and neighbors—has a theory about the murders. Among the theories: F. F. Jones, a prominent businessman, hired a crazed killer to eliminate Joe Moore because Moore's business was competing with his; Moore was having an affair with Jones's sister or sister-in-law and Jones and two other men killed the Moores; Joe Moore killed his family and then took the axe on himself; a preacher who had also been convicted of burning a barn (because God made him do it, he claimed) killed them. Featured on the Fox Family Channel's "Scariest Places on Earth" television show, the Axe Murder House has been a choice destination for "paranormal investigators" or ghost hunters, teenage thrill seekers, historians, legal, and judicial buffs. For a few bucks, you can tour the Olson-Linn Museum, a hodge-

A display at the Olson-Linn Museum, Villisca (the ax shown above is not linked to the infamous murders)

podge collection owned by Darwin and Marsha Linn, and the former Moore house, where the walls supposedly dripped with blood, children heard other children playing inside, and orbs of light dash around the bedrooms.

Expect a full briefing of the story before going to the house. You'll watch a short homemade video introducing you to the Moore family and a tape showing paranormal investigators discovering floating orbs, picking up electrical energy on their meters, and watching the temperature drop on their lasers. You can listen to a recording of an old radio program detailing the murder and scan newspaper clippings about the murder, the investigations, and profiles of suspects and detectives. Since the murders occurred, Villisca's population and vibrancy have sagged. When the Moores lived here, the town was a major railroad stop and retail center, and it had a vibrant town square and opera house. After the murders, families slept in houses together, their windows covered with chicken wire, and a man standing guard. Trust in their fellow residents dwindled.

Some visitors, upon arriving at the house, become too scared to go inside. Others march right on in and scoff at claims that the place is haunted. Walking into the house guided only by lamplight on a Saturday night some 90 years after the murder takes quite a bit of moxie, especially after watching a video of supposed paranormal events. Luckily, the Linns don't pull any sort of immature pranks (no one hiding behind doors waiting to jump out at visitors) and they don't impose their beliefs on their visitors. (For the record, though, they are skeptics: Darwin has never had any first-hand paranormal experience, although Martha was in a room once that became freezing cold and the hair on one of her arms stood up.)

The Linns, Villisca-area farmers, purchased the Moore house in 1994, restored it to 1912-era décor, had it placed on the National Register of Historic Places, and reopened it to the public in 1996. Since they restored the house to what they thought it would have looked like at the time of the murder, more people have reported seeing glowing orbs of energy in the house or felt chills. The genial Linns will show you around the house, recounting the murder and the facts about it. (All of the victims' heads were bashed in but covered with a sheet by, people think, the murderer; no money or jewelry was taken.) The Linns give you the lowdown on the investigations that followed and share explanations for why no neighbors heard the murders. (Investigators believed the murderer or murderers struck the family when trains passed through town shortly after 11 p.m.) The Linns share stories of alleged paranormal experiences that have been reported in the house, such as bubble orbs and chilly rooms. The scariest paranormal report occurred years ago when the house was being rented out and the woman living there woke up in the middle of the night to see a figure at the edge of her bed with an axe. Yikes!

This is not an in-an-out kind of visit. Expect to spend more than an hour in the house (and an hour in the museum). Yes, you will climb up the stairs to the bedrooms, step into a pantry, and attic—areas where some people think the murderer hid. Afterward you will be invited to sit on the edge of a bed or chair for as long as you'd like and discuss any experiences you had.

"I myself have never experienced any paranormal activity, but I can't say it isn't there or that what visitors experience didn't happen to them," Darwin says.

While you may not have a true-blue paranormal experience, shivers may run up and down your spine just from listening to the Linns talk and the drapes flapping in the night air (from open windows). To add visual effect, the Linns have placed dresses, drapes, or tablecloths in front of many mirrors and windows, much like the murderer had done.

The Olson-Linn Museum, your launching point for the Moore house, is a two-story sprawling and chaotic museum complete with shag carpet, a musty smell, and a mishmash of antiques. You'll see a rope maker (and get to make a piece), a soda bottle collection, barbed wire collection, matchbox collection, and a group of church pews and theater seats from Villisca. The Linns have quite a few automobiles that they have restored or are in the process of restoring, such as: an Atwood piano loader; a 1921 Ford Model T van; and a 1917 Cole ridden by a man whose mother scolded him for riding it, claiming that the air would be sucked out of his lungs because he was going so fast. Notice the coffin in the basement placed near antique dental equipment, a wheelchair from the early 1900s, and plenty of tractor seats on the wall. Not many of the items are labeled and most of them are scattered throughout the building haphazardly, but there are some rare finds, such as a stuffed turkey with a freeze-dried beak and a piece of the Skylab floor.

323 East Fourth Street, Villisca
(712) 826-2756
www.villisca.com (This is a Web site run by filmmakers working on a documentary about the murders.)
Open daily May through October from 9 a.m. to 4 p.m. Open January through October, Saturday and Sunday from 1 p.m. to 4 p.m. The Linns run weekend lamplight tours by appointment—a tour I highly recommend.
Admission charged

Index by Museum Type

Index

More Great Titles

FROM TRAILS BOOKS AND PRAIRIE OAK PRESS

ACTIVITY GUIDES

Great Cross-Country Ski Trails:
Wisconsin, Minnesota, Michigan, and Ontario   *by Wm. Chad McGrath*
Paddling Southern Wisconsin: 82 Great Trips by Canoe and Kayak   *by Mike Svob*
Paddling Northern Wisconsin: 82 Great Trips by Canoe and Kayak   *by Mike Svob*
Paddling Illinois: 64 Great Trips by Canoe and Kayak   *by Mike Svob*
Wisconsin Golf Getaways:A Guide to More Than 200 Great Courses
and Fun Things to Do   *by Jeff Mayers and Jerry Poling*
Wisconsin Underground: A Guide to Caves, Mines, and Tunnels
in and around the Badger State   *by Doris Green*
Great Wisconsin Walks: 45 Strolls, Rambles, Hikes, and Treks   *by Wm. Chad McGrath*
Great Minnesota Walks: 49 Strolls, Rambles, Hikes, and Treks   *byWm. Chad McGrath*

TRAVEL GUIDES

Classic Wisconsin Weekend Adventures   *by Michael Bie*
The Great Indiana Touring Book: 20 Spectacular Auto Tours   *by Thomas Huhti*
In Lincoln's Footsteps   *by Don Davenport*
Sacred Sites of Wisconsin   *by John-Brian and Teresa Paprock*
Great Iowa Weekend Adventures   *by Mike Whye*
Tastes of Minnesota: A Food Lover's Tour   *by Donna Tabbert Long*
Great Minnesota Weekend Adventures   *by Beth Gauper*
Great Indiana Weekend Adventures   *by Sally McKinney*
Historical Wisconsin Getaways: Touring the Badger State's Past   *by Sharyn Alden*
The Great Wisconsin Touring Book: 30 Spectacular Auto Tours   *by Gary Knowles*
Wisconsin Family Weekends: 20 Fun Trips for You and the Kids   *by Susan Lampert Smith*
County Parks of Wisconsin, Revised Edition   *by Jeannette and Chet Bell*
Up North Wisconsin: A Region for All Seasons   *by Sharyn Alden*
Great Wisconsin Taverns: 101 Distinctive Badger Bars   *by Dennis Boyer*
Great Weekend Adventures   *by the Editors of Wisconsin Trails*

HOME AND GARDEN

Creating a Perennial Garden in the Midwest   *by Joan Severa*
Bountiful Wisconsin: 110 Favorite Recipes   *by Terese Allen*
Foods That Made Wisconsin Famous   *by Richard J. Baumann*

PHOTO ESSAYS

The Spirit of Door County: A Photographic Essay   *by Darryl R. Beers*
Wisconsin Lighthouses: Photographic and Historical Guide   *by Ken and Barb Wardius*
Wisconsin Waterfalls   *by Patrick Lisi*

NATURE ESSAYS

Wild Wisconsin Notebook   *by James Buchholz*
Driftless Stories   *by John Motoviloff*

For more information, phone, write, or e-mail us.

TRAILS BOOKS

P.O. Box 317, Black Earth, WI 53515
(800) 236-8088 (e-mail: books@wistrails.com
www.trailsbooks.com